779-5089

DEATH FROM THE SKY!

Suddenly the Messerschmitts arrived, howling in at ground-level, machine guns chattering, cannon thumping, snarling in tight turns as they shot up the rear areas. The sand storm had died down and visibility was improving by the minute; yet only four solitary American planes appeared to take up the challenge presented by the numerous yellow-nosed enemy fighters....

KASSERINE

THE BATTLEFIELD SLAUGHTER OF AMERICAN TROOPS BY ROMMEL'S AFRIKA KORPS

CHARLES WHITING

JOVE BOOKS, NEW YORK

This Jove Book contains the complete
text of the original edition.

KASSERINE

A Jove Book / published by arrangement with
Stein and Day, Publishers

PRINTING HISTORY
Stein and Day hardcover edition published 1984
Jove edition / July 1991

ISBN: 0-515-10618-6

Jove Books are published by The Berkley Publishing Group,
200 Madison Avenue, New York, New York 10016.
The name "JOVE" and the "J" logo
are trademarks belonging to Jove Publications, Inc.

PRINTED IN THE UNITED STATES OF AMERICA

10 9 8 7 6 5 4 3 2 1

CONTENTS

ILLUSTRATIONS

A German Nebelwerfer
British troops probe for mines
Grenadier Guards reconnoiter near Kasserine
An American 37mm anti-tank gun and crew

LIST OF MAPS

Secure from actual warfare, we have loved
To swell the war-whoop, passionate for war.

—Coleridge

Time's wrong-way telescope will show a minute
man ten years hence, and by distance simplify.
Through the lens see if I seem substance or nothing; of
the world deserving mention or charitable oblivion.
Remember me when I am dead and simplify me
when I'm dead.

—Keith Douglas
(Killed in Action, 1944)

AUTHOR'S NOTE

They called it Operation Torch. Naturally the codename was taken from Shakespeare.[1] Were they not coming this Sunday of November 8, 1942, to liberate the French and to light a torch that one day would purify the whole of Occupied Europe with its sacred flame? Nothing but Shakespeare would do.

Now they prepared to land. They had brought their brass bands with them, their banners, their Class A uniforms. Their weapons they wouldn't need, of course. Hadn't they learned to chant the slogan saying who and what they were: *"Nous sommes soldats Américains! Nous sommes vos amis!"*[2]

Undoubtedly they would be welcomed as liberators by cheering crowds of excited citizens—they had seen it all in the movies that Hollywood had been feeding them for the last year or so. The occupied countries, with their heroic resistance movements, desired nothing more fervently than to be freed from those jack-booted, black-uniformed swine who bore that evil, crooked cross on their sleeves. So, as they clambered down the nets from their troopships all along the

11

French North African coast, they were confident that they would be welcomed with open arms.

Three days of severe fighting followed. One thousand of these naive young men, these "liberators," were killed; another one thousand were wounded. The first American soldiers to be killed in action across the Atlantic in World War Two were shot by men they regarded as their allies. It seemed that the French were not so eager to be liberated from the Nazi yoke.

In the end, the French grudgingly agreed to let themselves be liberated. They laid down their arms in Africa and got on with the business of living again, leaving these brash Anglo-Americans to go elsewhere—preferably as far away as possible—to fight the Germans, if that's what they wanted to do.

Life returned to normal in French North Africa. The brothels and the black market flourished. American dollars and English pounds poured into the local *caisses* and *crédits*. The Arabs continued to live their ragged, half-starved, miserable lives. The French prospered. The same administrators who had once served the Germans so loyally now worked for General Eisenhower, though not so loyally. The Allies were tactfully ignored. Let them play soldier out in the desert.

Now, on St. Valentine's Day, 1943, an American command met the Germans for the first time in battle in World War Two. Deep in the heart of North Africa, some 30,000 young Americans, most of whom had never before heard a shot fired in anger—under the command of an elderly, opinionated general, who had last seen combat a quarter of a century previously—faced up to an attack by no less a person than the Desert Fox himself. Rommel and his vaunted *Afrika Korps*, the veterans of two years of fighting in the desert, were coming for the new boys.

The result was predictable. Regiments were overrun; battalions broke and melted away into the desert; there was a mass slaughter of American armor. Drivers abandoned their vehicles in good running-order and fled. Hundreds of American soldiers surrendered without firing a shot.

The corps that had come to Africa with such youthful high hopes had suffered an overwhelming defeat. Nearly a quarter of those 30,000 men—6,500 Americans (plus another 4,000 British soldiers had come to their aid)—were killed, wounded, or taken prisoner. Nearly 400 armored vehicles, 200 artillery pieces, and 500 trucks and jeeps were lost.

At the very last moment, when it seemed that the whole Allied front in Africa would collapse, Rommel called off his attack. He was worn, sick, uncertain. He let them get away. But he had given the Americans a bloody nose. Now he could return to France to take charge of the anti-invasion army being set up there, confident he could beat the *Amis* if they ever dared to land there. Behind him he left a shaken, confused, deeply shamed American Army. Now it was up to them to learn the lessons of that terrible defeat and prepare for their next meeting with the Desert Fox.

This, then, is the story of Kasserine. It is the tale of youthful innocence sacrificed at the altar of the god of war by incompetent, complacent old men, who lived on to die in bed. The sacrifice was, as it always is in war, in the blood of youth.

prelude to a battle

*"Vive la France! ... Lafayette, we are here again—
for the second time!"*

—Major General Mark Clark, 1942

"**G**eneral—*the light!*" the young commander of the submarine called down from the conning tower urgently.

The tall craggy-faced American—whom Churchill liked to call his "American Eagle" on account of his beak-like nose—clambered up the ladder out of the hot fetid atmosphere of the sub onto the bridge.

Yes, there it was: a white light gleaming from a height just above the deserted, moonlit shore. It was the signal agreed upon. The coast was clear.

Now there was no time to be lost. The British submarine HMS *Seraph* was at her most vulnerable out here in the bay, only two miles from the Algerian coast. The American general whispered an order and the four officers who were to accompany him on this daring secret mission prepared to

15

board the frail wooden boats manned by three officers of the
commandos Special Boat Section. Two days before, the three
commandos had been shocked to find that they were landing
not "the seedy saboteurs" they expected, "but five members of
the U.S. Army's General Staff, led by no less a personage than
Eisenhower's deputy, Major General Mark Clark, the "American Eagle."[1]

But the three British officers had no time now for wonder.
They knew they could be spotted at any moment, and it was
two long miles to that foreign shore. With Lieutenant Livingstone—formerly of the Royal Ulster Rifles—in the lead, the
three boats set off in a V-formation.

At intervals, the commando officers stopped to scan the
shoreline with their field glasses, but it seemed quite empty.
If anyone were out there to greet them, he was keeping himself well hidden. Or maybe their mission had been discovered? If so, they were paddling right into a trap.

They were sliding quietly through the water, their paddles
dipping rhythmically into the inky sea. The first boat touched
the empty beach in a soft wash of gentle ripples. Livingstone
and his passenger, Colonel Julius Holmes of the U.S. Army's
Civil Affairs branch, took a quick look around. Nothing
stirred. They might have been the last men alive. Hastily the
former member of the sedate State Department, who had
never done anything quite like this before, flashed the agreed-
upon signal: the letter K with his flashlight.

Two hundred yards out at sea, General Clark spotted the
signal and nodded to the S.B.S. officer.

"There it is . . . let's go!"

The young officer needed no urging. It was not every day of
the week that he lay off an enemy coast, carrying the second
top man of the U.S. Army in the European Theater as his
passenger. The responsibility was almost overwhelming. He
set off paddling, while the American general, who was twice
his age, tried vainly to keep up with him. Minutes later they
were dragging their craft up the sand, intent on hiding it in
the black shadows among some bushes at the foot of the bluff.

Suddenly the little party of three British and five American officers tensed. A dark figure had detached itself from the trees to their left. The Americans whipped out their .45s and the commandos leveled their little Stenguns, hands suddenly damp with sweat, hearts beating furiously. Was it a trap after all? After the months of clandestine operations spreading over two continents, was everything going to end in failure?

But Colonel Holmes sprang to his feet, lowering his pistol. He had recognized the tall, heavy-set man with the broad Irish face who had stepped out of the trees into the moonlight; they had once been colleagues in the U.S. State Department. There was no mistaking Robert Murphy, who since late 1940 had been one of President Roosevelt's "personal representatives" assigned to carry out secret missions under his orders.

"Bob!" he cried, advancing on Murphy, hand outstretched in greeting.

Behind Holmes, lying in the sand, General Clark breathed a sigh of relief. Contact had been made. A few moments later the little party of American officers was surrounded by Murphy's fellow conspirators, French and American, while amid the enthusiastic exchange of greetings and mutual back-slapping the commando officers waited impatiently to get the boats under cover.

Robert Murphy turned to General Clark and held out his hand. It was an historic occasion, this secret meeting at midnight on a remote deserted beach; but at that particular moment, neither the civilian nor the soldier knew it.

"General," Murphy said simply, "welcome to North Africa."[2]

The reason why these five Americans found themselves in French North Africa on the night of October 22-23, 1942, went back over two years. Rising in the House of Commons on July 4, 1940, exactly two weeks after France had surrendered, the new Prime Minister, Winston Churchill, announced grimly that on the morning of July 3, the day before, Britain had committed an act of war against the French. "With aching hearts, but clear vision," Churchill said, the Royal Navy had gone into action to prevent the French Fleet, now officially neutral, from falling into German hands. Only two weeks before, the French and the British had been allies.

At Portsmouth and Plymouth, British sailors had seized French battleships, cruisers, and submarines. For the first time since 1815, Frenchman had fought Englishman. One British leading seaman had been killed and three wounded, while on the French side one officer had been killed and one seaman wounded. In Alexandria, too, French warships lying in the harbor had been neutralized—but, as Churchill told a hushed House, the worst was yet to come. At the French North African ports of Oran and Mers-el-Kebir, the Royal Navy had delivered an ultimatum: either the French ships that were anchored there would obey British demands, or they would be sunk within six hours. The French Admiral Gensoul had refused to comply. Accordingly, at 1753 hours that afternoon, the fifteen-inch guns of Admiral Somerville's battle squadron had opened fire on the trapped French ships, and torpedo bombers from the aircraft carrier HMS *Ark Royal* swept into the attack.

The results were horrific. One French battleship was sunk and another had to be beached; two destroyers and a seaplane carrier were also sunk. That hot July afternoon in North Africa, more than one thousand French sailors were killed and nearly the same number wounded by the men of the Royal Navy.

Churchill ended his solemn account of these events with the words: "I leave the judgement of our action, with confidence, to Parliament. I leave it to the nation, and I leave it to the United States. I leave it to the world and history."

With that he sat down, confident that he had shown President Roosevelt that the British were prepared to fight on; confident, too, that he would still be able to count on French support against Nazi Germany one day. For did he not have a tame Frenchman in London, already calling to his fellows to rally to his Free French Forces?

But the pudgy toothless old warrior, so full of spirit and fight in spite of his advanced years, had misjudged the personality and temperament of the French General. Although he was now totally dependent on Churchill for money and supplies, the Frenchman had plans of his own. General Charles de Gaulle—"that Joan of Arc," as President Roosevelt called him bitterly—was intent on escaping Churchill in London and setting up his own power base in French Equatorial Africa.

On September 23, 1940, a force of British warships and transport ships hovered off the great West African port of Dakar. By now de Gaulle had won most of French Equatorial Africa to his cause, but still the major French African port of Dakar held out against him. On this fog-bound autumn day, the general intended to intimidate the defenders into surrender. Not only did he have 2,000 Free Frenchmen under his command, but also a back-up force of three battalions of Royal Marines—just in case.

The first British and French planes from HMS *Ark Royal* swept in from the sea and, zooming down out of the thick fog, started showering Dakar with leaflets proclaiming de Gaulle's friendly intentions. The defenders' reaction was not so friendly. Everywhere antiaircraft guns opened up, stabbing the gray fog with angry bursts of orange flame, and from the harbor came the boom of the battleship *Richelieu*'s heavy guns.

De Gaulle was worried, but still determined. Telling his British audience that the defenders' gunfire was half-hearted, he sent two pinnaces ashore with spokesmen to explain his friendly mission. But as the spokesmen were landing, they were confronted by a grim-faced port commander who told them they were under arrest. The Free French made a dash back to their boats while machine guns opened up at them from both sides of the harbor and angry tracer cut the gray gloom. Both boats took casualties.

By now all hell was erupting. The French coastal batteries

started firing at the British warships anchored out at sea. But Admiral Cunningham, a tough old seadog, was not going to repeat the tragedy of Oran and Mers-el-Kebir. He ordered his crews not to fire back. For hours the French defenders pounded the silent British ships out there in the fog, until—at eleven o'clock precisely—the great guns of the *Richelieu*, France's newest and most powerful battleship, thundered into action. The British cruiser *Cumberland* was straddled by her shells; huge plumes of whirling white water hurtled into the sky on either side of her. Yet still the British did not retaliate. Then abruptly the *Cumberland* reeled. Black smoke started to mushroom from the cruiser. She had been seriously hit.

Admiral Cunningham's patience was wearing thin. He ordered a signal to be sent to the French: *"I am not firing at you. Why are you firing at me?"*

The reply was laconic and brutal in its simplicity: *"Retire to twenty miles distance immediately!"*

Admiral Cunningham had had enough; he gave the command for his ships to return the French fire. The British responded immediately. The two ancient battleships HMS *Resolution* and HMS *Barham* opened fire with their fifteen-inch guns.

Now Dakar's coastal batteries began to receive a taste of their own medicine and the fight developed into an angry brawl, casualties being taken on both sides. Once again Englishman fought Frenchman as if they were back in the days of Nelson and Napoleon.

De Gaulle, realizing that another Oran and Mers-el-Kebir tragedy was in the making, decided to abandon his attempt to capture the great West African port. He approached an angry Cunningham and asked him to signal the defenders that he was stopping the bombardment "at the request of General de Gaulle."

De Gaulle was attempting to save his face. That much was obvious to Admiral Cunningham—but he did not object. Well aware by now that Dakar could only be taken at the cost of heavy losses to his ships and crews, he agreed. One hour later, the British ships with their cargoes of French and British soldiers were sailing back into the Atlantic from whence they had come.

The expedition had been a total failure. Once again, in French eyes, Churchill's Britain had been shown to be the "perfidious Albion" of bitter French historical tradition. For his part, de Gaulle was now hopelessly compromised as a renegade, an opportunist Frenchman in English pay, who did not hesitate to shoot his own fellow countrymen.

Many years later de Gaulle would write in his memoirs: "The British being a practical people could not understand how and why the authorities, naval forces, and troops at Dakar expended such energy upon fighting against their compatriots and against their allies at a time when France lay beneath the invader's boot." But for de Gaulle it was no mystery. He knew why Frenchman was fighting Frenchman, and he blamed it on one person: the aged Marshal Pétain—one time "hero of Verdun," godfather of his own child, and now head of the puppet Vichy Government in unoccupied France. Pétain, wrote de Gaulle, "would never fail to misuse, against the interests of France, the courage and discipline of those who were in subjection to [him]."[3]

That had been in 1940. Slowly peace had returned to French Africa, remote from the fighting in Europe and in the Western Desert. A handful of French officials, protected by an army 150,000 strong and observed by 200 German and Italian officers of the Armistice Commission, continued to govern these immense territories as they had done for nearly a century. French North Africa seemed to disappear from the political map, a peaceful backwater in a world torn apart by war.

But one month after the United States entered the war in December 1941, and started to send the first American troops to Britain for the coming battle with Germany, the subject of French North Africa began once more to feature in the dis-

cussions of Anglo-American politicians and soldiers. For
Winston Churchill, who wanted to avoid the bloody cross-
Channel confrontation with Germany as long as possible,
French North Africa offered the ideal springboard for
launching an attack on what he termed "the soft underbelly of
Europe."

The French, however, had 150,000 trained soldiers plus
200,000 reservists stationed in that part of the world, and
Churchill, the supreme realist, knew from the experiences of
1940 in North Africa and Syria that the French would fight
back stubbornly if their empire were invaded. There had to be
some means of persuading them—peacefully—to join the
Anglo-American cause. But how was that to be done? Both
Britain and de Gaulle were hopelessly compromised in the
eyes of French officials and soldiers loyal to Vichy.

In the summer of 1942, just after his return from Moscow—
where Stalin, the Soviet dictator, had again insisted that the
Anglo-Americans should launch a Second Front in France
and take the heat off a hard-pressed Red Army—Churchill
invited the two most senior generals of the U.S. Army in
Britain to dinner at Number 10 Downing Street.[4]

Eisenhower and Clark were depressed about the future of
the planned operation in North Africa. Churchill, on the contrary, was highly elated. Wearing a smock and carpet
slippers, he gave his guests an excellent performance during
the meal. At one stage, he rose and went over to the wall and
rubbed his back up and down against it, like a dog with fleas.

"I guess I got them in Egypt," he remarked with a grin.

A little while later he rang the bell for his valet and asked
him to change his socks. Holding up one foot after another, he
allowed his socks to be changed for those of a lighter weight
without once pausing in his conversation.

The meal itself he ate with gusto, as an amused General
Clark noted. He bent so low over his bowl of soup that his
mouth was about two inches from the liquid, which he slurped
eagerly until his spoon was scraping the bottom of the bowl,
whereupon he bawled lustily for *"More soup!"*

But throughout the play-acting Churchill was hammering home his ideas on French North Africa.

"I want troops pouring into the new area," he growled at the two American generals. "I want them to come through the walls, the ceilings—everywhere! The French will go with us, if we are going to win, but they can't afford to pick a loser."

The hours passed. Now the drinking commenced. By midnight—with the inevitable brandy-and-soda in one hand, big cigar in the other—Churchill was saying: "When Stalin asked me about crossing the Channel I told him: 'Why stick your head in the alligator's head at Brest when you can go to the Mediterranean and rip his soft underbelly?'"

The drink had begun to have its effect on the two American generals. Clark's gloom had vanished. He told Churchill enthusiastically that they should have paratroopers landing with parachutes made of the Stars and Stripes banner, and aerial sky-writers buzzing across the North African sky inscribing the words, *"Vive la France! Lafayette, we are here again—for the second time!"*

But when that outrageous dinner party finally broke up at two in the morning, they were serious enough once more and a solemn Churchill warned the Americans: "Torch [the code-name for the attack on French North Africa] offers the greatest opportunity in the history of England. It is the one thing that is going to win the war. President Roosevelt feels the same way. We're both ready to help in any way we can. But the important thing, the first battle we must win is *the battle to have no battle with the French!"*

By the summer of 1942, there was a distinct possibility that Churchill's aim could be achieved. For the Americans—and they were the only Allies that the Vichy French would listen to now—had found a potential successor to the discredited General de Gaulle.

He was General Henri Giraud, an immensely tall, apolitical officer with gray hair and an old-fashioned handlebar moustache, who had fought bravely in World War One, knew

Africa well from the post-war colonial campaigns of the
1920s, and had commanded a French Army in 1940. There
was only one problem. Because he had refused to sign a
statement that he would never take up arms against the
Germans again, Giraud was currently imprisoned at Koenig-
stein Castle in the heart of the Third Reich!

But unknown to Robert Murphy, Roosevelt's special envoy,
who was desperately trying to find a substitute for de Gaulle
in unoccupied France,[5] Giraud had plans of his own. Wounded and captured by the Germans in World War One, he had
escaped from a German military hospital and returned to
active service. Now a quarter of a century later and in his late
forties he had decided to repeat that exploit, with the active
assistance of French Army Intelligence.

Locked away in his remote castle prison in Saxony, Giraud
had been carefully collecting the string with which the Red
Cross parcels intended for high-ranking French prisoners
were bound. At night in his cell, the former army commander
had patiently woven these pieces of string into a makeshift
rope. His progress was agonizingly slow, for it required five
or six yards of string to make one yard of rope. But Giraud,
animated by his burning desire to return to France, persisted
until his hands were red and burning from working the rough
twine. Yard after yard he fashioned the rope that would
enable him to escape: the first vital ingredient in his bold plan.

In the spring of 1942 Giraud was ready. Using the home-
made rope he lowered himself down the steep side of the
Castle, praying that the plaited string from the Red Cross
parcels would not break and send him plunging to his death
far below. But his handiwork was good: the rope held, and
later that same night Giraud was boarding the first of a series
of German trains that would take him back home. Operation
Marianne, as French Intelligence called the great escape
plan, was well under way.

And it succeeded. Giraud managed to reach the sanctuary
of unoccupied France in spite of the hue-and-cry raised by his
escape.[6] But his reception was far from warm. Although he
had not sworn an oath of allegiance to the head of the Vichy

Government (as had all other French officers still in government service) it was to Marshal Pétain that Giraud now
reported. Pétain was not pleased. He wanted Giraud to return
to German captivity. The *Boche* might take reprisals, he said;
there were still over a million French prisoners in German
hands. Hitler even sent a special envoy who tried, with
honeyed arguments, to convince Giraud that he should go
back. Premier Pierre Laval told Giraud he had poisoned
Franco-German relations. They all wanted him to give himself up.

Giraud refused. Bound by oath neither to the Germans nor
to Marshal Pétain, Giraud began to organize French resistance against the Germans, preparing for the day when he
confidently anticipated American forces would land in
France.

But the Americans were not coming to France just yet.
While Giraud found himself on the run again—only this time
from his own people—Robert Murphy made contact with
him. Would the General be prepared to assist the Americans,
Murphy asked. Guraud said he would. Did he have any loyal
followers in Africa, Murphy wanted to know—men who had
power and could swing the French Army behind them?

Giraud said there was only one senior officer in the whole of
French North Africa in whom he had implicit trust and who
would be prepared to act as his representative in any discussions there. That man was General Charles Emmanuel Mast,
deputy commander of XIX Corps, a French infantry corps
stationed in Algiers.

It was because of General Mast that "the American Eagle"
and his colleagues had come all the way from England by
submarine; he was the reason for this clandestine rendezvous
on an Algerian beach on the night of October 22, 1942.

Clark's mission was to discover whether General Mast
could help the Anglo-Americans to win Churchill's first battle: *"the battle to have no battle with the French."*

General Clark's first problem had been to hide the three
commando officers. Although the British Army would form

the major part of the attacking force on the North African coast, the French had to believe that this was a wholly American operation.

By the early hours of the morning of October 23, the Englishmen and their boats were hidden in a downstairs room off the courtyard of a white colonial villa. Clark warned them to lock the door after they had concealed their boats and not to show themselves when any French officers appeared.

Clark's next problem was to calm their host, Monsieur Teissier, the nervous landowner who was risking his life by letting the Americans use his house. For there were spies everywhere: Arabs working for the German Armistice Commission; French agents spying for Pétain; others working for de Gaulle in London; Arabs and Frenchmen working for anybody who paid them enough.

The blood-red ball of the sun had started to climb above the horizon when the distant sound of automobile engines indicated that General Mast and his staff were approaching. Turning to his own staff, Clark gave them a final warning: whatever the outcome of the talks with Giraud's representative, they must not reveal the date of the Allied invasion of North Africa; at all costs, this had to remain top secret until the very last moment. By now even the American new boys knew that French security was lousy.

So from the very start the Americans misled the French. They were going to make the French believe that they, the French, had months to prepare for an African D-Day instead of a mere sixteen days. Indeed, while the French and the American were still conferring, slow American convoys were already beginning to leave the United States heading for Africa. Nor were the French allowed to know the exact locations selected for the troop landings.

The French conspirators were going into this with their eyes blindfolded. But not for long. Soon—all too soon—the French would be misleading the Americans, too. On this fine October day, the seeds of a mistrust were sown that would bear a bitter fruit. America's first dealings with France would ensure that Franco-American relations would be poisoned for the next two decades—perhaps even for the rest of the twentieth century.

General Mast and his staff reached Monsieur Teissier's villa promptly at five in the morning. Mast, brisk but nervous (after all, he was committing high treason by meeting the Americans like this), said in his poor English: "Welcome to my country." Little did he know that his actions this day would ensure that within twenty-five years it would no longer be "his" country. He and Clark shook hands and then, with Robert Murphy acting as interpreter, they adjourned for *petit déjeuner*—coffee, bread and jam, and canned sardines.[7]

Mast was very sincere, or so Clark thought. He told Clark that he would do anything the Americans wanted; and then he asked, over the sardines, "With reference to a hypothetical landing, how would you do it?"

Clark swallowed hard and explained, lying as he did so; for he knew that Mast thought he was talking about a landing in Southern France and not in North Africa.

At nine, the staffs got together and began their discussions. Mast kicked off by asking how big the American effort would be. Again Clark was forced to lie. He told Mast poker-faced that half a million Allied troops would come in, supported by 2,000 planes (in fact 112,000 American and British soldiers were put ashore in the first landing).

Mast was impressed. He suggested that Giraud, his chief, should be picked up by American submarine in Southern France and brought to Africa to command the whole operation. Clark asked why. Mast replied that he was afraid of a *German* attack on North Africa soon.

"If they do attack," Mast swore vehemently, "we will fight immediately, no matter how little we have to fight with."

Clark has not recorded his thoughts on this reply, but he must have been feeling distinctly uncomfortable, knowing as he did that it was not the Germans who were going to invade soon, but the Anglo-Americans!

The discussions went on. At midday the generals adjourned for lunch: chicken in hot spicy sauce prepared by their scared civilian host, Monsieur Teissier. Thereafter Mast was forced to return to duty in Algiers. When Clark saw him again, Mast would have been deprived of his command and disgraced as a traitor who had sold North Africa to the Anglo-Americans.

In the middle of that long October afternoon, while the two staffs discussed the various problems they envisaged for the coming "invasion of Southern France," the telephone suddenly shrilled. Monsieur Teissier answered it and gave a shriek of alarm. The police would be arriving in a few minutes.

Instantly all was hectic confusion. Officers ran back and forth. Some of the Frenchmen of Mast's staff changed into civilian clothing with a speed that Clark had seen "exceeded only by professional quick-change artists." Mast's staff started to disappear: some headed for the car, which took off with a furious burst of brakes and protesting rubber for Algiers; others dived through the windows and vanished into the brushwood surrounding the villa.

Now only three of them were left—Murphy and another American, and a single French officer from General Mast's entourage. Suddenly Clark remembered the commando officers in the room off the courtyard; their British uniforms would certainly give the game away. He ran to warn them, just as the police car began to crawl up the steep drive to the house. (It later transpired that the gendarmes had been alerted by Monsieur Teissier's Arab servants that something strange was going on at the villa.)

Hastily the three British officers were ushered into a wine cellar—"empty unfortunately," as one of them recalled long afterward—where they were joined by the five Americans. The trapdoor was lowered on them and barrels were rolled on top, with dust sprinkled over the planks so that the entrance to the cellar was completely hidden. When the gendarmes burst into the villa, Monsieur Teissier's "guests" had disappeared.

Two hours passed. Bob Murphy and the two Frenchmen staged a convincing show for the suspicious gendarmes; they clanked bottles around and sang a little drunkenly, and Murphy—the staid diplomat, long happily married—indicated to the police with a knowing wink that they had women upstairs whom they would soon be visiting.

Down in the dusty darkness of the wine cellar, the eight officers crouched in nervous anticipation, expecting to be discovered at any moment. General Clark was tinkering with his carbine, clicking the mechanism up and down and muttering, "How does this work?"

"For heaven's sake put it down!" came a fierce whisper from one of the commando officers—not the usual manner of addressing a general, perhaps, but the commandos knew that the weapon was loaded.

Then Captain "Jumbo" Courtney of the commandos was seized by a fit of coughing. His companions tensed; if the gendarmes heard . . .

Courtney spluttered apologetically: "General, I'm afraid I'll choke, sir!"

"I'm afraid you *won't!*" Clark whispered back, and slipped him a wad of chewing gum to soothe his sore throat.

This quieted Courtney for a while. Later he remarked that American chewing gum seemed rather tasteless. Clark explained why: he had been chewing the gum himself to calm his nerves. The wad of gum he'd given Courtney had been in his own mouth.

At long last the gendarmes departed, and the eight men hiding in the cellar heard Murphy's urgent call from above.

"This is Bob. They've gone, but they'll be back."

"How long?" Clark asked anxiously.

"Just a little while. Better clear the house."

Clark decided that it was time to return to the little British submarine. He had achieved the main object of their mission: he had Mast's promise that he would help the Americans in any way he could, and that most French Army officers—though he couldn't vouch for the French Navy—would do the same. It would serve no purpose if he were captured now and the whole operation were compromised; and there was always the possibility that the French police were in the pay of the Germans. Treachery, it was clear, was standard operating procedure in French North Africa.

Urged on by a terrified Monsieur Teissier, who couldn't be rid of them fast enough now, the Anglo-American team retrieved their boats and made their way back down to the shoreline.

A stiff breeze was whipping up the waves, but Clark decided they would have to take a chance. He took off his trousers and his money belt—filled with gold coins worth several hundred dollars for bribes—and entered the water with Courtney just as the submarine surfaced only three-quarters of a mile offshore.[8] They stood waist-high in the sea, the undertow threatening to topple them at any instant, waiting for a lull between waves when they could launch their boat. Finally they managed to scramble into the boat; it looked as if they were going to make it. Then a huge wave crashed down on them, overturning the boat and flinging the two men into a swirling cauldron of foam.

The others plunged in to rescue them. To his chagrin, Clark heard one of the Englishmen cry: "Never mind the General—for heaven's sake get the *paddles!*"

Gasping for breath and soaked to the skin, the little party retreated to the cover of nearby woods to consider what to do next. From the villa there came word that the gendarmes had not yet returned. Clark decided to send a Frenchman, armed with a pocketful of gold, to bribe one of the Arab fishermen to take them out to the submarine in his boat. But the Arabs would have nothing of it; they were too frightened.

Clark began to worry. If he were captured the whole operation would be in jeopardy. The Germans would make short work of those troop convoys already in the Atlantic once they found out what was going on.

Someone suggested that they should try to obtain false

papers and a car and head for Spanish Morocco to the west, but Clark vetoed this idea. He radioed the submarine to stand by for another attempt, then retraced his steps back to the villa. His men were all cold, wet, and hungry, and the General decided that his first priority was to obtain dry clothing and food for them.

Monsieur Teissier was beside himself with terror. He wanted rid of Clark—at once! But Clark held out for clothes, bread, and wine. He got his way. He was just stuffing two bottles of red wine into his tight sweater—borrowed from the little Frenchman—when there was the sound of a car engine. The gendarmes were back.

Barefoot as he was, the General took off at the double. He dropped ten feet over a wall onto some shingle and yelped with pain as the pebbles slashed his feet. But at least he managed to save the bottles of wine. Now the eight American and British officers went to ground in the woods while the gendarmes repeated their search of Monsieur Teissier's house.

It was three-thirty the next morning before the police finally departed and the team could make another attempt to reach the submarine. Somewhere out there in the darkness, HMS *Seraph* was waiting for them. But the sea was just as rough as before, threatening to swamp their boats before they could reach the sub.

Then Courtney had an idea. When visiting the Gold Coast, he had once watched the natives launching their canoes in heavy seas. He explained his idea to the others: they would have to carry each boat out beyond the first line of surf, which was the most dangerous part, and hold it steady while two of them climbed into it.

First to go were General Clark and Captain Wright of the U.S. Navy. They flung themselves into the little boat and paddled furiously out to sea. The next pair were less fortunate. Time after time their flimsy craft was overturned by the angry white breakers; time after time the three British commando officers had to rescue the middle-aged American staff officers from the boiling surf, heave them back into their boat, and launch them again.

Finally they succeeded. All eight men were paddling out to the safety of the submarine, its conning tower clearly visible now, a stark black outline against the glittering sea. As the two commandos in the last boat were waiting to come alongside HMS *Seraph*, they glanced back at the land. Car headlights were bouncing along the coastal road, heading for the Teissier villa. The police were returning. The Americans and British had made it just in time.

Suddenly a huge wave caught one of the little boats and flung it against the submarine's hull. It broke apart and started to sink. Colonel Holmes—the former State Department man—grabbed frantically for support as the boat disappeared under the waves. A rating from the sub managed to get hold of him and hauled him up to safety, but the boat had sunk—and with it had gone a bag of vitally important documents that Holmes had been carrying.

Soaking wet and worn out after his exertions, General Clark now found himself in a quandary. He knew they had to get away before daylight, yet he didn't want to leave that bag behind. The documents it contained could, as Clark himself put it, "cause us and our associates ashore plenty of trouble." Among the bag's contents were some secret letters that Robert Murphy had given to Holmes to deliver in England; if found, they would reveal that the diplomat Murphy had been present at the secret rendezvous with General Mast. At the very least that would result in a major international scandal. So what was Clark to do? After all their efforts, was that stupid bag going to endanger the whole North African operation?

Lieutenant Jewell, the young English skipper of the submarine, made up Clark's mind for him. The sky was already beginning to glow a dirty white, indicating that dawn was not far off. They would have to submerge, Jewell said, before they were spotted by the police on the shore.

Reluctantly Clark agreed, and they went below. There, as the klaxons sounded and the pale-faced sweating sailors busied themselves with their tasks in the green-glowing gloom, Clark said to Jewell, "Haven't I heard somewhere about the British Navy having a rum ration even on submarines?" In contrast to the U.S. Navy which was "dry," Clark knew the Royal Navy was officially "wet."

"Yes sir," Jewell replied, "but on submarines, only in emergencies."

The craggy-faced, exhausted General forced a grin. "Well, I think this is an emergency. What about a double rum ration?"

"OK, sir. If an officer of sufficient rank will sign the order."

"Will I do?" Clark asked.

He would, and so the emergency rum ration—known as "Nelson's blood" to the eager matelots—was served to all aboard HMS *Seraph*, crew and passengers alike.

But even after the tense wearying events of that long day, Clark could not sleep. A couple of times he had to go to the "heads," bent almost double as he accommodated his height to the tight confines of the sub. What if those papers fell into the wrong hands, he kept thinking. In the end, he ordered Jewell to surface so that he could send a coded signal to Gibraltar, reporting the loss and urgently requesting Murphy to have the beach searched for that vital bag and its secret contents.

While Clark worried and fretted throughout that night and the following day, the submarine made steady progress toward Gibraltar, staying mainly on the surface to achieve greater speed. But Clark was growing impatient. He ordered Jewell to send a signal to Gibraltar requesting a flying boat to pick him and his officers up. At midday, the unwieldy-looking Catalina flying boat circled over the submarine and landed neatly on the sea beside it. Then, to the cheers of the crew, the Americans were transferred to the Catalina.

But although Clark put a good face on it, leaving the commando officers "with mutually cordial farewells and the promise of future meetings," he was a worried man. As soon

as the Catalina had taken off, he sent a long cable to his boss in
London, marked *"EISENHOWER EYES ONLY."* In it, he
described the successful rendezvous with General Mast and
stated that, in his opinion, "the bulk of the French Army and
Air Force [would] offer little resistance" to an Anglo-American invasion of French North Africa, although there would
be "initial resistance by French Navy and coastal defenses."
He mentioned the repeated raids by the French police, the
subsequent difficulties in embarking, and the loss of one boat.
The only thing that General Clark omitted to mention in his
cable was the loss of that all-important bag, the contents of
which might well compromise the whole operation. Now
there were exactly fifteen days to go before it all started and
Americans troops went into action in the West for the very
first time.

KASSERINE
First Blood

PART I

THE LANDINGS

Admiral Burrough berthed his flagship...and was glad to see that the harbor had suffered no serious damage and that a large crowd of all sorts were waving at him enthusiastically from every vantage point. It was an illusory view of a people, both French and Arab, whose main interest in the Allies was the profit to be made from them and who had no wish at all to be molested by war.

—Gregory Blaxland

one

On Saturday morning, January 26, 1942, a gray drizzly day typical of Northern Ireland, the flags were out at Dufferin Quay, Belfast. As the tenders started to nudge their way from the two transport ships, the *Straithaird* and the *Château Thierry*, which had braved the submarine-infested North Atlantic to bring the newcomers here, the band of the Royal Ulster Rifles started to play "The Star-Spangled Banner."

Slowly the dignitaries began to move forward in the drizzle, ready to welcome the first man ashore. They were the "top brass," the most distinguished figures in the whole of the province: a Duke, a Prime Minister, a Secretary of State for Air, a clutch of general officers—even the Inspector-General of the Royal Ulster Constabulary, whose men would soon have their hands full trying to contain the youthful exuberance of these "cousins from across the sea," as Mr. Churchill was currently calling them.

The Secretary of State for Air, Sir Archibald Sinclair, a tall lean man dressed in a black suit and wearing a stiff wing-collar, looking every inch an upper-class English gentleman,

39

addressed the new arrivals from the quay. From the prairies and towns of Iowa and the American Northwest they had come thousands of miles, he told them, not to sojourn among strangers but among grateful friends. Their safe arrival marked a new stage in the war.

Now the first American soldier to set foot on British soil since 1918 came ashore: a slightly bewildered Private First Class Milburn H. Henke from Hutchinson, Minnesota, of General Ryder's 34th Infantry Division. His hand was shaken, photographs were taken, the band played, the onlookers cheered, while he stood there a little overwhelmed by it all, with his old-fashioned World War One helmet tilted to one side and weighed down by his personal equipment.

Suddenly the welcoming dignitaries were startled to hear another military band playing—and then the soft shuffle of rubber-soled boots on the quayside, so unlike the harsh stamp of hobnailed British ammunition boots. As one they turned in surprise. A whole company of the 34th Infantry had somehow escaped the reception committee and were already marching smartly off to their new camp. Instead of being the first American soldier to land on British soil, PFC Henke was probably the hundred-and-first. Not only that, it turned out that Henke was of German origin. The first American "cousin from across the sea" had more relatives beyond the German Rhine than in the Mother Country!

Those first GIs of the 34th Infantry arrived in Britain at the low ebb of the war for the British. This was the third year of the war: a gray time in a gray age. Up to now the British forces had not achieved a single real, lasting victory. It had been defeat after defeat. Even as the hard-pressed Eighth Army was fighting for its very existence against Rommel in the Western Desert, a new enemy had appeared on the scene, scoring one success after another in the Far East. Hong Kong had fallen, Malaya had been overrun, and the great bastion of Singapore was about to be taken by the Japanese, with the greatest surrender of British troops ever recorded.

At home all was gloom, too. Due to the U-boat blockade

applied by German Admiral Karl Doenitz, rations were at their lowest ever. Butter was limited to two ounces per person per week. A civilian could count himself lucky if the weekly one egg per person ration was honored. There were long queues outside butchers' shops for offal. Even the traditional staple of the working class, fish-and-chips, was hard to come by. Doenitz's wolf packs were everywhere, sinking even fishing smacks. So the poor ate "scallops" (fried slices of potato) with their chips, instead of the traditional "one o' each."

Now, in Northern Ireland at least, the gloom was shattered by the arrival of thousands of well-fed, cheerful, noisy young men, who roared around in their jeeps and were as liberal with their money as they were with "the goodies" (as they called the wonderful foodstuffs they brought with them in such plenty).

"Ireland would be OK if only it had an umbrella over it," they would joke about the seemingly constant drizzle of Ulster—but the girls were all right; they seemed willing enough.

In Ballymena, County Antrim, so the story went, the first romantic encounter between an amorous American and an attractive colleen floundered due to the difficulties of the language.

"Say, honey," the sergeant asked hopefully, "what do you do about sex over here?"

"Oh," she supposed to have replied, "we do be having our tea about that time!"

But as more and more GIs of the U.S. V Corps started to pour into this remote backward province—still lit by gas for the most part and heated by turf—that particular barrier was speedily overcome, and public VD clinics, advertised by large notices giving details of these Early Treatment Stations, soon became a familiar feature of small-town living in Northern Ireland.

Naturally enough, perhaps, British soldiers stationed in Northern Ireland detested these men who would soon be their comrades-in-arms in the fighting in North Africa. The Yanks wore smart uniforms, with a collar and tie, as if they were "officers and gentlemen" in the British Army. They also wore soft rubber-soled shoes rather than heavy hobnailed boots like those worn by British soldiers; and instead of the poncholike cape of the Tommy, they were issued with a tidy fawn civilian-type raincoat to be worn in Ulster's persistent drizzle. Above all, the pay of the ordinary GI was nearly five times that of the average British soldier. No wonder, so the British thought, they got all the girls.

As soldiers, however, the British thought the Yanks were hopeless. They called their NCOs—sometimes even their officers—by their first names. They didn't march with "Bags o' swank!" and plenty of "Swing them arms there!" as did the British Army; they seemed to saunter along in a casual easy-going style. When they mounted ceremonial guard outside their camps in the evening, there was none of the traditional British Army "bull," commands of "Old guard!" and "New guard!" soldiers slapping their gleaming rifles in clouds of green blanco powder. Instead they leaned casually on their rifles, chewing gum, and smoking, even in the presence of the "OD" as they called officer of the day, the orderly officer (the Yanks seemed to abbreviate everything). The general opinion of the British troops in Ireland was that if this "shower" was typical of the whole of the U.S. Army, then "Thank God for the bleeding Royal Navy!"

The GIs weren't impressed by the Tommies either. To them the "Britishers," as they called them, were too class-conscious, their traditional respect for authority verging on servility. More importantly, this was the third year of war and the British Army had still not beaten Adolf. In early 1942 those brash young soldiers of the U.S. V Corps took little trouble to conceal their contempt of the British Army, with its long run of defeats since Dunkirk.

The GI's crack that he wanted a pint of beer "as quick as the British got out of Dunkirk" was widely quoted—but not the Tommy's answer: "Is that how the Yanks swam at Pearl

Harbor?" When that sentimental favorite of the time "There'll Always Be an England" was played at dances or on the giant Wurlitzer organ at the local cinema, the GIs would snigger: "Sure—as long as we keep it there for you!" The only real British victory of the war, the over-publicized "Battle of Britain" fought against the German Luftwaffe in 1940, was used by the Americans in a snide, cynical manner to mean their own personal battle—to conquer as many British girls as possible!

But as the tensions mounted between the soldiers of the two new Allies and over 30,000 GIs arrived in Ireland—including the U.S. 1st Armored Division, which one day would suffer such a terrible defeat in North Africa—a new commander landed in London, whose task it was to weld the British and American Armies together (and, for that matter, those of another half-dozen allies) and lead them into their first battle against the Germans. General Dwight D. Eisenhower had arrived!

For three days now, the girls had been waiting for the American brass to arrive. Each day they had reported to the motor pool in Central London at five-thirty in the morning and had waited till well after midday. But the whole of Britain was fog-bound and the authorities were not going to risk the lives of these important American generals by flying them down from Prestwick, Scotland, where they were stranded. But on the fourth morning the girls were informed that some "Very Important Persons" (as they were beginning to call high-ranking personages in London) were coming down by train and would be arriving at Paddington Station, although no one knew exactly when.

So the girls went to Paddington and waited again, Betty and Shiela and Kay, wondering which general they would get to drive, for an army driver's prestige depended on the rank of the uniform in the back seat. Betty already knew that her passenger was a three-star general, but there were also two lowly two-star generals among the party, and Kay Summersby, an Anglo-Irish divorcee with red hair and green eyes, guessed that she would be landed with one of them. In particular she had a feeling that her passenger might be one Major General Eisenhower.[1]

Standing patiently by their Humber staff cars in the courtyard of Paddington Station, with crowds of men in khaki and Air Force gray trudging by, laden with kit and weapons, Kay Summersby turned to her friend Shiela, an American girl married to a British officer.

"Surely *you've* heard of General Eisenhower?"

Shiela considered for a moment, then shook her head. "Eisenhower? No, never heard of him."

And neither had anyone else in London that day, when he made his first visit to the capital prior to becoming the Supreme Commander, responsible not only for the American Army in Europe but also for the British, the Canadian, and all the other Allied armies that would be involved in the coming invasion.

In that spring of 1942, the officer who would soon be known to half the world as "Ike" was still completely unknown outside the tight circle of the U.S. military. Even the previous autumn, when his star was already in the ascendant and he was photographed for *Life* magazine, the caption beneath the photo read, *"Lt. Col. D. D. Eisenberger."* As Eisenhower commented wryly, "At least the initials were right."

Now Eisenhower, with his ready grin, his liking for Westerns, mush with chicken gravy and hominy grits, who had never heard a shot fired in anger and had never commanded anything larger than a company in the whole of his long Army career, was in England to lick into shape the first American Army sent to Europe since 1918.

It was going to be a tough job, and Eisenhower knew it. On July 1, 1939, the total enlisted strength of the U.S. Army had been a mere 130,000 men (and this included the U.S. Army Air Corps, still not a separate service). By August 30, Congress had authorized the mobilization of the National Guard, followed six weeks later by the introduction of the draft, and thousands of young Americans flocked to the colors. By the time of Pearl Harbor some 1,500,000 Americans were in the Army.

They had swamped the handful of regular officers and noncoms available for training them, most of whom had never seen action themselves unless it had been in the trenches twenty-odd years before. It was not surprising, therefore, that the troops whom Eisenhower was now going to command in Britain were ill-trained, ill-disciplined, and emotionally unprepared for what was soon to come. Moreover, their senior officers were often over-age and overweight, while the younger ones were cynically dubbed "ninety day wonders" on account of the shortness of their training.

In that first month of his new command, Eisenhower flew to Northern Ireland to inspect the U.S. V Corps, taking with him General Mark Clark, who would be commanding the U.S. II Corps in England once it arrived from the States. There, the two major generals watched an exercise between British troops and Ryder's 34th Division. Eisenhower said he was pleased by what he saw, but Clark, who had been wounded as an infantry captain in World War One, was more critical. He thought the Americans "seemed fat and podgy in contrast to the lean, hard look of the British soldiers." He came to the conclusion that the II Corps "was going to have a period of gruelling training after it arrived in the United Kingdom to prepare for battle."[2] Unfortunately for the II Corps, Clark never managed to achieve that aim.

Throughout that spring and early summer of 1942, while the politicians and chiefs-of-staff in London and Washington bickered and fought and schemed about where exactly Eisenhower should employ his troops, and while Stalin in Moscow cried out for a "Second Front" in Europe, Eisenhower set about getting his Americans ready for the battle soon to come.

The first essential was constant, intensive training. Time was short. This new war demanded hard, trained soldiers. But Eisenhower recognized that the U.S. Army could never

turn the average American into a Prussian-type automaton;
so every commander, he said, should make sure that each man
under his command thoroughly understood "the reasons for
the exertion he is called upon to make . . . Any commander
should be summarily relieved who neglects this important
phase of training intelligent, patriotic Americans."[3] It was
equally important to maintain a high morale—but this could
not be achieved by pampering the men or lowering discipline
to permit easy living.

But in the end, as events would prove, Eisenhower failed.
Time was too short, the task too great, the political entangle-
ments forced upon him as Supreme Commander in London
too intense.

Writing after the Battle of North Africa was finally won in
the summer of 1943, American ex-journalist Engineer-
Captain Ralph Ingersoll, who had gone through the whole
bitter campaign, summed up his thoughts about the training
of the GIs who had fought in Africa: "It is the practice at home
to put troops through rigorous exercises called maneuvers.
During these maneuvers soldiers do sleep on the ground and
get wet in the rain. But maneuvers are for so many days, for so
many weeks, and at the end of them there are nice warm
barracks and the day-rooms and the U.S.O. to go back to and
in which to sit around and beef about how tough it all was.
This is an odd thing for a soldier who so intensely disliked his
own basic training to say, but if I were to pray for a miracle, it
just might be that every barracks in the United States would
burn down! Then the American Army in training might start
learning to live as it will one day have to live, with the sky for a
ceiling and the ground for a floor . . . An army trained that
way would be an army that was at home the day it arrived in
the field."[4]

The British soldiers under Eisenhower's command were, by
contrast, very well trained. Indeed, for the two years since
Dunkirk, the British Army in the UK had done little else but
train and drill. By 1942, an impartial observer of the British

Army might have thought the war had been forgotten and that the Army was concentrating on turning its wartime conscripts into regular peacetime soldiers. "Bull" (for "bull-shit") reigned supreme. As the cynical soldiers observed: "If it moves, salute it; if it doesn't, paint it!"

For months, years even, they had been drilled in the three-hundred-year-old tradition of the British Army, so that by now they went through the drill with the precision of professional chorus-girls. They marched everywhere: "*Swing them arms there! . . . Bags o' swank now! . . . Show 'em who yer are!*" They marched to eat. They marched to defecate. They marched to be entertained. They marched to bathe. They marched to fornicate—and they marched to ensure that there were no unpleasant results of that fornication. "On the command one, you will lower yer slacks. On the command two, you will take yer John Thomas[5] in yer right hand. On the command three, you will present it to the M.O. for inspection. Right, now—*One! . . .*"

And they polished, too. For hours on end, squatting on their bunks in their ancient unheated barracks, they scraped (illegally) at the thick serge of their battledress trousers with an old razor blade so that the flatiron could give them a crease; they "boned up" their heavy boots with red-hot spoons and toothbrush handles till they gleamed like mirrors; they "bulled" their badges and brasses until they could see their faces in them. And above all they blancoed; it seemed that their barracks were permanently enshrouded in the green fog of that obnoxious powder with which they cleaned their webbing.

By 1942 when Eisenhower became their Supreme Commander these British soldiers—regular and wartime conscripts—were tough, hard, well-trained men, who had been drilled to such an extent that they carried out orders given to them by superiors without the slightest hesitation.

But the British soldiers did have something in common with the new boys over from America: the great majority of them had never heard a shot fired in anger. A few of the older

ones had fought at Dunkirk, but that was about it. Neither
had their commanders, the men who would soon be leading
them into battle in North Africa, had any recent experience in
battle. General Evelegh, commander of the 78th Infantry
Division, had been just old enough to serve for a few weeks in
France in 1918 before being wounded. Since then he had seen
no action. General Keightley, commander of the 6th Armoured Division, had been too young to serve in World War
One and had been on the staff in 1940 in France. Their corps
commander General Allfrey had last seen action in 1932,
when he had won the D.S.O. quelling a rebellion in far-off
Kurdistan.

So—like Eisenhower, Clark, Patton, Ryder, and the rest of
the generals who would command the fighting troops in
North Africa—the British generals' experience of war was
either nonexistent or dated back nearly a quarter of a
century.

To send soldiers like these into action against the Germans,
hardened by years of desert fighting or the bitter struggle in
Russia, was a recipe for disaster.

In early July 1942, Eisenhower received his first personal
publicity in a national magazine. But the critical tone of the
article spoiled any pleasure he might have derived from the
event. The editors of *Life* began their story on Ike with this
forthright commend: "The U.S. Army, nearly eight months
after Pearl Harbor, has yet to deliver an offensive land attack
on any enemy anywhere." In another article in the same issue,
Life claimed that Russia was buying time for the Western
Allies at a cost of "tens of millions of its people." As the writers
pointed out, "Compared with this awful sacrifice, the war
effort of the Anglo-Saxon nations is so far pitifully puny."

Eisenhower would have agreed with these comments, but
his hands were tied. In Washington and London they were
still wrangling over exactly *where* to attack. In London,
Churchill favored North Africa. In Washington, General
Marshall —Head of the U.S. Army, to whom President

Roosevelt left a great deal of freedom on military matters—
preferred an effort focused on France. As for the American
naval chiefs, in particular Admiral King, they favored
neither North Africa nor France. They wanted America's
major effort to be concentrated on the other side of the world,
in the Pacific against the Japanese.

On July 16, General Marshall and his senior officers
arrived in England to thrash the whole matter out. The discussions went on till July 22. On that Wednesday, an unhappy
Marshall cabled Roosevelt that he and the British were dead-
locked. Roosevelt cabled back that Marshall had four options:
he could launch an attack on French North Africa together
with the British, or he could send the Americans in alone;
alternatively he could send American troops into Egypt to
fight under Montgomery, or run an operation through Iran
into the Russian Caucasus as a direct means of helping the
Soviets. *But he had to have American troops in action before the
end of 1942.*

The heat was on, not only from the press back home, but
now from the President himself. Marshall knew that public
opinion and the politicians were going to force his hand. He
held out for two more days, but on July 24 he gave in. Operation Torch was on.

Eisenhower would not attack across the Channel into
France but across the Mediterranean and the Atlantic into
French North Africa. For the first time since the French and
Indian wars of the eighteenth century, there was going to be a
joint Anglo-American offensive. All Eisenhower's work of the
previous six months, ever since he had been first appointed to
Marshall's staff, could now be tossed into the ashcan. Now he
had to start planning a completely new invasion and he had
only three months to do so.

Operation Torch proved to be a tremendous undertaking. The
naval phase alone was enough to take away the planners'
breath. Three separate but coordinated assaults were to be
made by 107,453 soldiers, who had to be ferried across

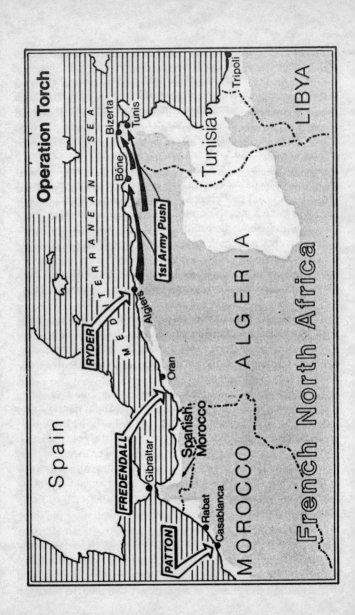

submarine-infested waters from distances of up to 4,500 miles in 111 transports escorted by no less than 216 warships.

From the United States would come a certain General George S. Patton, 57-year-old veteran of World War One, who had still not been loosed on the unsuspecting world. He would assault the port of Casablanca and capture French Morocco with some 40,000 men. His force would be named the Western Task Force.

From England would come the Center Task Force, commanded by General Fredendall, another 57-year-old who had last fought in World War One. But unlike Patton, Fredendall would have no luck. Four months after his II Corps had successfully assaulted Oran, he would be sent home "to train troops," to receive a hero's welcome—and to disappear from the pages of military history.

Finally there was the Eastern Assault Force, under General Ryder of the 34th Division, another veteran of World War One; their task was to assault the port of Algiers and ensure that Algeria fell into Allied hands. It was only here that British troops would take part in the landings, in the shape of the commandos and one brigade of the British 78th Division. But once the initial assault was successfully completed, the grandly named British First Army (at this stage it numbered only brigades), under General Sir Kenneth Anderson, its third commander since its inception, was to race five hundred miles eastward to capture the port of Tunis, prevent it from falling into German hands, and seize Tunisia, the most easterly French colony, for the Allied cause.

The problem of logistics, immense as it was, was gradually overcome by Eisenhower and his staff in London. But there was still the problem of the French. They had fourteen divisions, however poorly equipped, spread out over the three colonies, which outnumbered the Anglo-American effort by some 50,000 men. They would be in fixed positions; they knew the country; and they were supported by more than five hundred aircraft. As a worried Eisenhower wrote to General Marshall in the middle of September, two months after the

great decision had been taken: "If this Army [the French]
should act as a unit in contesting the invasion, it could . . . so
delay and hamper operations that the real object of the expedition could not be achieved, namely, the seizing control of the
north shore of Africa before it can be substantially reinforced
by the Axis."[6]

Clark's secret meeting with Mast in October seemed to
solve the problem. But in early November General Mast was
informed exactly *where* the Americans were going to land,
and he reacted angrily. As a very worried Robert Murphy
said in his cable, asking for the invasion to be postponed, the
French General was very surprised at the Americans' intentions and considered that such short notice amounted almost
to "an ultimatum of hostile action."

After all he had been through in order to reach an accord
with Mast, Clark blew his top.

Stamping up and down in his office, he dictated a vitriolic
message for Washington to send to Murphy. Mast should be
told, he said, "that we are coming as planned; that all hell and
the North African Army can't stop us; that if he uses the
information already furnished him on the operation as to the
time of its execution to our disadvantage either by regrouping
his troops to more effectively stop us, by disseminating the
confidential information Murphy has entrusted to him, or
otherwise betraying our cause, *we'll hang him higher than a
kite when we get ashore!*"[7]

Now there was no turning back. Everywhere in French
North Africa secret preparations were being made for the
arrival of the Americans.

The American OSS (mocked in Washington as the "Oh-So-
Shush-shush" or "Oh-So-Secret," the forerunner of the CIA,
which was well supplied with money for bribes, had "resistance" groups everywhere, assigned to beachheads and drop
zones. Those groups were equipped with flares to guide in the
invaders.

At Oran, an OSS agent removed demolition charges in a

tunnel connecting the port with the naval harbor of Mers-el-Kebir. Elsewhere, members of the genuine Resistance prepared to assassinate the two hundred German and Italian officers of the Armistice Commission.

At the five illegal radio stations operated by the OSS— *Yankee, Franklin, Pilgrim, Lincoln* and *Midway*—they waited for the BBC to transmit the vital signal: *"Allo Robert . . . Franklin arrive . . ."*

As soon as Mast and his staff heard these two phrases, they would spring into action to defuse any French resistance to the Allies, at least among the Army. For Mast now knew that the Americans had sent a submarine to bring Giraud from France to Gibraltar, and thence to North Africa, where he would take over Supreme Command not only of the French North African Army but of the American Army too. (So far Mast knew nothing about the British First Army.) Appeased by this news, Mast was prepared to co-operate once again.

In London the tension mounted. Eisenhower was bid "God speed" by the King himself. He spent a last weekend at Chequers with Churchill. On the Sunday evening he gave a small dinner party at his hideaway, Telegraph Cottage; it was his farewell party for his most intimate friends.

On the Monday, a typical dull gray November day in London, Kay Summersby drove Eisenhower to Addison Road Station, where he would catch a train to Southampton. From thence he would be transported by Flying Fortress bomber to his forward headquarters at Gibraltar.

"Well, Kay," Eisenhower said, "tomorrow's the day."

There was a flutter of good-byes in the blackout, a few tears, shouts of "Good luck!" and "God speed!" and then the train bearing the staff and their chief disappeared into the night.

Kay Summersby—who now enjoyed a much more privileged position than a mere civilian "chauffeuse" and knew that she would soon be going to North Africa herself—spent the following day mooning around Ike's office at 20 Grosvenor Square. The atmosphere in the near-empty office was "that of a theater after the show's over," she said.[8]

Suddenly the phone rang. It was General "Beetle" Smith, Eisenhower's red-haired, hot-tempered Chief-of-Staff. They had arrived safely at Southampton, but the Flying Fortresses at the nearby Bournemouth airdrome were grounded; the weather was "too lousy" to fly. So the whole party was on its way back to London for the day.

Eisenhower was hidden back at Telegraph Cottage with his principal staff officers. All of them were nervous—as bad as expectant fathers, as one irreverent officer expressed it to Kay Summersby, and she herself felt "as nervous as a pregnant nun."

Black coffee disappeared by the pint. Everyone chain-smoked. Even the usually imperturbable Eisenhower was edgy. Dinner was silent and glum. In the end, the whole party traveled into London to Wardour Street, the heart of the capital's commercial film industry. To calm their nerves, they were going to be given a private showing of a new movie straight from the States: the latest Bob Hope and Bing Crosby comedy, costarring Dorothy Lamour.

The lights dimmed. The high-ranking audience started to relax. The music commenced and the titles rolled. No one laughed, so it is recorded, when they saw the name of the movie being shown in secret in this VIP sneak preview. It was *Road to Morocco!*

two

General George Patton—one day to be known to the world as "Blood and Guts" (*"yeah, our blood and his guts,"* his Third Army GIs would quip bitterly)—went to war again in a defiant mood. Day by day, as that October of 1942 drew to a close, the tall graying general, who had last seen action in 1918, prepared for his departure to battle.

On October 20, Patton made out his will, enclosing a letter to his wife that was to be opened "only when and if I am definitely reported dead." With it there was another note for his brother-in-law, lawyer Frederick Ayer.

The note to Ayer did not make very encouraging reading. Patton was going into battle with no illusions, in spite of the dramatic language it was couched in: "The job I am going on is about as desperate a venture as has ever been undertaken by any force in the world's history." He asked Ayer to look after his family if anything happened to him.[1]

Next Patton went to see the President. Unlike most of his brother officers in the Regular Army, Patton was independently wealthy, and he had friends in high places. The President was puzzled when Patton put on one of his customary shows of bombast: "Sir, all I want to tell you is this," he declaimed. "I will leave the beaches either a conqueror—*or a corpse!*"

Paying his last respects to General Marshall, Patton repeated the same statement; but that craggy-faced introvert knew his "Georgie" Patton, and this time Patton's fine words met the skeptical reception they deserved.

"Black Jack" Pershing, commander of the American Expeditionary Force in World War One, was next on Patton's visiting list. General Pershing, once so tough and ramrod straight, was now confined to a hospital bed in the Army's Walter Reed Hospital. At first, the man under whose command Patton had had his first taste of action—in Mexico back in 1916—did not recognize Patton. But in the end he did, and just before he left, Patton kissed Pershing's hand and asked for the old man's blessing. "Black Jack" (he had acquired his nickname when he commanded black cavalry soldiers at the beginning of the century) told Patton to kneel. Patton did so. Pershing squeezed his hand weakly and whispered, "Goodbye, George. God bless you and keep you and give you victory."[2]

A final visit to the War Department in Washington, a last lunch with the long-suffering Mrs. Patton, and he was off by plane to the port of Norfolk, Virginia. On October 23, 1942, he boarded the force flagship, the cruiser *Augusta*, which was going to be his home for the next two weeks—until his 40,000 men finally "hit the beaches" in faraway French Morocco. At 0230 hours the next morning, the great invasion fleet slipped anchor and headed for the open sea. Patton was on his way to war again.

The fleet made a grand sight, spread over many miles of glittering blue sea. Thirty transports and cargo vessels, surrounded by forty destroyers, weaving in and out like sheep dogs. Beyond them, the heavy cruisers: the *Cleveland*, the *Brooklyn*, and the *Augusta* with General Patton and the naval commander Admiral Hewitt aboard. And, dimly glimpsed in the distance, the battlewagons: the *Texas*, the *New York*, and the newly commissioned *Massachusetts*. Overhead, Navy dive-bombers and Wildcat fighter planes roared and zoomed upward as they were launched from the *Ranger's* flight deck to provide the great convoy's eyes and ears in these dangerous waters of the North Atlantic.

But where were they going?

During the day, the soldiers of the 9th Infantry and 2nd Armored divisions who were going to make the initial landing were either asleep—the ships were so overcrowded that the men slept on a rotation basis, hammocks being assigned to the men for eight hours at a time—or too busy to worry. The officers kept them scrambling up and down rope ladders rigged fore and aft of the transports till they could climb them like monkeys. But at 1700 hours sharp the cry would go through the ships, "Close all battle ports!", whereupon the ships would immediately settle down into a total blackout, with the final order of the day crackling over the loudspeaker like a bugler blowing taps, "The smoking lamp is out on all weather decks!" Then the sweating young men—crowded tight in the fetid holds littered with weapons and equipment, the bunks reaching up four, even six high—began to talk. *Was it Africa they were heading for? But where? Egypt, perhaps, to help the Limeys? Nah, once out in the middle of the Atlantic, they'd change course and start to sail round the Cape for . . . Yeah— head for where?* The choice was limitless.

On the evening of Tuesday, November 3, 1942, while Eisenhower and Kay Summersby were enjoying the antics of Hope and Crosby in that dingy Wardour Street cinema in far-off London, the troops were finally told where they were going. One former fighter pilot from World War One, Major Charles Codman—a "retread," as the older officers called back into service were rudely designated—later recalled how the news was broken on board the transport ship *Ancon*.[3] The loudspeakers crackled metallically and a voice announced that Major Gardner, commander of the troops aboard the *Ancon*, would read a message from the commanding general.

"We are now on our way to force a landing on the coast of northwest Africa," Major Gardner told them, reading the address that Patton had prepared. "Our mission is threefold: first, to capture a beachhead; second, to capture the city of Casablanca; third, to move against the German wherever he may be and destroy him . . . We may be opposed by a limited number of Germans," he added, admitting that it was not known whether the French African Army would contest their landing. And the message ended in ringing, typical Patton style: *"The eyes of the world are watching us . . . God is with us . . . We will surely win!"*

No one cheered.

Meanwhile, as the convoy plowed steadily across the heaving Atlantic, Patton predicted to his staff officers that "the goddam Navy" would mess things up "as usual"; according to him, "Never in history has the Navy landed an army at the planned time and the right place!"

By now, the troop ships carrying the two assault forces that would be coming from the British Isles were preparing to sail or had already sailed from the more distant Scottish port of Greenock.

With the men of the 34th Infantry Division and that most famous of all American Army units, "the Big Red One," the U.S. 1st Infantry Division, who would be landing at Oran and Algiers, there were two British units: the 6th Commando Unit (including Randolph Churchill, Churchill's son, acting as Intelligence officer) and Brigadier Cass's 11th Brigade of the 78th Division, known as "the Battleaxe" on account of its divisional insignia.

Colonel McAlpine's 6th Commando Unit was as unblooded as the American units with which it was sailing, apart from a few raids on the coast of France, and the commandos were not particularly heartened by the address that General Ryder made to them and their comrades of the U.S. Rangers. A painfully thin, gray-haired, slightly stooping man, Ryder was commanding general of the 34th Infantry Division and overall commander of the attack. He had last seen action as a battalion commander in 1918. Now in his late fifties, he was some ten years older than most of the British generals, and given to the same sort of rhetoric as Patton. Pointing the pipe he affected at the tough young Americans and Britons, he proclaimed: "Some of you will not make the beaches! *But you will be immortal!*"[4]

With that the ships' sirens began to shrill, anchor chains clattered up out of the water, and slowly the great convoy started to move off, while the troops started wondering about whether or not they would achieve immortality. It was, as the chronicler of the commandos put it, "a subject of much speculation during the voyage."

On November 1, they found out. On that Sunday morning, the infantry commanding officers were handed sealed envelopes by the ships' captains and ordered to open them so that they could brief their officers and men. The contents of the envelopes came as a bombshell, even to those suffering now from chronic sea sickness.

Here they were in mid-Atlantic, due to assault the shores of a country of which they knew nothing save that it was neutral, and the British troops were part of an American division whose commander and men were enigmas to them. All that most of the commandos and Cass's infantry—the Lancashire Fusiliers, the East Surreys, and the Northamptons—knew about the Yanks was that they chewed gum, had funny ideas about discipline, ate buckets of ice cream (which the English hadn't even seen since 1939), and were grossly overpaid.

Ryder did try to relieve the situation. He appointed two of his officers aboard each transport ship to tell the British troops about the U.S. Army, and in particular about the 34th "Red Bull" Infantry Division.

But the infantrymen of the 2nd Lancs and the 1st East Surreys, both regular battalions, weren't particularly interested in the divisional history of the 34th. They'd heard enough regimental histories, sitting to attention in their barracks of a Wednesday afternoon, "making do and mending," sewing on buttons and darning socks while a corporal recounted the daring exploits of their forerunners. They were seasoned troops, who had done well in France. Moreover, some of them suspected that this operation might turn out to be another "Fred Karno's" as Dunkirk had been—a total mess, in other words. And it was no use their officers reassuring them that the Lancashire Fusiliers had won "six Victoria Crosses before breakfast" at the Gallipoli landings back in 1915, for that invasion, just like this one, had been the brainchild of "Old Winnie"—and what a slaughter that had been!

But Cass's infantry need not have worried. They weren't going to be slaughtered—at least, not yet.

Deep in the bowels of the Rock of Gibraltar, Eisenhower and his staff waited tensely for news of the landings. They were housed in a 500-yard-long tunnel bored through solid rock, with offices opening off the end. Eisenhower and his deputy, Clark, who had done so much to make Operation Torch possible, were closeted in an office only eight feet square, containing two desks and a cot on which one of them could sleep if necessary.

Not that either man was particularly inclined to sleep while all three invasion convoys plus the back-up convoys (including Kay Summersby) were at sea. Even if the Mediterranean were not the "Axis Lake" that Mussolini proudly proclaimed it was, this could still be a very dangerous stretch of water, as Ike would soon find out.

But the danger presented by Doenitz's U-boats to his convoys was only one of Eisenhower's problems. On his arrival, the governor of Gibraltar, General Mason-MacFarlane,[5] had greeted him with bad news. A British officer had been picked up dead by the Spaniards—and he had had the complete plans of Operation Torch "in his back-pocket"! Admittedly the Spanish authorities had returned the body later, complete with documents. But what if Spanish Intelligence, known to be in the pay of Admiral Canaris's *Abwehr*,[6] had passed the information on to Berlin? And what if Hitler then ordered the divisions he had stationed in France to drive through Spain—

with or without the consent of General Franco, the Spanish dictator—and into Spanish Morocco? The whole operation could be at risk.

There was also the question of the quality of Eisenhower's troops, untried in battle and commanded by generals whose last experience of combat command had been nearly a quarter of a century before. Much later he would write of his doubts, as he sat there deep below the Rock: "The key to success was the quality of leadership we had provided for our troops. The men were well armed and partially trained by now, and as Americans they had both the initiative and the ingenuity that, fed by courage, could decide the course of battle—if their leaders, from platoon to division, were men who could inspire them to their best. *The outcome was far from sure.*"[7]

General Clark, who shared that tiny office with him, had his own worries. He was particularly concerned about the attitude of the French. Everything depended upon Giraud arriving in time at the Rock and agreeing to control the various French military and civilian factions in French North Africa. But where the hell was Giraud, fretted Clark, and would he agree to do what the Allied commanders wanted?

On November 5, just before leaving England, Clark had received a message that Giraud would board the submarine *Seraph*, now commanded by U.S. Navy Captain Wright, in the Gulf of Lions. Since then nothing had been heard of the little sub that had taken Clark on his own wild adventure to Algeria the previous month. Had it been sunk?

On the morning of November 6, Clark received a visit from British Admiral Sir Andrew B. Cunningham—known behind his back, because of his initials, as "old ABC." He strode into Clark's office dressed in a turtleneck sweater and gumboots, radiating confidence and encouragement. He laughed at Clark's fears about Giraud.

"He's thrown his coat over the fence," he snorted. "He'll do what he is told!"[8]

Eisenhower joined in the discussions. The question was

brought up of whether General Mast would carry through the
plan agreed upon in October, if Giraud were delayed or
refused to go along with Ike's plans.

Again Cunningham pooh-poohed the Americans' fears. "He
must," he said decisively. "He's gone too far to draw back."

Clark and Eisenhower began to feel better. Their optimism
was further boosted when a signal arrived from Captain
Wright at midday. It read, *"Task done . . . radio failing."*

Giraud, who had escaped from Germany and had been on
the run for nearly six months now, had ended his long odyssey.
He was on his way to Gibraltar.

On the afternoon of November 7, with his convoys ready to
start landing soon, Eisenhower had what he later called "one
of my most distressing interviews of the war."

Giraud was received by Eisenhower and Clark in their
underground office. He was dressed in rumpled civilian
clothes, his cheeks were more sunken than ever and his beautiful handlebar mustache was drooping lamentably. At first
sight he hardly seemed "a figure that would fit easily into the
important niche in history that might be awaiting him," as
Clark later commented.[9]

The tall Frenchman was patient and dignified as they all
exchanged formal greetings. But the Americans soon found
that Giraud was stubborn, too.

Outside their office, the red lamp was switched on to indicate that Eisenhower did not want to be disturbed and, with
Colonel Holmes as interpreter, they got down to business.
Eisenhower did all the talking at first. He explained that he
had prepared a message stating in vague terms that the
U.S.A., anticipating a German attempt to seize French North
Africa, was intervening first. Giraud's role was merely to
agree to the statement, "I resume my place of combat among
you" (the French Army).

Giraud sat up and the Americans waited.

His first words shocked them. "Now," he said formally,
"let's get it clear as to my part. As I understand it, when I land

in North Africa, I am to assume command of all Allied forces and become the Supreme Allied Commander in North Africa."[10]

Clark gasped. Eisenhower managed to keep a poker-face. Here was this French General, who had been out of circulation for two years, demanding his own post to command troops in an invasion of which he knew nothing, except that it would be taking place very soon. "There must be some misunderstanding," Eisenhower said cautiously.

There was no misunderstanding.

For the next three hours the Americans worked on Giraud. As Clark reasoned, Mast might have promised Giraud anything and everything to persuade him to support the scheme to wrest French Africa from Pétain. Now the chickens were coming home to roost. Giraud simply refused to sign the statement.

In the end they gave up. Giraud was sent away to have dinner with Mason-MacFarlane. Clark and Eisenhower, worn out by the discussions, grabbed something to eat, had their bedrolls moved into the office and prepared for a long night as messages started to flood into their little headquarters. The warning order had just come in that Operation Torch would commence on the following morning.

Ryder's force had arrived. From seven miles off the coast, they could see a myriad of tiny lights twinkling along the shore on both sides of Algiers. It was obvious that they had achieved complete surprise. The French were not expecting them—or perhaps they were; perhaps they were just waiting for them to step ashore peacefully, with flags flying and brass bands playing!

Brigadier "Copper" Cass, the fiery little man commanding the British 11th Brigade, who had won a second D.S.O. in Norway in just such an operation as this back in 1940, was taking no chances. Punctually at 2350 hours he set off with his assault companies, two from the Surreys (on the right) and two from the Northamptons (on the left), their small packs bulging with two days' worth of rations—bully beef, sardines, and, naturally, being British soldiers, "compo char"[11]—just in case. Behind them the follow-up companies, waiting to descend into the scramble nets, began to sing, softly but jubilantly, for they had just heard the first details of Montgomery's great victory over Rommel at El Alamein. Now they felt they were going to achieve a similar victory on this side of Africa.

Further north, closer to the great port of Algiers itself, MacAlpine's commandos were also preparing to disembark. The commandos had undergone a surprising transformation. They had been forced to part with their beloved green berets. Now they all wore the American basin-shaped steel helmet, together with liner, and American olive-drab uniform complete with the Stars and Stripes sewn on the shoulder. For the next twenty-four hours, the 6th Commando had become pseudo-Americans in order not to offend the delicate sensibilities of the French, for whom they had come so far to "liberate from the Nazi yoke."

Now the Americans of Ryder's 39th and 168th Regimental Combat Teams prepared for their landings, too. Unlike the British, who had seen some action, many of the American officers who crouched there in the glowing darkness, queuing for their turn to board the assault boats, had waited a whole lifetime for this moment.

Year in, year out, throughout the depressed thirties, when the U.S. Army had been almost forgotten, starved of money and equipment, regarded by civilians as a last refuge for fools, reactionaries, and the work-shy, they had "soldiered on." They had plodded through the routine of peacetime soldiering, hidden away in some remote garrison town. They had sweated through morning parades under the harsh Texas sun, choked through the humid heat of Florida on maneuvers, hiked through the dust-bowl of the Midwest. On Saturday nights at the Post's Officers Club, they had listened to the same old people making the same boring small talk; they had regularly drunk themselves into trouble; they had made the usual passes at someone else's wife. On Monday mornings, with aching heads, they had been faced with the same old charges: drunk in public, brawling in a bar, insubordination to a noncom. Year in, year out . . .

Suddenly in 1941, these permanent "first looeys" and captains, who were already beginning to think about pensions, carpet slippers and leisurely rounds of golf, were magically transformed into majors, "bird colonels," even brigadier generals. Now they found themselves commanding hundreds or even thousands of men, where before it had been only scores. But these draftees they commanded were unknown quantities to them after the hard-bitten "old heads" of the Regular Army. These conscripts were "drugstore cowboys," "canteen commandos," products of "greetings from Uncle Sam," who had stumbled into their draft boards with farewell hangovers, their women's tears still damp on their jackets, and had become what Hanson W. Baldwin, the military writer of *The New York Times*, described at the time as "a partly organized rabble of khaki-wearing civilians."

The regular officers had been training these same "drugstore cowboys" for two years now, first in the States and then in Northern Ireland. They had taught them all they knew. Yet there was one thing they could not teach them, for their own experience of it was limited to what they had read about in books or heard from the lips of older men: *how to stand up and react under fire!*

This was the moment of truth—for themselves as well as for their soldiers. At 0130 hours precisely, they would be going into action for the first time. So they waited in that velvety darkness beneath the stars of Africa while the password was given out, whispered from man to man in voices that were suddenly dry and strained. The password seemed appropriate enough for that Army. It was straight from the comic books, the famed cry of that masked fighter for honor and justice in the Old West, "the Lone Ranger." The password was *"Hi-ho, Silver!"* And the answer was *"Away . . . !"*

The lights were also blazing at Fedala, near Casablanca in French Morocco, where Patton's main thrust was to land, and the swell, which the Navy had worried a great deal about, was only moderate. Contrary to Patton's gloomy prediction, the U.S. Navy had brought his force to the right spot, dead on time: at exactly seven minutes to midnight. Now there were four hours to go before his men landed.

From the bridge of the *Augusta* Patton could see the whole city shimmering with light; he could even make out the old Arab quarter, around the wall of which the European city had grown in a semicircle. The city's broad palm-lined avenues were clearly defined by the street lights. All was calm, peaceful, and harmless. It was clear that the French were not expecting him, save for those few who were in the plot to take over the country without a shot being fired.

Dressed in gleaming riding boots, custom-tailored breeches, and his famous lacquered helmet, Patton kept out of the way of the naval officers as they prepared to launch the first four scout boats, equipped with powerful infrared flashlights and small radio sets, which would direct the main landings. He knew that at this stage of the business he was superfluous. He would come into his own once his soldiers had landed on the beach. Yet, as his biographer Ladislas Farago records: "Those crucial last hours subdued him and made him sentimental almost to the point of tears. He felt intense pangs of concern for the men in the scout boats on their suicide mission."[12]

But his men were in good heart, in spite of their commander's fears. As Sergeant Jim Webster of the 1st Battalion, 504th Engineers, put it, they were expecting to be welcomed "with brass bands." If anything had gone wrong, they reasoned they would have known it by now.

The man in command of Patton's old division—"Hell on Wheels" (the 2nd Armored)—General Harmon had a similar "comforting feeling." At Safi, where he was to land, the lighthouse was still shining away brightly, indicating that those on shore were still unaware of their approach. That silver white beam shining out to sea, almost illuminating the stationary invasion fleet every few seconds as it swung round, made

Harmon feel at ease. For he knew his troops were opposed by 1,000 French soldiers and four 130mm coastal guns with an estimated range of 19,000 yards. Harmon had fought alongside French soldiers in World War One and he had a healthy respect for the efficiency of French artillery. Hadn't old "Black Jack" Pershing's American Expeditionary Force armed themselves with the French seventy-five's because they were the best cannon available in those days?

Midnight approached. Still all was calm. Inside the bowels of the hot, malodorous transports and warships, the sweating radio operators hunched over their sets, finely adjusting the dials, while French-speaking officers stood by, trying to pick up local French stations that might give some clue to the French defenders' intentions.

With dramatic suddenness, at precisely midnight, the unmistakable voice of President Roosevelt, broadcasting from Washington and being translated into French as he spoke, came on the air. The operators and French-speaking officers looked at one another in consternation. What the devil was going on? They were soon enlightened.

"Allo Maroc... Allo Maroc... Le Président des Etats Unis s'est addressé cette nuit..."[13]

And there it was—that fine, rich, confident drawl, well-remembered from his fireside chats. "My friends, my friends who suffer night and day under the crushing Nazi yoke, I speak to you as one who in 1918 was in France with your army and navy... All my life I have held a deep friendship for the people of France. I know your farms, your villages, your cities. I know your soldiers, your professors, your workers... We arrive among you with the sole objective of crushing your enemies. We assure you that once the menace of Germany and Italy has been removed we shall quit your territories. I appeal to your realism, to your self-interest, to French national ideals. Do not, I pray you, oppose this great design. Lend us your help wherever you can, my friends, and we shall see again that glorious day when liberty and peace once more reign over the world. *Vive la France, éternelle.*"[14]

That powerful ringing appeal ended in a flurry of rapid French, and over the fleet a rocket exploded, fired by one of the destroyers, scattering across the African sky a firework semblance of "Old Glory."

General Harmon cursed his president. Well, the French certainly knew they were coming now. That comforting beam from the lighthouse suddenly went out.

Colonel Holmes could translate no more. It was midnight and he was exhausted. Now Clark took over, with his fractured French, and he no longer attempted to be polite to the stubborn French general, who had now returned from his dinner with Mason-MacFarlane. Giraud was still obstinately insisting that he should take command of the North African operation, although it was already beginning. He was simply not prepared to accept a subordinate role.

"But what would the French people think of me?" he kept saying. "What about the prestige of Giraud? What about my family?"

While the others slumped wearily around in the cramped underground office, Clark began to get tough. He told Giraud that he could take over all French forces in North Africa in due course, but he could not be appointed Supreme Commander. He knew nothing of the plan, the men, the operation.

"After all," he pointed out, " *we* made all the military preparations."

But, proud and completely unrealistic like so many of the French generals that Clark would be encountering over the next couple of years, Giraud drew himself up to his full six foot three and said, "Then I shall return to France."

"How are you going back?" Clark asked softly.

"By the same route I came here."

"Oh no you won't," Clark snapped grimly. "That was a one-way submarine. You're not going back to France on *it!*"

For a while the discussion died away. Outside in the corridor, telephones had started to ring and excited clerks were hurrying back and forth. Something was happening. But

Clark and Eisenhower were too preoccupied with the problem at hand to notice.

It started to dawn on Clark that perhaps Giraud was not so unimaginative as he looked. Perhaps he was playing a waiting game. "He wanted to see how things would work out in our invasion," Clark recalled later; "he was planning to stall along for a couple of days and then, if all went well with our attacks, come around to our viewpoint."[15]

Clark tried again. He attempted to put over the idea that Giraud should not let his personal ambitions and interests stand in the way of the best interests of France. But even this ploy failed. In disgust Clark turned to a weary Colonel Holmes, who was slumped in one corner.

"Tell him," he barked in his best parade-ground voice, face flushed with anger, "If you don't go along, General, you're gonna be out in the snow—on the seat of your pants!"

Eisenhower, always concerned to find a middle way, intervened. He suggested that as they were getting nowhere they should all turn in for a few hours sleep. When Giraud agreed and went, Eisenhower and Clark sent a long message to Washington, expressing their "bitter disappointment" at Giraud's attitude. They ended the message on a very pessimistic note: *"Latest news that we have been able to gather indicates that we may expect considerable resistance, which, if true, shows that Mast, operating in the name of Giraud, has not been very effective. The Chief-of-Staff of the Oran division has just reported that their plans have been discovered and that an intense alert is being conducted."*[16]

Then, just before the two commanders turned in for an hour, completely exhausted, they received their first message from Patton. In it he reported his anger at the Roosevelt speech, but also that the surf at Casablanca wasn't as bad as expected. Nothing was going to stop *him* from landing, Patton said; if he couldn't land on the west coast, he'd find somewhere else to land—even if it was in neutral Spain!

As Clark recalled many years later, "We liked the sound of that message."

Finally they slept, Ike and the American Eagle, tossing uneasily in their narrow cots, while up above the first German reconnaissance plane droned toward the Rock, trying to find out what was going on and why there were so many ships passing through the Straits.

They had done all they could. The actors all knew their parts, the scene was set, the drama could begin . . .

three

By now half the commandos' assault craft were sinking or having engine trouble. The commanding officer himself, Colonel MacAlpine, was heading for the beach in a craft half under water, while the rest of his men were busy making use of their newly acquired American helmets, baling for their very lives. Everything was confusion. The commandos' boats were spread out all over the place, most of them hopelessly lost; only a fifth of the assault craft had made contact with the launch that was to have led them to their landing site.

Suddenly searchlights flicked on all along the shore. Icy cold fingers of light began to part the darkness. A heavy machine gun started to chatter like an irate woodpecker. An instant later cherry-red flame stabbed the night. The French were firing at them!

The confusion increased. Carried well off course, three assault barges under the command of Major A. Ronald, who had won the Military Cross in one of the first commando raids at Vaagso, found themselves chugging along the Ilot de la Marine, the most heavily fortified part of Algiers harbor. A furious barrage of shells bracketed the three little craft. All around them the water heaved and tossed in a white fury. Ronald's barge was hit. Several men were killed, including the major. Beneath a pall of black smoke, the boat began to drift helplessly ashore, with its cargo of corpses lying sprawled in the wild abandoned postures of those who have met a violent death. Once again, Frenchmen were killing Englishmen.

The staff had planned that the commandos would land by 0100 hours that Sunday morning. But it was already three o'clock and still the first of them had not yet reached the shore through the hail of gunfire that hissed across the eerily glowing bay.

The commandos' troop leaders spent increasingly desperate hours searching for a suitable landing spot. Finally some of them made it. "Made a rough landing," one commando wrote in his diary the day afterwards, "losing special equipment. A rocket pierces the bottom of the barge and she sinks. Sailors scream, but we can't wait, and push on up the cliff. Have landed by a huge Roman bath, all floodlit."[1]

Now the first of the widely scattered commandos were beginning to struggle ashore. Pushing inland, they headed for Fort Duperré, west of Algiers, from whence the French were bombarding the invasion fleet with heavy guns.

The second-in-command of 6th Commando, Major McLeod, separated from his commanding officer, decided to push on alone. Fortunately the natives were friendly; the French troops, dug in where they landed, did not fire upon the bedraggled commandos in their soaking wet American uniforms. "Had our reception been anything but friendly," the Major noted drolly, "it is extremely unlikely that this account would ever have been written."[2]

But if, as it seemed, the French Army was not prepared to fight the invaders from the sea, the French Navy—with bitter memories of Mers-el-Kebir in its collective mind—apparently could not restrain its impulse to attack. Fort Duperré, at the western extremity of the long narrow hillside city, was manned by *les pom-poms rouges* (French sailors, so called on account of the red pom-poms on their hats), and they fought back defiantly.

Armed only with light machine guns, the commandos could make no impression on the fort. They dug in around the walls and started sniping. Captain Lieven, a Canadian, produced a megaphone and called on the French to surrender. His answer was an angry burst of white, hurrying tracer bullets.

Gradually, more of the commandos were finding their way to the objective, joining their comrades beneath the fort's walls, while their officers radioed urgently to the fleet for further assistance.

Advancing down a little road, the men of No. 4 troop bumped into a lone French civilian on a bicycle. He nearly fell off his bike when he saw these heavily armed strangers with blackened faces appearing out of the gloom. To one man at least, the invasion had come as a complete surprise. As the Frenchman later told the officer commanding the troop, he couldn't decide how to greet them: "Heil Hitler!," "God save the King!," "God bless America!"—or "Three cheers for the blacks!"[3]

Now a full-scale artillery duel was taking place between the invasion fleet's covering destroyers and the guns of Algiers' forts. French planes had already scrambled from the closest field, at Maison Blanche. Some had taken off without orders, manned by pilots who had fought against the British before, in Syria or over Gibraltar, and who proudly bore the insignia of their "kills" against the RAF on the fuselage of their planes.

But the Seafires and Seafuries of the aircraft carriers *Formidable* and *Victorious* were waiting for them. As flak peppered the pre-dawn sky, they swung into action against the French. A bitter dogfight commenced. Two French planes went streaming to the sea, trailing white glycol fumes behind them.

Now, while the destroyer HMS *Zetland* engaged the French batteries at Cape Matifou, two other destroyers

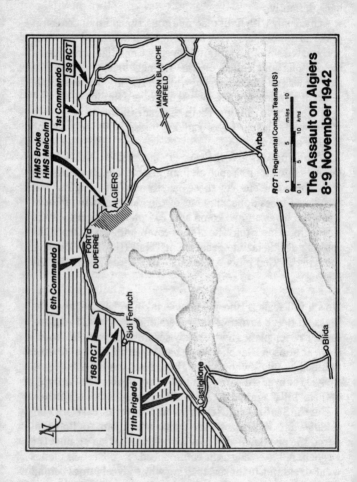

39 RCT

1st Commando

HMS Broke
HMS Malcolm

MAISON BLANCHE
AIRFIELD

ALGIERS

FORT d'
DUPERRÉ

6th Commando

Sidi Ferruch

168 RCT

11th Brigade

Castigliane

Arba

Blida

RCT : Regimental Combat Teams (US)

0 1   5   10
     miles
0 1 5   10   kms

**The Assault on Algiers
8-9 November 1942**

N

rushed forward to the attack: the *Broke* and the *Malcolm*, carrying Ryder's 135th Infantry for the frontal assault on Algiers. The aim of the infantry was to capture the vital port installations—Algiers was going to be the main supply port for Anderson's First Army—before the French could sabotage them.

Three times the *Malcolm*, the lead ship, tried to break into the southern entrance, but in vain. She was subjected to heavy fire from the defenders; all around her the water boiled and heaved, shooting upwards in angry white spurts. Then, on the last attempt, she was hit—and so badly damaged that she began to draw water immediately. Her captain gave up. Under cover of smoke, the *Malcolm* limped back out to sea, her troops still unlanded.

Now it was the *Broke*'s turn. The slim gray shape of the destroyer hurtled at top speed toward the boom barring the entrance to the harbor. Her sharp prow crashed into the boom and split it in two. She was through! Now, swinging to port, the *Broke* started to land her troops at a nearby quay. The Americans swarmed ashore with alacrity; they had had enough of sea warfare. Hurriedly they spread out along the dock to secure the power station and oil installations while the French gunners concentrated their fire on the *Broke*.

The young captain of the destroyer shifted his berth. The field guns, firing over open sights, and the nearby batteries followed him. He shifted his berth again, and then again, while on the shore the Americans were pinned down by ever increasing French machine-gun fire. In the end the destroyer's captain gave up. The French gunners couldn't miss now and he was taking severe fire. He gave the order for the ship to withdraw, taking with her those of the Americans capable of reembarking but leaving 250 men still trapped among the debris of the quay.

The *Broke* made it, only to sink while being towed the following morning. As the bells from Algiers' Roman Catholic churches started to peal, summoning the faithful to their prayers this Sunday morning, the 250 Americans of the "Red Bull" Division, who had trained so long for this moment—the liberation of the French from "the crushing Nazi yoke," as their President had put it only hours before—raised their hands in surrender. *To the French!*

What had gone wrong? Where was General Mast, who had virtually guaranteed that there would be no opposition to the invaders in Algeria?

A little before eight o'clock, the alarming news was received from Vichy via a radio broadcast that Admiral Darlan, Pétain's heir apparent, was in Algiers and was personally directing the defense. His son Alain had been stricken by polio and he had rushed to French North Africa to visit him in the hospital.

The news broke like a bombshell in Gibraltar. A five-star political admiral Darlan hated Britain with a passion. All his life, the stocky, vain little sailor had been an Anglophobe. He maintained that the British had always been envious of the French fleet, that they had opposed it ever since the famous Naval Conference of 1922, that their one aim was to emasculate his fleet. And this was the man the Anglo-Americans somehow had to persuade to join their side.

In the city itself, while American soldiers were being shot and killed by Darlan's men, Roosevelt's special envoy, Robert Murphy, hastened to meet the little French admiral, together with his commander-in-chief General Juin.

Darlan turned purple when he heard that the Americans were invading French North Africa. "I have known for a long time that the British are stupid," he spat, "but I have always believed that the Americans are more intelligent. Apparently *you* have the same genius as the British for making massive blunders!"[4]

Murphy set to work to get Darlan to agree to a ceasefire. It was going to be a tough job.

At Oran, Fredendall's infantry landed at three separate points. Once again, the initial problem was one of navigation and fighting the sea. French Army resistance was slight. There was some firing, admittedly, and the men of "the Big

Red One," trying as always to be the first American formation to join battle (hadn't they fired the first shots of World War One in 1917 in France?) took a few casualties. But there was no serious opposition to their landing or that of the 1st Armored Division. Indeed, French resistance was something of a joke.

One young lieutenant, single-handed, succeeded in capturing a whole battery of French seventy-fives and marched its officers and men back to American lines at the point of his tommy gun.

Later General Terry Allen, commanding general of the 1st, who was about to give the young officer a decoration, asked him how he had done it.

"You remember, sir, that your orders were not to fire on a French soldier unless we were absolutely sure that he was unfriendly. I thought, how can I tell for sure? Then I remembered that we had a countersign, so that if they were friendly French they should know the reply."

Allen stared at the lieutenant in disbelief. "You thought," he said slowly, "that you had better challenge the battery that was firing in order to make sure that it was unfriendly?"

"Yessir," the young officer replied brightly, "and that is what I did. I cupped my hands and hollered, and when they did not have the right answer I knew I should have to take them prisoner."

"What did you holler at them?" Allen asked faintly.

The lieutenant looked perplexed. "Why—you remember the countersign, sir? It was 'Hi-ho, Silver!' And they should have answered 'Away!' So I cupped my hands and hollered 'Hi-ho, Silver!' at them."

"And then?"

"Oh, then they put their hands up right away. They surrendered, sir."

The young officer did not get his Silver Star.[5]

But now the French Navy was joining in the battle for Oran, and the fun stopped abruptly.

Two ex-U.S. Coast Guard cutters, renamed *Walney* and *Hartland*, manned by British sailors and flying both the White Ensign and Old Glory, now attempted to rush the port of Oran itself. Their object was to land Rangers. Under the command of a retired Royal Navy man, Captain F. T. Peters, who would win the Victoria Cross and the American Distinguished Service Cross this day, the two cutters raced into the harbor. Searchlights flicked on everywhere. Tracer zipped from the shore—red, white, and green—like a flight of angry hornets. Someone aboard the *Walney* appealed through a loud-hailer in French for the firing to stop. But the French sailors had spotted the hated White Ensign of the Royal Navy, which had destroyed so many of their own ships at nearby Mers-el-Kebir, and they simply intensified their fire. Undaunted, the two cutters set up a smokescreen to hide the *Walney* as she made a dash at the harbor boom.

The French sloop *La Surprise* raced to meet her. At the very last moment the British skipper swung to one side as the sloop attempted to ram his ship. At point-blank range, the sloop raked the length of the *Walney*. The British ship, her engines wrecked, now drifted helplessly in the harbor while a French destroyer and submarines took her under crossfire. The crew and the Rangers huddled for cover as shells slammed into their dying craft; there was nothing else they could do. A blazing hulk, her decks a shambles, her superstructure a mass of holes, she drifted on a little while longer, but finally she went under. The handful of survivors—including Captain Peters, who had only a few more days to live—were taken prisoner by the French.

The *Hartland* had already been hit before she groped her way through the smokescreen into the harbor. Once inside, the French destroyer *Typhon* started shelling her at point-blank range. The ex-Coast Guard ship didn't have a chance. Her superstructure riddled like a sieve, her mast dangling, metal twisted into smoking, grotesque shapes, she was brought to a standstill. A plucky tug rushed up in an attempt to save her—to no avail. The French pounded the *Hartland* with all they had. On fire from stern to stem, all her passengers and crew dead or wounded, she blew up.

The butcher's bill was mounting.

It was now three o'clock in the afternoon and Darlan was weakening. So far, the little French admiral with watery blue eyes and petulant lips had not agreed to any general ceasefire in French North Africa; like Giraud in Gibraltar, he was still playing both sides of the field, seeing how things would go and how the Germans, whom he had once supported so wholeheartedly, would react. React they would, and speedily—that he knew. But he was prepared to arrange a local surrender at Algiers to General Ryder.

Murphy didn't wait for Darlan to have second thoughts. He had heard that Ryder was already ashore, on a beach some ten miles from Algiers, so he borrowed a car from Darlan and raced off to find Ryder.

The first person Murphy met on the debris-littered beach, with here and there a still shape stretched out under a blanket, rifle planted bayonet-down in the sand to indicate the presence of the body there, was Randolph Churchill. He seemed to know of Murphy and told the flattered American diplomat that the British Foreign Office could use a few men like him.

Finally Murphy found Ryder and explained that Darlan had agreed to arrange a local ceasefire if Ryder would come to his office in Algiers.

But General Ryder seemed more concerned about his personal appearance than stopping the war. Before he would allow himself to be led to Murphy's car, he announced that he had to change into a clean uniform and said he had to send a message to Gibraltar.

So an impatient Murphy waited, fuming, while Ryder sat down on a rock to dictate the message to an aide. It seemed to take him an age to dictate a single paragraph. In the end Murphy took him by the arm and steered him firmly to the car.

Ryder was met by Admiral Darlan, General Juin, and fifty other French officers. Just as he entered the room with Murphy, American planes came over and dropped a stick of bombs, shaking the house to its foundations.

An ecstatic smile spread over Ryder's skinny face. "How wonderful!" he exclaimed. "This is the first time since World War One that I have been under fire!"

His pleasure was not shared by the French. A moment of icy silence followed.

But a short while later both parties had signed a preliminary ceasefire. The fighting in Algiers was over. Both the Rangers and Ryder's "Red Bull" Division had taken scores of casualties, as had the commandos. In fact, the only Allied unit not to have taken casualties was the one that had been prepared for the worst, Brigadier Cass's battle-experienced 11th Brigade. The 11th had lost only one man: an over-eager officer who had jumped too soon from the assault craft, landed in deep water, and drowned.

But the erstwhile French allies had suffered casualties too. General Mast was already in hiding, a warrant out for his arrest. Elsewhere throughout Algiers, Juin's soldiers were arresting Mast's fellow conspirators on a charge of treachery. The whole would-be "resistance" movement was in complete disarray, with the Americans now seemingly dealing with their enemies—Darlan and Juin, those supporters of Pétain.

It was at this moment that General Giraud in Gibraltar decided to throw in his lot with the Americans and agreed to fly to French North Africa.

In Oran the fighting still continued. Over the city the air battles continued, with fighters twisting and snarling in tight turns as they maneuvered for position and the final "kill." On the ground the soldiers of "the Big Red One" advanced doggedly against stiff resistance. The French threw in an air attack against them, but Spitfires from Gibraltar came zooming out of the sky and broke up the French attack formations, screeching past at treetop height, cannon and machine guns spitting fire. A French column preparing to counterattack the 1st Division was caught completely in the open. Afterward the pilots boasted that in this, their first action, they had knocked out ten French tanks and twenty-five trucks laden with infantry.

Now, with the guns of the Royal Navy's *Rodney*, *Aurora*, and *Jamaica* thundering from out to sea, a general assault was launched on Oran by the 1st Infantry Division and the 1st Armored Division. The French broke. By noon on November 10, Oran had surrendered, and it was all over in this part of French North Africa.

The men of the 1st Armored had never lacked self-esteem. As the fighting died away, the soldiers of the 1st Battalion of that division went about clapping one another on the back, shaking hands, and loudly congratulating themselves on their victory. But their commanding officer was not so sanguine. Lieutenant Colonel John Waters—he was married to Patton's favorite daughter—called his men together and lectured them.

"We did very well against the scrub team," he declared. "Next week we hit the Germans. Do not slack off in anything. When we make a showing against *them*, you may congratulate yourselves."[6]

But there would be no congratulations for the men of the 1st Battalion. Little did Waters know, when he spoke those words, that within four short months his battalion would be virtually destroyed and that he himself would be on his way to Germany to spend two long years in a prisoner-of-war camp.

The beach at Fedala, Morocco, was a shambles. Major General Lucien K. Truscott, looking youthful and aggressive in his riding breeches, leather jacket and silk scarf, jumped out of his stalled jeep and strode across to the beachmaster's command post. What was going on, he wanted to know.

In the darkness, stabbed here and there by the scarlet flash of French guns, the beachmaster knew as little as the commanding general. Craft intended for Blue Beach were landing on Green Beach, and vice-versa; there was no sign of the tanks of Truscott's 3rd Infantry, and he could barely see the transports out at sea waiting for his instructions.

Receiving this report, Truscott cursed and commandeered the beachmaster's halftrack. Then this ex-cavalry crony of Patton's did what every red-blooded soldier should: he rode to the sound of the guns. As the halftrack groaned its way up the beach, he ordered two light tanks and a tank destroyer to follow him—but his long military career almost ended there and then. Just behind him, one of the gunners opened up with a long burst of machine-gun fire, missing Truscott's head by a hair's breadth. Grimly the general pushed on, telling himself it had been a long time since World War One; he had forgotten that such things happened in combat.

When he reached his forward positions, the news was bad. French infantry and tanks had overrun the infantry road-blocks on the Rabat Road to his front. Only a few survivors had struggled back. Truscott rapped out his orders, telling his officers to form some sort of cohesive front, and then set off back to the beach, with firing breaking out on all sides. It was clear that Roosevelt's message had been a failure. The French were fighting back.

The beach was still as bad as ever. "As far as I could see along the beach," Truscott recalled after the war, "there was chaos. Landing craft were beaching in the pounding surf, broaching to the waves, and spilling men and equipment into the water. Men wandered about aimlessly, helplessly lost, calling to each other and for their units, swearing at each other and at nothing."[7]

Truscott squatted there, feeling very lonely and chilled, dying for a cigarette although it was against blackout regulations to light one. In the end he succumbed to temptation. Instantly little red glows appeared all around him as his men followed suit.

Sitting there, his cigarette half-finished, wondering what to do next, Truscott was startled to see a strange-looking figure lumbering up to him out of the gloom. It stopped, and a voice cried in an alien accent, "Heyyuh, gimme a cigarette."

Green Beach at this particular moment was no place to

stand on dignity. Obligingly, therefore, the general handed the stranger a cigarette.

"Goddam—all wet! Gimme a light, too," demanded the man with the funny accent.

Truscott held up his own cigarette, and as the stranger put it to his face, two of Truscott's staff appeared out of the darkness, thrust tommyguns into the man's stomach, and yelled the password for the night: *"George!"*

But they did not receive the expected answer—*"Patton!"*

"George?" came the indignant response. "George, hell! Me no George. My name Lee—Cook, Company C, 540th Engineers ..." The stranger, it turned out, was a Chinese-American.[8]

The commanding general, squatting there on the wet sand in the darkness, shook his head in wonderment, not knowing whether to laugh or cry.

Patton was preparing to go ashore. He was dressed in his best—more as if he were about to go on parade instead of into combat. There wasn't a crease in his uniform, his boots gleamed, and his famous lacquered helmet was adorned by outsize stars that shone in the morning sunshine. Only one thing was missing—his pistols.

"George!" he barked at his colored orderly, Sergeant Meeks. "Where are my pistols?"

"In the boat, sir," Meeks answered, indicating the launch that was about to take him ashore.

"Get them!" Patton ordered, striking a martial pose for the benefit of the watching sailors.

Meeks did so, and Patton began to strap them on in the very same instant that the *Augusta*'s main battery thundered into action. A French cruiser and two destroyers had broken through the Navy's defensive screen and were trying to get at the U.S. transports. The blast blew the bottom out of the launch and Patton's belongings disappeared into the Atlantic.

Patton grabbed the pair of oversize binoculars that Meeks was holding for him. "Goddamit, George!" he cried in that squeaky, high-pitched voice of his. "It was a close shave—the

pistols I mean. I hope you have a spare toothbrush with you I
can use to clean my foul mouth. I don't have a thing left in the
world . . ." he flashed a wicked glance at Admiral Hall,
standing nearby ". . . thanks to the United States Navy!"[9]

It was nearly four hours later before Patton could finally go
ashore. He did it in style, smoking a big Havana, pistols at his
side, as he stepped for the first time onto the soil of Africa,
every inch a conqueror. There was only one slight flaw: his
.45s were empty. He had no ammunition for them!

Major Codman, soon to be Patton's personal aide, watched
in blank astonishment as his future boss strode up the beach
toward an infantryman who was lying face downward in the
sand, tommygun next to him.

Patton snatched up the gun. "Ya-ah!" he yelled at the prone
figure.

The young soldier half turned and shielded his eyes from
the light. "Go 'way and lemme sleep."

Patton thrust the barrel of his own tommygun into the
soldier's stomach. That did it. The soldier finally opened his
eyes and his gaze traveled slowly up the remarkable figure of
a man standing before him, his face registering growing
amazement as he took in the cavalry boots, the deep-chested
torso, the helmet with its two stars . . .

"*Jesus!*" he breathed in awe.

Patton ordered him to get up and gave him back his weapon. "I know you're tired," he said. "We're all tired. That makes
no difference." He laid his hand on the boy's shoulder. "The
next beach you land on will be defended by Germans. I don't
want one of them coming up behind you and hitting you over
the head with a sock full of shit!"

The young soldier grinned, and Patton strode off, followed
by his grinning staff.[10]

The Patton legend had started.

But still the real fighting continued, the kind that isn't
recorded in the admiring biographies of great commanders.

Up front with his men, General Harmon found that they were being sniped at remorselessly from some cliffs. He located the source of the firing and twice sent patrols to the small house from which it appeared to be coming. Both patrols came back reporting that the house was occupied by "a harmless old man and woman." But casualties were mounting, and Harmon was in no mood to observe the Hague Rules of Land Warfare. Several men had been hit just in front of him. Angrily he called up a tank and ordered its commander to advance to within ten feet of the house "and blow it off the map!"

A few minutes later the house disappeared in a ball of angry yellow flame, the walls tumbling down in a furious rush of masonry and stone, leaving the "harmless old man and woman" dead. Infantry pushed forward into the smoking debris and discovered a trapdoor under the living room rug. Tentatively an officer raised the trapdoor. Behind him his men tensed, grenades poised in their hands ready for tossing into the black pit below. But there was no need. A French officer emerged, followed by thirty of his men, all with their hands raised, faces blanched and apprehensive, blinking in the sudden light.

Harmon contained himself, luckily for the French. Instead of shooting them, he ordered them to be taken back to the divisional "cage."

Now, with French resistance at Safi over, Harmon ordered his tankers to head north toward Casablanca. The night was pitch-black as his Combat Command B set off in the lead, rattling along a narrow, high-crowned road from which it was easy to slip into the deep ditches on both sides. The tanker crews were tense and apprehensive, the drivers straining every nerve not to skid into the ditches and thus get left behind. They weren't scared of the French, but they had heard exaggerated tales of the wandering Arabs of the area. They slit the throats of stragglers, it was whispered from man to man, and then "cut the dick" off anyone unfortunate enough to fall into their hands. As Harmon recorded later, "We had no stragglers."

But Colonel Dewey, in charge of the column, had many more real and immediate problems to tackle. Time and time again the vehicles rumbled to a halt, and he would hurry forward to find out what the source of the trouble was. More than once a leading vehicle had stopped, and the men had simply gone to sleep.

But at two o'clock that night, Dewey was called forward to find a group of awed tankers standing in a circle in the middle of the road. This time Harmon was with him. All that Harmon could see was a solitary light further up the road. He pressed on, and gasped.

At the side of the road, standing on an enormous rock against which there was propped a placard proclaiming *"Egalité—Fraternité—République Française,"* was an elderly Frenchman, his chest covered with combat ribbons.

Harmon stared at him open-mouthed, his own broad face illuminated by the lantern the Frenchman held aloft as he spoke to the troops, who did not understand a single word of his flowery rhetoric.

Harmon, who had fought in the Argonne in 1918 and spoke some French, asked him what the devil he was doing there.

The Frenchman replied that he had been ordered to set up a barricade. It was a *barricade symbolique,* he explained— which was true enough, for the Americans could either push around the rock or roll it away.

Harmon smiled wryly: the old man and his rock seemed to typify the French attitude to the invasion. Then he asked the old man why, if he wished to halt the Americans, he carried a lantern.

The Frenchman replied simply that he wanted to provide enough light so that the young Americans did not injure themselves at the *barricade symbolique.*

Harmon's beefy soldier's face cracked into an understanding smile. The old man had only been trying to do his duty as a good soldier should. He was lucky he hadn't been shot by the trigger-happy young men of "the Hell on Wheels." Gently he sent him back home to his wife; then he got on with the grim business of total war, so far removed from such quixotic gestures.

At first light, Harmon received a message from Patton. It was marked "urgent." It directed Harmon to attack the southern exits to the city of Casablanca at 1100 hours that morning. That meant immediate action. The column was still fifty miles from the city, and they were running out of gas. Harmon's mind raced, but before he could decide what to do, the problem was solved for him. Another message arrived from Patton. The French in Casablanca were going to surrender! All attacks were to be stopped "at once." [11]

A few hours later, after motoring through the great city that would soon find a place in American hearts—not because so many Americans had died fighting to capture it, but because of a sentimental movie starring Humphrey Bogart and Ingrid Bergman—Harmon rolled to a stop outside Patton's HQ at the beautiful Miramar Hotel.

Patton, immaculate as ever, looked at the dusty, unshaven General and cried, "Where in hell have you been all this time?"

That same afternoon, Patton concluded what he called "a gentleman's agreement" with the French, scrapping the official State Department treaty in that high-handed manner of his that would eventually bring about his downfall.

Speaking in French, he told the assembled French generals: "I propose until final terms are arranged by higher headquarters that you return all your men with arms to your proper stations, that you take your sick and wounded with you, and your dead . . ." [12]

The apprehension in the Frenchmen's faces began to disappear. Patton's terms were not harsh, and they certainly satisfied French honor—which now, all of a sudden, seemed so precious to them.

Patton paused, staring around at their faces. "There is, however," he said gravely, "an additional condition upon which I must insist."

The French abruptly froze. Was this going to be the sting in the tail of the beast?

Patton let them squirm for a moment. Finally he broke his silence, and a broad grin creased his face. "It is this—that you join me in a glass of champagne!"

It was a scene that might have been taken from one of those romantic early-nineteenth-century military paintings. The end of the battle, with gallant opponents saluting each other as the one surrendered his sword to the other, while the wounded (bloodstained bandages wrapped around their heads, not with their guts hanging out like gray pulsating snakes) looked on, supported by brave little drummer-boys.

But pictures can never tell the whole story. Behind this jovial scene lay the unpicturesque dead. On the Anglo-American side alone, there were over 1,000 of them, 500 each from the British and American armies. They had come to liberate the French from the yoke of Nazi tyranny, or so they had been told. But it appeared that the French had not wanted to be liberated after all. Hollywood had got it wrong. The French liked their lives as they were, occupied by the Boche or not. As reward for their services in the liberation of French North Africa, more than one thousand Anglo-American troops received exactly six feet of African soil (that is, if their bodies were ever found)—and were speedily forgotten in the interests of Franco-American solidarity.[13]

PART II

THE FIRST TEAM

We did very well against the scrub team. Next week we hit the Germans. Do not slack off in anything. When we make a showing against them, you may congratulate yourselves.

—Lieutenant Colonel John Waters, November 1942

four

On the morning of November 11, the same day that saw the end of hostilities in French North Africa, all was hectic activity at the Luftwaffe bases of Naples and Trapani. Heavily laden Junkers 52s rose, one after another, into the bright hard blue sky and began to fly south. Field Marshal Kesselring, the German Commander-in-Chief in Southern Europe, was already reacting to the new threat to Rommel's rear. Scratching together whatever troops he could find, he was flying them to Tunis to capture the city before the Allies did.

Some of the troops he found in Italy were draftees, hurriedly formed into battalions, but the men sitting in the old three-engined "Auntie Jus" (as the troops called the Junkers) were no ordinary "stubble-hoppers" fated to be simple cannon-fodder. These men in their camouflaged coveralls and rimless helmets were the elite, the best soldiers Germany had to offer in 1942: they were the paras of Colonel Koch's Parachute Regiment Number Five.

They were young, many of them under twenty, and new to battle, but they were volunteers, trained to drop by parachute, and they were commanded by veterans, "the turret-breakers" as they called themselves: officers and NCOs who had swooped in by glider to land right on top of the Belgian fort of Eben-Emael in May 1940 and captured it in a bold *coup-de-main*. All of them, too, had been through the hell of Crete a year later, which had decimated the ranks of the German Parachute Division.

For the last few months these men had been training to capture Malta by a parachute assault. Now they found themselves being flown hurriedly to Africa. It was a flight into the unknown; even Colonel Koch knew only that a single German officer by the name of Colonel Harlinghausen had flown to Tunis airport thirty-six hours before, accompanied by two Messerschmidt fighters, and taken possession of it. But there were more than 14,000 French troops in Tunisia, commanded by a General Barré. What would they do when they were confronted by a whole regiment of heavily armed German paratroopers coming in to land on that same airfield?

Forty Junkers flew the regiment across to Africa, with Colonel Koch in the leading plane. As land loomed up on the horizon, Koch toyed with the Knight's Cross that hung from his neck and listened to Dr. Waitzel the regiment's medical officer, grumbling about the surprise mission.

"A nice piece of shit this is," Waitzel complained to the adjutant, Lieutenant Wolf, who nodded his agreement.

As commanding officer, Koch knew that he had to improve the morale of his officers. He forced a smile. "Don't be so down in the mouth," he called across to the doctor. "It'll make a change to hit the *Amis* in the trap, won't it? Beside, there'll be Chesterfield cigarettes and biscuits. Won't that be something?"

Waitzel's reply is not recorded, for at that moment the pilot of the lead plane called out, "Tunis . . . we're landing!" Automatically the commanders in their individual planes cried, *"Fertigmachen zur Landung!"* and the young soldiers duly prepared themselves for an assault landing.[1]

But this time the paratroopers wouldn't be needing their

chutes. One after another, the "Auntie Jus" touched the soil of Africa and rolled uneventfully to a stop. Stuka dive-bombers already filled the French hangars. Half a squadron of Luft-waffe fighters were gassing up on the runways, and light flak guns were dug in ready for action, the gunners searching the western sky from whence the *Amis* would come.

Only one thing was troubling Koch as he strode away to report to Harlinghausen. All around the airfield French sol-diers of General Barré's division were dug in, helmeted, and their weapons at the ready. Now he wondered just how long they were going to remain there, watching the Germans build up their strength, before they acted. But the tough young airborne colonel, whose regiment was going to prove such a thorn in the flesh of General Anderson's First Army until it was finally abandoned to its fate by Hitler in the spring of 1943, need not have worried. The neutral French, who on this day were tamely allowing the rest of their country to be occupied by Hitler, were going to prove better allies to the Germans than their cobelligerents, the Italians.

General Clark was angry. He had arrived in Algiers that day to find American policy for the French in ruins. Giraud, who had finally given in and flown to the city before Clark, had intended to broadcast to the French, asking them to support himself as the new governor and commander-in-chief of the armed forces, authorized by the Allies. But his arrival had proved a total flop; instead of making his broadcast, Giraud found himself forced to go into hiding, just like his supporter Mast.

It now seemed to Clark that there wasn't a single French-man in North Africa prepared to cooperate with him without the authority of the Vichy government. He would have to do a deal with the arch-traitor, Admiral Darlan.

Prior to the great invasion, as Clark knew, Churchill him-self had told Murphy that if he could meet Darlan, much as he loathed the man, "I would cheerfully crawl on my hands and knees for a mile if by doing so I could get him to bring that fleet of his into the circle of Allied forces."[2] But Clark also knew that once the press back home got hold of the story that he was making agreements with the man who had backed Hitler, who had had Jews imprisoned by the thousand in France and French North Africa, and who had stubbornly refused to come out for the Allied cause, there would be all hell to pay. Like all the senior American generals, Clark was well aware of the power of the press to make or break military reputations.

All the same he had to get that fleet, which Churchill had spoken about and which was currently stationed at Toulon, near Marseilles. More immediately, he wanted the French in Tunisia to oppose any attempt by the Germans to land there.

Now, on the morning of November 10, towering above the nervous little admiral, Clark blustered and threatened, desperately trying to get the Frenchman to cooperate.

"You've told us repeatedly that you want to free France," Clark snapped, "but you've given no visible indication or decision in support of us or the Allied cause. There are two ways you can demonstrate your good faith—by summoning the French fleet to a North African port and by ordering the governor of Tunisia to resist the German invasion."[3]

Darlan objected. "I have no authority to summon the fleet," he complained, though he went on to say that he felt sure the fleet would "follow orders to scuttle itself rather than be seized by the Germans."

Clark wasn't so sure. "There is a danger," he said, "that there will be no time to scuttle the fleet—and in any event, that will be an act against the Allies as much as against the Germans."

But Darlan still refused to comply. In the end a furious Clark stormed out with an angry "Good-day!" slamming the door behind him.

That afternoon, however, Darlan called Admiral de la Borde at Toulon and asked him to send the French fleet to North Africa. De la Borde's answer was laconic in the extreme. *"Merde!"* he said.[4] The French fleet was not coming.

Later Clark returned. He thrust the telephone into Darlan's

hand and told him to call Admiral Jean Esteva, the governor-general in Tunisia, and order him to fight the Germans. Rather to Clark's surprise, Darlan obeyed.

As Darlan spoke to Esteva, 500 miles away in Tunis, Clark and Robert Murphy listened in on the conversation.

"Esteva," Darlan asked, "are you willing to become an American?" Nervously Esteva replied, "Yes—but when are they coming?" He meant Anderson's First Army, already beginning its race across North Africa towards Tunisia.

Darlan lied; the Allies would be arriving soon, he said. Obviously relieved, Esteva said he would order General Barré to resist any further German buildup.

Clark left Darlan nervously puffing his awful pipe, feeling very relieved. Darlan was beginning to cooperate, and Tunisia was won for the Allied cause without a single shot having been fired. Outside he ordered the guard he had slapped on Darlan's residence the day before to be removed; there would be no more trouble from the five-star admiral with the watery blue eyes and shifty face.

Clark was wrong. At five o'clock the next morning, while far away in Italy Colonel Koch was receiving his final briefing before embarking on his flight to North Africa, Clark was shaken out of an exhausted sleep (he had slept hardly at all in the last seventy-two hours) to be told the bad news by a worried aide. Darlan had revoked his order to Esteva to resist the Germans.

General der Panzertruppe Walther Nehring received his new orders in Rome just as he was about to fly back to Rommel's *Afrika Korps* to take up his old post, in spite of the open wound in his right arm—the result of driving over a British mine in August. He was to fly immediately to Tunis and take over command of something called the XC Army Corps. Nehring had never heard of a German corps of that name, nor had the handful of staff officers he was to take with him to North Africa. This was not surprising; the XC Corps did not as yet, exist—save perhaps in Adolf Hitler's mind.

But General Nehring was not accustomed to questioning

orders. Dutifully he flew to Tunis, only to find that his "corps" consisted of a battalion of parachute engineers commanded by Major Witzig (another one of those famed "turret-breakers" of 1940), plus Colonel Koch's paratroopers and a handful of infantrymen who had been landed by sea. His communications had to depend on the vagaries of the French telephone service—and his command vehicle was a hired French taxi cab!

Not exactly impressed by his new "corps," Nehring nevertheless set about the defense of Tunisia in the usual dynamic manner of the trained German staff officer. He did not trust the French, in spite of Admiral Esteva's "neutrality," and he knew that he had to gain Bizerta, the great port to the north of Tunis—it would be vitally important for the reinforcements he expected. But how could he and his handful of paratroopers capture a place that was defended by 14,000 French sailors and soldiers?

Again boldness paid off—helped by French indecision. While General Barré was planning to fight the Germans and carefully withdrawing his troops to the west, the direction from which the Anglo-Americans would come, Admiral Derrien, commander at Bizerta, was dithering. One day Derrien was declaring that the Germans and Italians were his enemies; the next day he was advocating strict neutrality.

Privately Derrien told his staff: "I have seven citations and forty-two years of service, and I shall be known as the admiral who delivered Bizerta to the Germans."[5]

He was. On November 12, the Germans started landing in force and Derrien's 14,000 men stood tamely by and let it happen.

Now it was Barré's turn. Nehring tried to trick him into coming to meet him in Tunis, but the wily old French General would have nothing of it. Then Derrien applied pressure on his fellow countryman. That didn't work either. In the end, the Germans sent a deputy minister to see Barré in his remote farmhouse outpost. The minister told Barré that his own government—in other words, the Vichy government—had

ordered all French troops in French North Africa to resist the
Anglo-American invaders, and he asked Barré to clear all
routes leading west so that the Germans, France's new ally,
could advance and stop the enemy.

Barré did not refuse outright. He explained that it would
take a few days for him to confer with his chief—Juin—in
Algiers. The German minister told him he had just six hours,
till seven o'clock that night; if he had not made his decision by
then, General Nehring would be forced to take action.

At eleven o'clock, German planes bombed Barré's headquarters. Twenty minutes later, German artillery started to
shell the headquarters and Koch's paratroopers began to
advance under its cover towards the farmhouse. Barré hesitated no longer. He ordered his soldiers to return fire.

Once again, after an interval of two years, Frenchmen were
fighting Germans.

But it was too late. By the end of the first week of Nehring's
command in North Africa, his handful of troops had occupied
all key points in the major cities, including the ports of Tunis
and Bizerta. They had also arrested all known and suspected
Allied sympathizers, disarmed virtually all of the French
troops who were left in Tunisia, and were preparing to move
out against the Anglo-Americans advancing from the west.

There were 5,000 German troops in the country by now.
They had tanks and air superiority and a stable base along the
coast. Every day a complete new battalion was flown in.
Nehring's XC Corps was rapidly beginning to take shape. The
time had come to engage the enemy and stop that headlong
race for Tunis.

The Allies had beaten the "scrub team," as Colonel Waters
called it, but now they were going to meet the "first team."

The 1st Battalion of the Parachute Regiment made its first
combat jump on the morning of November 16, 1942. Its objective was a road junction at Beja, a key point some ninety miles
east of Tunis, thus catapulting General Anderson's First

Army within striking distance of the great city. As the Battalion's transports began to take off for its first combat operation, a number of the "Red Devils" who had been ordered to stay behind were observed running after the aircraft, borrowed parachutes in one hand, personal weapons in the other. Some twenty of them were hauled aboard by their cheering comrades.

As the battalion historian observed, "It is not every man who will disobey orders to parachute into battle."[6] But then these weren't ordinary men; these were the soldiers of the Parachute Regiment, volunteers to a man, who had survived the long selection process of their regiment, overcoming their daily fears in order not to have those terrible three letters stamped onto their papers: "RTU" (Returned To Unit).

They landed in soft plowed earth, with only a few casualties, and, forming up immediately, marched toward the village of Souk el Arba where they first met the French of General Barré's withdrawing division. Not only that, the whole village turned out to fete them, with flowers, champagne, local wine, and kisses from an elderly man sporting a row of combat ribbons from World War One.

The paratroopers pressed eastward until their liaison officer, Major des Voeux (who had broken his leg), located General Barré himself. Looking sharp in his immaculate uniform and colorful gold-braided *kepi*—though seeming "incredibly old" to the young paratroopers—Barré seemed very downhearted.

Colonel Hill of the 1st Parachute Battalion decided to cheer him up. He marched his 500-odd soldiers around and around the little town where Barré had located his headquarters, first in their helmets, then in their red berets, to make the French think that the British were here in strength.[7]

But the elderly general wasn't convinced. It would take something in the nature of a miracle to impress the French, who had known only defeat and abject surrender to the Boche.

The paras duly provided that miracle. The next morning, under the command of Major Cleasby-Thompson, a detachment of engineers and paras were ordered forward to the village of Sidi N'Sir, where they were to contact the local French commander, said to be pro-British.

The "village" consisted of one solitary white house on a hill and a yellow-painted railway station. The station was occupied by gigantic black Senegalese soldiers with yard-long bayonets under the orders of cloaked and field-booted Frenchmen. According to one of the para officers, remembering the incident long afterward, those big Senegalese regarded "our little fresh-faced parachutists in their green smocks" with complete indifference.[8]

By sundown the following day the Senegalese and their French officers thought differently. Leaving the village, the paras pushed on toward the little town of Mateur, stopping fifteen miles short of it as the African night descended with its usual startling suddenness. They bought eggs and sheep from the local Arabs, feasted on the food and fell into a deep sleep— abruptly broken by a burst of sten-gun fire from one of their sentries. The Germans were coming!

Three armored cars and three scout cars were rolling toward them. Hastily the paras prepared an ambush. As it happened, this was ideal countryside for ambushes; as one paratrooper recorded later: "On one side of the road the hills rose steeply; on the other, the ground was extremely boggy."[9] The sappers mined one end of the road, while the paras made arrangements to "close the door" with more mines at the other end of the road, once the German column was in the trap.

Tensely the paras waited. Two young officers, lieutenants Mellor and Kellas, crouched in a ditch at the side of the road clutching Gammon bombs, sticky bombs that would adhere to anything against which they were thrown. They could clearly hear the motors of the German vehicles groaning up the road in low gear, but they still were out of sight.

Suddenly an Arab appeared, dressed in the usual rags and riding sidesaddle on a skinny-ribbed, fleabitten donkey, going in the direction of the German column. The two officers in the ditch ducked, well aware that most Arabs supported the German cause or would sell anyone to anyone if the price were right. Should they kill him now? But the Arab rode harmlessly over the mines laid in the road without spotting them and disappeared from sight.

A few minutes later the first German vehicle appeared. Cautiously the six-wheel armored car ground toward the hidden paras, its aerials swinging in the breeze like silver whips. The men sat rigid with expectation. They had orders not to fire until the first German hit the mines. Their fingers curling around the triggers of their weapons were white-knuckled with tension. Sweat greased their faces. Any minute now it would be starting; for the first time in their lives they would kill their fellow human beings.

Abruptly the front end of the armored car rose into the air, a ball of angry yellow flame exploding beneath it. The next instant its ugly smoking snout had rammed the rock wall. The trap was sprung. Mellor and Kellas didn't hesitate. They leaped out of the ditch and flung their bombs. Two more scout cars behind the first braked to a halt in a slither of dust, flames already spreading across their steel plating, the paint bubbling in ugly blisters.

Now the team manning the single three-inch mortar went into action. There was the obscene snarl and plop of a mortar round being fired. It rose straight into the sky, a whirling, fat, black bombshell, seemed to hang there for a moment, then came racing back to earth, exploding in a violent eruption of dirt and pebbles behind the end of the column.

Like a trained collie worrying reluctant sheep, the mortarmen forced the German column ever closer to where the burning, wrecked armored cars lay. Another vehicle was hit and two Germans sprawled dead in the road. Now the paras' fire was hitting the Germans from both sides of the trap, as they crowded closer and closer together, the slugs howling off the vehicles' armor with the crews huddling there fearfully. Soon the enemy had had enough. It was all over within minutes. The rest of the Germans who were not already dead surrendered.

Later that day, Cleasby-Thompson and his triumphant paras returned to the village of Sidi N'Sir where the cloaked French officers and the Senegalese giants were no longer so disdainful of these "fresh-faced" newcomers. The French were convinced the paras had some sort of secret weapon that could deal with the heaviest of German armored vehicles. It was recorded that their commandant now became "wholeheartedly pro-Ally."

Two days later, American soldiers fired their first shots of the war against the Germans. While the British paras probed forward along the road that led to Bizerta, with two brigades of "the Battleaxe" Division following them and assisted by elements of the U.S. 1st Armored Division, they heard a great roar of motors to their rear. For one terrible moment the paras thought the Germans had pulled off one of their characteristic outflanking exercises and were going to attack them from behind. But they need not have worried.

A long column of artillery vehicles hove into view, all bearing on their sides the white star of the Allied invasion force. The paras relaxed. They were Yanks!

They were the men of a mixed artillery battalion of General Ryder's 34th Infantry Division. Waving gaily and shouting mock insults at the British, the "Red Bull" men sailed past the paras, cannon bouncing up and down on the potholed road, and disappeared over the rise to the front.

Again the heavy African silence reigned, the eerie brooding stillness of that vast empty continent. But not for long. Suddenly there came the sound of rapid firing from behind the rise. The Americans were attacking. After two years of training and waiting, the Yanks were going into action at last.

A little while later the same column reappeared, heading west this time, the dusty GIs flushed with triumph and full of themselves. A battery commander stopped to explain: it had occurred to them, he told the paras, that no American had actually fired at a Kraut thus far in the war, so he and his fellow battery commanders had had a race to see who could be

the first. In fact, they hadn't seen any Germans; they had
chosen Medjez church as a target instead, and, boasted the
American, they had "clobbered" the innocent church "well
and truly."[10]

With that they were gone again, leaving the Tommies—
who would soon be fighting a bitter slogging match with real
visible Germans—unimpressed. "Bleeding Yanks," one was
heard to grumble to his mate, "don't even know they're bleeding born!" But they soon would. The quick triumphs and easy
victories were about over.

In the last week of November, Colonel Waters and his men
finally faced up to the "first team." They were assigned to the
British armored covering force, working with the two forward brigades of "the Battleaxe" Division. Their task was to
establish what the British called a "tank-infested area" over
fifty square miles of ground. Waters did not know exactly
what this meant, but he didn't ask too many questions; he was
a West Pointer after all.

So he led his battle of Honey tanks forward, making laborious, churning progress through the gluey clay soil, confident
that his 1st Battalion of the 1st Armored Division was the best
in the whole of the U.S. Army; and that although his Honeys,
armed with 37mm cannon, looked puny in comparison with
the Crusaders and Valentines of the British 17th/21st
Lancers who were working with him, they were fine tanks
just the same. He was soon to be disillusioned.

Waters' column was descending into a deep valley in which
was located a stone farmhouse, held by the enemy, when the
Stukas spotted the Honeys. For one long moment the gull-
winged German dive-bombers seemed to hover there, stark
black against the blue of the November sky. Suddenly the
leader waggled his wings. Next instant the pilot threw his
plane out of the sky. The noise was hideous. Sirens howling,
engine going all out, the Stuka diving at a ninety-degree angle
seemed to be heading straight for destruction. As if in a tight,
black chain, the rest of the squadron followed.

The startled American tanke.s woke up to the danger. The gunners grabbed the antiaircraft machine guns attached to the outside of their turrets by spring-up cradle. There and then they discovered the first deficiency of the Honey. As the frantic-fingered gunners took a bead on the Stukas roaring down in their death-defying dive, they discovered that the vibration of their machine guns worked loose every fifth or sixth slug. All along the winding column of stalled tanks, gunners cursed and ripped open the breeches of their machine guns as the damned things jammed.

The Stukas leveled out, sirens screaming like banshees out of hell, and a myriad of black eggs began to fall from their blue, evil bellies. Only one American gun was still working, the one mounted on the command half-track. The Stukas' 250-pound bombs exploded the length of the column, sending the light tanks whipping back and forth as if struck by a sudden tempest. Fist-sized silver slivers of shrapnel flew everywhere. Crouched inside their tanks, the crews could hear the metal howl off their steel plating, as the world trembled and heaved.

Then it was over, and the tankers popped their heads out to a transformed world. The scrubby trees had been cleaned of their branches, stripped as bare as new matchwood. Great, brown, steaming craters lay on both sides, like the work of giant moles. Here and there a still khaki-clad shape lay crumpled on the earth like a bundle of abandoned rags. But not one single tank had been hit!

Now the men of Waters' Company C raced through a village at thirty miles an hour, using the Honeys' tremendous speed to best advantage, whipping off shells to left and right like western gunslingers. Roaring out the other side, they left behind them a trail of shattered blazing German Army Volkswagens and destroyed trucks. Fearing that the Germans had been alerted, the Americans pushed into a grove of olive trees for cover and, working their way through the dark green trees, emerged at a ridge. The driver of the little tank in the lead braked instinctively, then whistled slowly through his teeth in disbelief.

Spread out on the plain below him was a temporary airfield, packed with German aircraft, just ready for the taking. It was a cavalryman's dream. The men of the 1st Armored didn't waste the opportunity. Swiftly the company commander formed up his seventeen light tanks in line abreast on the ridge, while below on the airfield the German ground crews worked on their planes, completely unaware that murder and mayhem were about to descend upon them.

The American tanks charged as one, straight across the airfield toward the dipping sun. Abruptly the flat surface of the field was transformed into fountains of red and yellow earth as they opened up with their guns. Flying stones and dirt rose up in ugly spouts, through which the racing tanks dodged and weaved, sometimes disappearing altogether in cascades of acrid-smelling dirt and thick black smoke.

The men of the 1st Armored were enjoying themselves. It was as easy as falling off a log. They went through the Germans like "shit through a goose," as one recalled later,[11] shooting up the German planes as their frantic pilots tried to get them airborne to escape the blazing massacre.

A dozen or so planes started to roll and bump down the pitted field, but the Honeys gave chase. It was just like a scene from an adventure movie, a real cliff-hanger, as the planes raced forward with the tanks rumbling after them, guns barking. In the end only two German planes got away; the other eleven were left on the field, burning wrecks, their tracer ammunition exploding, the white and red shells zigzagging crazily into the burning sky.

The two fighter planes that had escaped soon gained height and started to turn in a tight curve, preparing to swoop back and attack. The tankers meanwhile had turned their attention on the hangars, crowded with other planes. Again, whooping madly like Red Indians, the tankers whipped back and forth, peppering flimsy fuel stores and temporary hangars with their shells and incendiary bullets, as the Honeys swerved around the airfield delivering scarlet fountains of death. Plane after plane was hit, its undercarriage crumbling until it sagged to the ground like a crippled bird. But now the two Messerschmitts that had escaped were coming back, zooming in at ground-level, violent, angry lights rippling the length of their wings. It was time to go. Speedily Company C began to pull back, leaving behind them a lunar landscape of craters and ash, dotted with burning and wrecked planes— thirty-six in all, at the cost of two men killed by the Messerschmitts. The 1st Battalion of the U.S. 1st Armored Division had been well and truly blooded. They had won their first battle against the "first team."

It was a fine November morning when the men of the 1st Battalion met German tanks for the very first time. They had billeted themselves around one of the abandoned farms in the Chouigui Pass area, stoutly built almost like a small fort to keep out the marauding Arabs, and were enjoying their time out of war. Despite the fact that their Thanksgiving dinner had been British compo rations washed down with strong tea, and even though they had been reduced to smoking leaves rolled in "Army Form Blank," as the British called toilet paper, they were in a good mood. Had they not beaten the Germans and knocked a damned nice hole in the Luftwaffe's strength in North Africa? Now they were within twenty-four hours' drive of Tunis and its fleshpots. Hell, before the week was out—and it was already Thursday—they might well be wallowing in dames and booze!

Second Lieutenant Freeland A. Daubin of the 1st's Company A was particularly pleased with the world as he sat in the command halftrack, "shooting the breeze" with the maintenance officer and the "first shirt." In his prejudiced opinion, Company A was the best outfit in the best battalion in the best division in the whole of the U.S. Army—and he belonged to Company A![12]

While the three men talked, the sentries up front had turned their attention to some small dark shapes moving along the ridge road to their front, close to the next farm, which was still in German hands.

"Movement on the road!" one of the sentries finally called out, knowing that the only other tanks in this area belonged to the British on their left flank—and these small dark shapes didn't look like British tanks.

Immediately half a dozen pairs of binoculars flashed up and focused on the movement on the ridge road.

Daubin let the first strange vehicle slide into the gleaming, calibrated circle of glass. He swallowed hard. The tank was carrying a massive gun, the like of which he had never seen in his whole career with the Armored Corps before. It seemed to hang in front of the tank nearly a good three feet. What the devil was it?

There was a sudden tearing noise, like an immense piece of canvas being torn apart, and as the first huge high-velocity shells began exploding all around the 1st Battalion, Daubin's heart sank. He knew now who they were. Those tanks were German Mark IV Specials, easily capable of knocking a Honey out at a range of 3,000 yards, while the Honey's 37mm popgun was reckoned to be effective only up to 1,200 yards (and as it turned out, even this figure was wildly optimistic). The result, in simple arithmetic, was that the Honeys would be within the range of the German guns for 1,800 yards before they could hope to do any damage on the Mark IVs.

Undaunted by that terrible thought, the tankers ran for their Honeys. Camouflage nets were thrown off. Drivers scrambled into their seats. Gunners and commanders whipped down into the turrets. One after another the big radial airplane engines roared into life, filling the morning air with blue smoke and the sweet stink of gasoline. They were ready to attack.

Meanwhile the assault gun platoon—three snubnosed 7mm gun howitzers mounted on White halftracks—moved forward to tackle the Germans. They rumbled across the valley trailing long wakes of dust behind them and came to a halt just as the first German tanks emerged from an olive grove. By this time the tense sweating gunners had ranged in. At a thousand yards they opened up with HE (high explosive).

For a few moments the German panzers hesitated, milling around in the sudden fog of war, as the howitzers laid down a tremendous barrage. But HE had no real effect against the thick steel hide of the Specials, save that it might have rattled their crews. But not for long. The first Mark IV came scuttling out of the black smoke, its long overhanging gun swinging from left to right like some primeval monster scenting out its victim.

Waters got on the radio. He was not going to sacrifice his thin-skinned assault guns—their armor was only proof against machine-gun bullets. He recalled them. The gunners responded immediately by setting up a smokescreen, the little dischargers hurling the smoke bombs between them and the Panzers. A thick white fog began to rise, blinding the enemy gunners. The three assault guns ran for safety.

Now the Honeys raced into action. Their only hope was to catch the German monsters from the flank, where their armor was at its weakest. Perhaps they'd be able to knock off a track or weld the German's turret solid to his chassis with a lucky shot.

Daubin's platoon rattled forward with the rest, his tank going all out. A small Italian tank loomed up in front of him. He banged the driver in the small of his back with his foot—the signal to halt. The Honey slammed to a stop. The gunner didn't wait for orders; he pressed the firing device and two rods of white solid shot hissed toward the unsuspecting Italian.

As the little enemy tank rocked to an abrupt stop, a round of HE howled toward it. In a flash, the stalled vehicle was burning from end to end.

"Look at that Ginzo burn!" cried a jubilant Daubin and his crew.

For what seemed an age, the Americans were mesmerized by the sight of their burning opponent, as the paintwork blistered like the symptoms of some loathsome skin disease and gleaming silver rivulets of molten metal started to drip to the charred ground like steel tears.

But the Germans were coming ever closer, ready to take up the challenge. Daubin suddenly realized the danger, and ordered the tank to move on. The Honey raced into a small dried-up stream bed, ideal protection for the under-gunned American tank; now it could get within killing range of the Germans.

Daubin spotted his victim. The gunner opened fire from a hull-down position—standard operating procedure. But what happened next was definitely *not* S.O.P. as taught in the tank training schools back in the States. Daubin's shells glanced off the Mark IV's tough hide like glowing ping-pong balls. The 37mm shells simply would not penetrate. All they managed to do was gouge great silver scars the length of the German tank's plating.

And Daubin was not the only one. Colonel Waters' tankers were finding the same thing everywhere. Suddenly the men of the 1st Tank Battalion realized that they were in very serious trouble indeed.

"The Death or Glory Boys," as the British public called them, did not hesitate. The men of the 17th/21st Lancers, whose badge was a Death's Head with the proud motto *"Or Glory"* beneath, had always been at the forefront of an attack ever since they had been formed nearly 300 years before.[13] They charged into the Germans' flank just as they opened fire on the American Honeys.

The Lancers had last been engaged in battle with the Americans back in the late eighteenth century when they had fought *against* them. They had been besieged by the colonists at Boston, captured Long Island, ridden 1,500 miles into the Deep South, engaged in a personal skirmish with no less a person than General Washington himself when they had ridden with Tarleton's Legion, and 25 of their survivors had surrendered with Cornwallis at Yorktown. Now, after nearly 250 years, they were fighting on the side of the descendants of those same upstart Americans!

But the British six pounders and two pounders—"peashooters," as their biographer R. L. V. ffrench-Blake called them contemptuously[14]—were hardly any more effective than the American 37mms. Yet the impact of that sudden charge into the Germans' right flank had the desired effect. The Germans started to pull in their horns. The pressure on the Americans eased somewhat. As the Lancers advanced to recapture the ground that Waters' men had lost, the Germans finally decided they had had enough, for the time being at least. Some of them began to withdraw, leaving a dozen smoking or burning Mark IV Specials behind them. But not all. Among the dried up creeks and wadis, a few still lurked, making the Americans pay the price for their bold charge against the steel monsters.

Second Lieutenant Daubin was one of the few lone Americans bravely trying to stave off the inevitable. At the range from which he was engaging the Mark IV, not even poor cross-eyed Ben Turpin of silent movie days could have missed. But Daubin's shells simply bounced harmlessly off the German tank as it advanced ever closer on the valiant little Honey.

Now it was only fifty yards away. The young officer braced himself inside his turret for what was to come: the German shell ripped the sky apart—*and missed!* Striking the nearby wall of the wadi, it showered Daubin's turret with dirt and pebbles. But the Mark IV lumbered steadily on toward him, only thirty yards away now, climbing a small mound. Daubin decided his luck wouldn't last much longer. The time had come to retreat—and fast.[15]

To his horror, the young officer discovered he couldn't reach the driver with his foot. The latter was half buried in empty shell cases. Daubin leaped down beside him.

"Reverse!" he cried urgently above the roar of the Honey's engine.

The driver seemed absolutely calm. Daubin couldn't understand it. They started moving back down the wadi; now the Honey was beginning to climb the bank. They were going to make it. They were going to escape.

But it wasn't to be. The Mark IV fired at point-blank range. The world disintegrated before Daubin's horrified gaze. Thereafter everything happened in confused fragments, like a newsreel film glimpsed at intervals. *Wham*—and a shower of hot shrapnel... Daubin, for some inexplicable reason, lying on the ground, gasping for breath and knowing he was bleeding to death... The gunner, blind, stunned and badly injured, crawling out of the tank on all fours to collapse in the dirt... The loader running for his life, arms working like pistons, to be cut down by a cruel burst of machine-gun fire ... The Honey ablaze, flames licking up everywhere along its structure, moving off under its own power, a ghost tank, kept going by some mechanical freak till it had creaked around the bend to disappear, leaving him there to die...

But young Daubin didn't die. He would live to fight again in North Africa, Sicily, and Italy. He would live, too, to learn the reason that his shells had been so ineffective against the German monsters. The ammunition that he and the other Honeys should have been using that day was still rattling around somewhere in the utter chaos and confusion that was the Army's major supply port, Algiers. The 1st Tank Battalion had been firing shells meant for use in peacetime exercises.

five

The troopship was torpedoed just after it had sailed past neutral Tangiers, the first land that the seasick nurses had seen since leaving Scotland. For five days the battered old ship SS *Strathallen* had fought waves sixty feet high. All the furniture had had to be tied down, but even so, the piano in the ship's lounge had broken loose one night and slammed across the parquet floor into the wall, with a crash of mahogany and a twanging of piano wires. "Oh my God—*The Lost Chord!*" groaned Kay Summersby down below in the cramped cabin she shared with Ethel Westermann, a nurse, and Jean Dixon, a Washington girl whose British husband had been killed in the RAF.

But the rough seas of the Atlantic were soon forgotten as they sailed into the calmer waters of the Mediterranean. Tomorrow the *Strathallen* would dock at Oran, and Kay knew she would be reunited with Ike. The girls planned a last night party, and after packing their luggage they went to join some friends "in a party as gay as any peacetime celebration aboard a cruise liner."[1]

It was one-thirty in the morning when Kay and the other girls returned to their cabin. She kicked off her shoes and was just beginning to take off her tie—pictures of her new life in Algiers flashing by her mind's eye, "where all the women looked like Hedy Lamarr and the men spoke like Charles Boyer"—when it happened.

The German submarine's torpedo slammed into the side of the troopship. Kay was hurled against the bulkhead. The lights flickered and went out. For a moment there was absolute silence, broken only by the hiss of steam escaping from the *Strathallen*'s ruptured boilers. Quietly Ethel Westermann said, "This is it, kids."

The three girls grabbed their coats and struggled up onto the deck, already beginning to tilt to port alarmingly. As Kay recorded after the war, "There was no confusion, no panic." The faces of the nurses and women auxiliaries, who made up many of the troopship's passengers, were "sleepy, presenting a half-sheepish, half-astonished expression," as if they could not realize that this was happening to *them*.

Boats were lowered hastily, and the Lascar crew helped the women into them. Swiftly Kay Summersby's boat began to pull away from the stricken, sinking ship, through water filled with soldiers, yelling for help, swimming around aimlessly in the darkness. Kay grew angry at the Lascars because they refused to pick up the soldiers, but finally their white coxswain cursed and cajoled them into action and 20 soaked soldiers were hauled aboard, including one with a broken leg, who gasped out the horrible news: "Whole boat turned when they lowered it . . . Lots of nurses and officers drowned!"

But now the rescue ships were close at hand. A lean gray shape hove out of the darkness, and an English voice called through a megaphone that the whole area was infested with U-boats. They couldn't be picked up until morning.

Dawn came. The sun came out and wet clothes began to steam and dry. The soldiers talked of food. The women applied their lipstick. Finally the destroyer of the night before appeared once more and took the survivors aboard, to feed them hot tea and meager emergency rations. Later that afternoon they were landed at Oran. Kay Summersby had reached Africa, which was going to be her home—and Ike's—for over a year, the most eventful year in both their lives.

The soldiers marched away, leaving Kay and her companions wondering what to do next and how they were going to find clothes in this strange place. In the end, still wearing her wrinkled skirt and torn nylons, Kay pushed her way into the American headquarters there and demanded to see the officer in charge.

"Look here," she cried in exasperation, "I've just been rescued from a torpedoed ship. I want to call General Eisenhower and tell him his staff is safe. And I want to get orders what to do next." She ended with that malicious English middle-class phrase: *"Do you mind?"*

The name Eisenhower worked like magic. The colonel in charge got her through to Eisenhower's headquarters right away.

Eisenhower spoke to her personally, then Clark, the Deputy Supreme Commander. Twenty-four hours later Kay Summersby was aboard Eisenhower's personal B-17 bomber heading for Algiers. As General Everett Hughes, that inveterate American chronicler of scandal and tittle-tattle at Eisenhower's headquarters, remarked in his diary: "Ship with five WACs, thirty navy nurses, 200 English nurses [has been] torpedoed. Bedell[2] flew to Oran, took over the WACs; the five were promoted to captains at 2,000 dollars p.a., the nurses got nothing except English battledress."[3]

Already the saturnine-looking general, who had a way with a woman—and a bottle—himself, had noted in that diary of his: "I suspect from the females that Ike is taking [to N. Africa] that Butch[4] has his eye on a bit of . . . for the CG."[5]

Kay Summersby and the WACs had arrived.[6] The cozy period of housekeeping in Algiers, over four hundred miles from the front in Tunisia, could commence.

On the same December day that Kay Summersby first

entered the old St. George Hotel, high on the cliffs above the
city of Algiers, Eisenhower wrote in self-disgust to an old
friend in the States: "I think sometimes that I am a cross
between a one-time soldier, a pseudo-statesman, a jack-
legged politician and a crooked diplomat . . . I walk a soapy
tight-rope in a rain storm with a blazing furnace on one side
and a pack of ravenous tigers on the other."[7]

Presiding at the daily conferences in the old hotel, with its
high ceilings and freezing rooms, Eisenhower was so beset by
political, military, and personnel problems that he regularly
ended squabbles among his French, British, and American
subordinates with a curt, angry, "Anyone who wants the job of
Allied Commander-in-Chief can have it!" The saying, which
had begun as a joke back in November, was now deadly
earnest as the front in Tunisia bogged down and the problems
piled up here in Algeria.

The French under Darlan still were not cooperating fully
with their Anglo-American allies; they were dragging their
feet, complaining that they lacked weapons and supplies,
although they possessed the biggest army in Africa, some
fourteen divisions in all. Not only that, Darlan still insisted on
court-martialling all French officers who had aided the
Allied landings as "traitors." If that were not enough, those
French troops who were in the line—General Koeltz's corps
serving on the British First Army's right flank—refused to
take orders from the British. Koeltz took his orders directly
from General Juin—Darlan's man—although General Giraud was now officially commander-in-chief of the French
Forces in Africa.

There were local problems, too. After the fall of France, the
local authorities had placed severe restrictions on French
North Africa's Jewish population, as was done in Vichy
France. There, the Minister of the Interior had ordered all
Jews to be rounded up and, in due course, sent to German-
occupied Europe, where many thousands of them perished in
concentration camps. Now that same minister of the interior,
Marcel Peyrouton, was appointed governor general of Alge-

ria by Darlan. It was no use Murphy protesting that Peyrouton was better than his reputation. Eisenhower knew he stood for repression and collaboration in the eyes of liberals in the States and the Gaullists in England.

The Arabs were another source of trouble. They wanted food and clothing, and the more educated ones wanted something else as well—they wanted liberty from the French. Already, Intelligence reported, the Arabs were making approaches to the Germans in Tunisia; virtually everywhere that German troops operated they were assisted by the local Arabs. The Nazi yoke seemed preferable to the Arabs to that of France. Both Clark and Murphy impressed upon Eisenhower that the prime need was to keep order in Algeria. Only established French officials who knew the country and the language could do that.

So again Eisenhower, harassed and unwell by now, had to compromise. Just as had been the case with the Jews and with those officers who had actively attempted to aid the Allied cause, Eisenhower allowed things to stay as they were. The French, under the command of the two men who were hated as Vichy collaborators, would continue to repress the Arabs and, ruling through the various Arab puppet "beys" and "kings," crush any attempt at independence.

Churchill thought the American was too naive for French North African politics, but Eisenhower sent him a cable: *"Please be assured that I have too often listened to your sage advice to be completely handcuffed and blindfolded by all of the slickers with which this part of the world is so thickly populated."*[8] To General Smith, still in London, Eisenhower wrote a letter asking him to impress upon the British the fact that the Allies were still very weak in Africa. Without French help the situation would be impossible. Allied strength was building up but, he wrote, "it will be a long time before we can get up on our high horse and tell everybody in the world to go to the devil!"[9]

Wheeling and dealing that December like the "jack-legged politician" with whom he had compared himself, somehow or other Eisenhower managed to satisfy—or half-satisfy—everyone except his boss in Washington. On December 22, 1942, with the front in Tunisia hopelessly bogged in the mud, rain, and mountains, Marshall cabled Eisenhower sternly: *"Delegate your international diplomatic problems to your subordinates and give your complete attention to the battle in Tunisia!"*[10]

At the front it rained: a cold gray drizzle that, together with the fog on the dripping heather-covered mountainsides, made the place look more like Scotland than Africa. For weeks it had continued to drizzle while Anderson's men attempted to batter through the mountain passes that barred the road to Bizerta and the final prize, Tunis. But Koch's paratroopers, Witzig's airborne engineers, and the tankers of Fischer's 10th Panzer Division managed to hold them, throwing back attack after attack.

They had all taken their turn, those handful of British and American units that made up Anderson's grand-sounding First British Army: paratroops, commandos, the PBI ("Poor Bloody Infantry") of the Battleaxe Division, the tankers of the 6th Armoured Division, and those of the 1st Armored's Combat Command B. And every time they had been repulsed by the Germans dug in along the mountainsides overlooking the "bloody djebels" as the weary, bitter soldiers cursed those dank, wet valleys in which death reigned.

All the infantry battalions were down to half strength. The Hampshires, for example, who had gone into action 800-men strong, returned with exactly six officers and 194 men (of whom 100 had not taken part in the fight). The tankers, British and American, suffered, too. Their "popguns" were simply no match for the German 75mm and dug-in 88mm cannon, to say nothing of the new monster that had appeared on the battlefield here for the first time—the 60-ton Tiger tank, armed with an 88mm gun, the armor of which could not be penetrated frontally by any existing Allied gun.

Slowly but surely, the steam started to go from Anderson's

drive. His men had been in contact with the enemy virtually every day since the landings; now they began to weary and bog down in the thick goo of the Tunisian mud. The mud, the lack of supplies—which had to come from Algiers 500 miles away, being shipped there all the way from Britain—and the paras of those two tough "turret-breakers," Koch and Witzig, were proving simply too much for the Tommies and their Yank friends of the U.S. 1st Armored.[11]

The mud was so bad that, for two miles behind the front, all supplies had to be brought up by mules, and the 250 casualties being evacuated daily had to be taken out by the same laborious means. That mud, thick, sticky and bottomless, was graphically described by the Australian war correspondent Alan Moorehead. "The dead were buried in the mud and the living were in it up to their knees. They were wet to the skin all day and all night. They had mud in their hair and mud in their food. When the mud dried, it set like iron and had to be beaten off the boots with a hammer or a rifle-butt. Before the astonished eyes of the commander, tanks went down to their turrets in mud. A spell of a few fine days made no difference—the mud was there just the same, and if you sent out a squadron of tanks you never knew whether or not they would be caught in another downpour and so abandoned to the enemy."[12]

But it wasn't only the mud. The nights were bitterly cold, with snow and frost glittering on the mountain peaks. A. B. Austin, the *Daily Herald* correspondent, heard one Louisiana GI complaining in "his high-pitched Huckleberry Finn drawl" that: "Folks back home think Africa's warm. They should be here at night. *Brr!* If there was rain, the puddles should be crackling!"

"I have never been as cold ever since as that winter of 1942 in Tunisia," ex-captain Eric Taylor of the 78th Division could recall forty years later. "All the infantry had up front was a hole and what they could carry or loot from the abandoned French farmhouses. At night we crawled into our holes, wrapped in anything and everything we could find, including rugs and carpets looted from the farms and tarpaulins stolen from the gunners. For a couple of hours, one could manage to keep fairly warm, but by two or three in the morning the biting mountain cold would steal into your very bones and you would be praying for dawn and first light, trembling like a puppy in your hole, with the stars looking down icy and unfeeling."[13]

But those young men of forty years ago were hardy creatures. They had gone through the Depression of the 1930s and had always known lean times. The war and its shortages and then the Army had toughened them even further. Now hundreds of miles from civilization they lived a strange life, unthinkable to their folks back home. If they were tankers, they led a nomadic existence; if they were infantry they lived like cave-dwellers.

"We stood to mostly just before dawn," remembers ex-Trooper Frankland of the 17th/21st Lancers. "It was forbidden to brew up during the hours of darkness and we would be standing there above the 'flimsies' (primitive stoves) filled with petrol and earth, matches at the ready, trembling just to get the first brew of char of the day started."[14]

There was always somebody who could not wait. "There'd be the soft whoosh of petrol exploding, a spurt of blue flame and suddenly, all around, blokes would be lighting their fires and putting the dixies on top of them to boil up the char (compo tea with a can of condensed milk added). Out would come the compo rations, forty-two tins of various meals for fourteen men, together with seven fags per person, a bar of bitter chocolate and some boiled sweets, plus "Army Form Blank" ready for the next operation after the first brew-up. And always someone'd say as we worked on the cans with our jack-knives, 'Which tin has got the cunt in, mates?'"[15]

Soon the freezing morning air would be heavy with the smell of cooking, "armoured pig" (Spam) and "bully" (corned beef), as the men fried their breakfast on the "flimsies." Then biscuits would appear, dripping with plum-and-apple jam, the only sort they had, to be washed down with a mug of steaming hot "char."

Breakfast over, men would be seen striding purposefully into the countryside, "Army Form Blank" in one hand, a spade in the other. They were "taking a shovel for a walk" as they called it; for all of them were suffering by now from "gippo tummy," which resulted in "the quick sits": the virulent three-day bout of dysentery that was epidemic. A wash, a shave in cold water with a plastic razor that left the face red and sore for the rest of the day (for this was the British Army; one shaved before one went out to meet the enemy), and they were off again, "swanning about" in the wadis and the "bloody djebels," hoping to catch "Old Jerry" off guard.

Like their comrades of Montgomery's Eighth Army, a thousand miles or more to the east, they were creating a vocabulary all their own.

Unless there was a big attack going on, the infantry "lay doggo" most of the day, cramped in the "funk-holes" or "wanking pits" as they called the slit trenches, talking about "bints" (girls), "desert chickens" (bully-beef), and the "flying dhobi wallahs" (Arab laundrymen) who seemed to appear out of nowhere whenever there was anything of value to be picked up. For hours on end they would lie there, shivering and smoking (if they were lucky, for cigarettes were in short supply), keeping an eye on the gray December sky because the Luftwaffe still dominated Tunisian airspace, and waiting for the real business of the day.

Just before night swept across the valley floor like the wings of a great silent black bird, they would cook their rations, wash if they could, and then assemble ready for yet another fighting patrol.

With the German *Fallschirmjäger*, the paras of Koch's and Witzig's regiments, dominating the heights, and the Luftwaffe all powerful during daylight hours, shooting up everything that moved—in one week alone the 78th Division had lost 250 supply men delivering rations—offensive action could only be successfully taken at night.

The infantry respected their opponents. As the divisional historian of the 78th wrote just after the war, "The German troops in North Africa were highly trained, skilful, courageous and at their best in defensive, delaying fighting." But in between the German positions and the British positions there were "huge unpoliced areas as big as England behind and on every side, peopled by French farmers, some of doubtful friendliness, and by Arabs some of whom spied for one side now and for the other at another time, and who stripped the dead of their clothes."[16]

Into these "unpoliced areas" the fighting patrols slipped, on the look-out for trouble—at least, their officers were. Invariably they would find it: a hissed challenge; an angry, frightened cry; a sudden flare hurtling into the night sky, bathing the crouched figures in its eerie glowing red light; a burst of fire; the crump of a hastily flung grenade. *COMBAT!*

Later they would be limping back to their own lines, ever fearful that one of their own lads, a little more trigger-happy than the rest, might finish them off even now. Usually they would be dragging their wounded with them, and maybe also a prisoner or two, a bewildered, terrified "Hans" or "Fritz" who would face interrogation.

There was no comfort anywhere for the infantrymen, no little luxuries to ease their bleak existence. Drink played no part in their lives—it was only officers who got a ration of one bottle of whisky and one of gin each month. Sex was simply a matter of boasting talk, fond memories, and, if they had the energy in those miserable dank conditions, the caresses of the "one-armed widow." The only civilian women they ever saw were the occasional Arabs—filthy, ragged, and downtrodden, looking at twenty as if they were three times that age.

Of course, the Arabs were always there, even in the most unexpected places, at the summit of some vital djebel or at the bottom of a garbage pit, scavenging as usual. But the natives were simply spectators as far as the Anglo-Americans were concerned. The Arabs waged war "with oranges, eggs, dates, almonds, and shoeshine boxes," as the *Stars and Stripes* recorded at the time, "rather than with hand grenades and howitzers." Admittedly there were Arab snipers in the hills, "snipers who seemed to be harmlessly tending the stunted dwarf Barbary cattle or riding inoffensively with their families on overloaded small donkeys," as BBC war correspondent Howard Marshall noted, although he also commented that "The Arab's main capacity seemed to be for squatting on his haunches wrapped in filthy robes, endlessly contemplating the infinite."[17]

Filthy the Arab certainly was. One new arrival, Artillery Lieutenant John Guest of an antiaircraft unit, was shocked by the natives' way of life. Writing that December to a friend back in Britain, he said: "They live in what look like hollowed-out dunghills; they scratch the earth for food, scrounge, scavenge, scratch themselves and potter about on tiny donkeys, their feet almost touching the ground on either side . . . The rags they dress in are beyond description—hundreds of small pieces crudely stitched together and displaying horrible sores on their legs, arms and chests . . . But they are a nuisance. You can't leave anything unguarded. Morality doesn't enter into it—stealing and scrounging are just their livelihood."[18]

The Arabs were "a nuisance": this was a sentiment agreed upon by all the frontline troops, British and American. Near Tebessa, where the U.S. II Corps was based, they brought large sections of the communication network to a standstill by cutting fifty-yard lengths out of the insulated Signal Corps wire to use as clotheslines. They stole the troops' barracks bags to make into trousers, cutting slits in the bottom of the bags for leg holes and using the draw cords as belts. Wherever the soldiers built screens around their "crappers" and "thunderboxes," the Arabs sneaked up at night and stole them; they used the material to make cloaks for the men and rough sandals for the womenfolk. As the GIs cracked to each other: "The Arabs have broken through and are bringing up vital supplies—of rugs and shoeshine boxes!"

One cynical staff writer of the U.S. Army newspaper *Stars and Stripes* summed up the Arabs: "The truth will some day have to be told to our children. We, their fathers, will confess that the North African campaign never really ended. When leaving this continent, will go the story, we fell in disorgan-

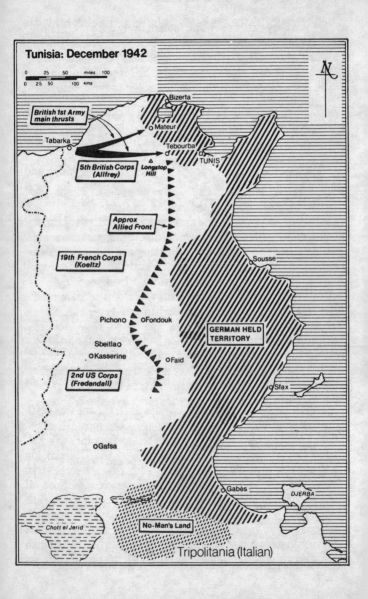

Tunisia: December 1942

0 25 50 *miles* 100
0 25 50 100 *kms*

British 1st Army
main thrusts

Tabarka

Bizerta

Mateur

Tebourba

TUNIS

5th British Corps
(Allfrey)

Longstop
Hill

Approx
Allied Front

19th French Corps
(Koeltz)

Sousse

GERMAN HELD
TERRITORY

Pichon

Fondouk

Sbeitla

Kasserine

Faid

2nd US Corps
(Fredendall)

Sfax

Gafsa

Gabès

DJERBA

Chott el Jerid

No-Man's Land

Tripolitania (Italian)

ized retreat with the Arabs on our heels; and we left behind to our opponents great stores of cigarettes, candy and GI clothing. '*Baraka!*' say the Arabs, meaning 'blessings' . . ."

But if the troops at the front lived a harsh, tough, brutal life, which ended all too often in sudden death, there was plenty of *baraka* for the lucky ones who manned that long administrative tail reaching all the way back to Algiers and Supreme Allied Headquarters. "A peacock!" Churchill called it contemptuously. "All tail!"

Chocolate, candy, and cigarettes would buy everything and anything—even "white meat" as the GIs called the local French women. As far back as Casablanca they sang the dirty little ditty called "Stella" to the tune of "Abdul Abul-bul Emir" whose first verse went:

"Now every young tanker who was in Casablanca
Knows Stella, the Belle of Fedala,
A can of 'C' ration will whip up a passion
In this little gal of Fedala."

And it was true. In the big cities—particularly Algiers, with its famous Kasbah—the brothels flourished for "the guys who brought up the Coca-Cola" as cynical frontline GIs called them: "*One* guy in the line and *five* guys to bring up the Coca Cola!"

But there were other women available too, if one was sufficiently flush with black-market money—and most GIs of the Service of Supply had something to sell on the black market. Like their fathers a generation earlier, the GIs quickly learned the necessary phrases for picking up the local girls: *Bon jour, bébé!* and *Voulez-vous promener avec moi?* Soon all the English-French dictionaries in the big cities to the rear were sold out, though as the *Stars and Stripes* recorded, language didn't present an insuperable barrier. Chortled one private to its reporter on December 9, 1942, while the British First Army was fighting for its life under the counterattacks of Koch's paras in the rain-sodden mountains, "These French gals understand the sign language. I had a date with one the other night and she didn't know no English and I didn't know no French, but she sorta knew what I was after."

It was not surprising. The GIs had a lot of money to spend. In that same issue of December 9, the *Stars and Stripes* correspondent reported from Oran: "American soldiers stationed here and French civilians living here are having a wonderful time getting acquainted. So far everything's been as rosy as a honeymoon in Utopia, with the French trying hard to explain how glad they are to have us here and the Americans reciprocating by spending *beaucoup* francs and by passing out unheard of quantities of such previously unobtainable tidbits as chewing gum, candy bars and cigarettes."

There was iced beer, plenty of Algerian wine, citrus fruit aplenty, a local version of the *Folies Bergères*, three o'clock movie matinees, the Red Cross, the USO, the NAAFI—everything. So it was this whole tremendous infrastructure of well-fed, happy soldiers that kept supplies trickling forward (sometimes) to the handful of hungry, wet, frightened men fighting at the front, which was fortunately so far, far away. For this was the country of the "feather merchant" and the "canteen commando," where officers strode around in their "pinks" and gleaming boots, where soldiers wore ties and saluted anything that vaguely resembled an officer, even if the "officer" turned out to be a French postman.

Kay Summersby was rapidly finding her feet in this exciting new world of Algiers. The shops were chic and modern. Some things were in short supply, but there were plenty of French perfumes, lipsticks, and cosmetics—things virtually unobtainable in wartime London.

Fighting off the ubiquitous Arab children begging for candy and gum, she managed to find "a few pairs of panties and bras" to replace those she had lost when the troopship went down. They were, she commented long afterwards, "very French."[19]

Now she was ready to celebrate Christmas 1942 with Ike and the rest of the "headquarters gang." For they were all there now in Algiers: "Beetle" (General Bedell Smith), "Tex" (Colonel Ernest Lee), "Butch" (Lieutenant Commander Harry Butcher), "Mickey" (Eisenhower's servant), and all the rest of them—even the dog Telek. From faraway Morocco, where he was now living like an Eastern potentate in a splendid house, Patton had sent them two live turkeys for their Christmas dinner, their crates so large that Mickey had been forced to collect them in a jeep from the airfield—they had, naturally, been given priority clearance. "Rank hath its privileges," as the GIs said.

But Kay was fated not to eat Christmas dinner with Ike this year. Back home, the press was attacking Eisenhower on all sides because of "the Darlan deal," as it was being called. He could not risk incurring Marshall's displeasure, too, by letting the military situation get out of hand. After all, Marshall had made him in 1941; he could just as well break him in 1942. It was time for Eisenhower to go to the front at last.

On Tuesday December 22, Lieutenant Commander Butcher wrote in his diary: "We are off to the front tomorrow at 6 A.M., the Allied Commander-in-Chief preferring to make it a Christmas at the front. Expected back here Saturday night. I am going along . . . Taking a Cadillac and a Packard in case the Cadillac breaks down . . . All the aides are jealous, and I am glad. This is written for their benefit, as they are privileged . . . to torture themselves by reading this stuff."[20]

It was all going to be very jolly, with packed lunches, flasks of coffee and bourbon, rugs for the Supreme Commander—he was still feeling under the weather—and an escort of armored scout cars "fore and aft" as amateur sailor Butcher put it. At last the Supreme Commander, who had not yet heard a shot fired in anger in two wars, was going up to "the sharp end."

six

The Arabs called it Djebel Almera, the Red Hill. Few if any of the German, American, and British soldiers who fought and died there ever knew this, but if they had known, they would surely have agreed that it was an ironically appropriate name. For before this Christmas week of 1942 was over, Djebel Almera would be red with their blood.

To the general public back home in the States and the United Kingdom, the feature became known as Longstop Hill. The significance of that nickname meant nothing to the Americans, either soldiers or civilians, unacquainted with the terminology of English cricket. The Germans thought "Longstop" meant the furthest the *Amis* and Tommies would ever penetrate their lines—which was true in a way; they were going to hold it till almost the very end.

But the British had named it for its strategic and tactical importance. Before anyone could send an armored thrust toward Tunis, Longstop Hill had to be captured, for it marked the boundary of their view down the Medjerda Valley. It was not an impressive hill. Looking at it from Medjez-el-Bab, the observer saw a long, low, hog-backed eminence, rising out of the valley at right angles to the much more impressive line of rock-crested mountains that rose immediately to the north of it, 2,000 feet or more compared with Longstop's mere 900 feet.

Yet from the top of Longstop one commanded the whole of the Medjerda Valley and most of the plain toward Tunis. On a fine day you could see salt lakes near Tunis, twenty-five miles away. You could also see the main road to Tunis along which the armor would have to advance to capture the capital. Up here you could range your gun batteries on a given spot in the valley below and stop any attack eastward in its tracks. Before Anderson's First Army could attack, Longstop Hill would have to be captured.

And that, in spite of the rain and the mud, was what General Anderson intended to do. He would send his only armored division, the 6th, hurrying down the road to Tunis by way of Massicault, while his battered 78th Infantry Division would guard the left flank against a German counterattack. But first Longstop had to be taken on that left flank.

The tankmen of "the Mailed Fist" Division as the 6th was called (on account of its mailed-fist divisional insignia) regarded the new plan with the utmost gloom. The top brass might be sanguine; the men were not. In front of their positions, as they waited for the day of the attack to come, they could see ample evidence of the victory of "General Mud": a line of rusting U.S. Shermans and Honeys stuck in the mud, lying directly under the muzzles of the German 88mms hidden in the wooded hills above. On December 6, the U.S. 1st Armored Division had been sent reeling by a surprise German attack, losing 18 tanks, 41 guns and 132 other vehicles, as well as 900 American and British soldiers.

The Battleaxe Division had similar doubts, but they were not going to lead the main attack against Longstop. That unenviable task fell to the "new boys": the 1st Guards Brigade and the U.S. 18th Infantry Regiment's 1st Battalion, the pre-

mier battalion of the premier U.S. infantry division, otherwise known as "the Big Red One."

In name at least, they were both elite formations. The Coldstream and the Grenadier Guards had traditions going back
nearly 300 years. Apart from that Scottish regiment that was
so old it nicknamed itself "Pontius Pilate's Bodyguard," they
were the two oldest regiments in the whole of the British
Army. Drill and discipline had made them the best turned out
soldiers in the whole of French North Africa. They would go
into their first real action with creases in their khaki trousers
and their ammunition pouches still squared out with card-
board, as if they were about to mount guard on Buckingham
Palace itself. But they were not just parade-ground soldiers.
They were well trained and tough, and mostly well led, in
spite of the average Guards officer's reputation as a poor
leader of men in actual combat. Despite all the heel-clicking,
slapping of rifle butts, rigid salutes, and the ritual "Permission to speak, sir?" when addressing an officer, they would be
more than a match for General Fischer's *Grenadiere* of the
10th Panzer Division, waiting for them on Longstop.

The 1st Battalion of "the Big Red One" was perhaps not as
disciplined or as well trained as the Guards, but it had the
same high opinion of itself. Indeed, some might have called
them downright cocky. But the 1st had always been like that,
ever since the days of the Civil War when it had been formed.

"No mission too difficult. No sacrifice too great. Duty first!"
That was the proud boast of the 1st Infantry Division. In
World War One, it had been the first outfit to land in France
and, on the morning of October 23, 1917, one of its artillery
sergeants had fired the first shot of the U.S. Army against the
Hun. Now, although those artillerymen of the 34th Infantry
Division had this time beaten them to the draw, they would
show the Kraut that they were just as good as those old doughs
of "the Big Red One," with their old-style pancake helmets,
who had fought the enemy into the ground. Sure, the British

Guards were okay, but they weren't the good ole "Big Red One." And as they went into their first real battle with the Germans, they were confident that nothing could stop them.

General Anderson had estimated that by December 22 he would have four-fifths of his army ready for battle in the forward area, with supplies for eight to nine days of hard fighting. D-Day for the armored thrust would be Christmas Day. Before that, Longstop Hill would have to be cleared.

Now everything depended on the weather. Unless there was fine weather for at least a week, the ground would never harden sufficiently to carry tanks. Fortunately, for six whole days now the weather had been good; the sun had baked the surface of the ground. But underneath there was three to four feet of oozy clay. One light shower and it would turn into the same old frustrating mud that had bogged down the tanks before.

On the twenty-second it was still fine. General Allfrey, commanding V Corps, ordered the great attack to commence. As the tanks of the British 6th Armoured Division rumbled into their start positions, the barrage—if one could call it that—began. This was not the barrage of El Alamein of the previous October, with a thousand guns firing for hours on end. The attack on Longstop commenced with a quarter of an hour's bombardment by sixteen field guns and a few mediums of the Royal Artillery, just enough to alert the *Grenadiere* to the fact that something was happening in the valley below.

It was a bright moonlit night as the Coldstream Guards started their approach. Now the only sound was the muffled tramp of their boots and the croak-croak of frogs in the wadis. The plan was simple. One company would capture the col connecting Longstop with the main range of hills to the left. Another would clear the top, after Longstop had been thus isolated. A third would secure the railway halt, a collection of miserable one-story buildings, east of Longstop. Finally, Colonel Stewart-Brown (invariably, as a Guardee, the Cold-

stream's commanding officer had a double-barreled name)
kept one company in reserve.

Now the guardsmen were splitting up into their companies,
edging their way through the cold, heartless moonlight
towards their various objectives, bodies tensed for that first
high-pitched, hysterical hiss of the German spandau machine
gun. They began to climb the steep hillside. It was tough
going. Everywhere there were rocks and thick-growing juni-
per and rosemary shrubs. Laden down as they were with
equipment and ammunition, they found themselves gasping
for breath. But over the German positions, red and green
signal flares started to shoot urgently into the bright moon-
silvered sky. It wouldn't be long now.

Even though they had been expecting it, that first angry
burst of tracer made the young guardsmen jump. It came
from the shadows of one of the ravines to their right. In an
instant the whole hillside burst into frenetic action. Scarlet
flame stabbed the darkness of the hollows. Tracer zipped
back and forth. Suddenly all was controlled chaos. Officers
crying orders, waving their useless revolvers. Noncoms bel-
lowing red-faced at their men. Guardsmen, all weariness
forgotten now, the adrenaline pumping new energy furiously
into their bloodstreams, hurrying forward at the crouch, the
bullets cutting the air all around their tall skinny frames.

At the Halte d'el Heri, the little railway station in the
middle of nowhere, the Germans had dug themselves in well;
they had barricaded the buildings, turning them into a mini-
fortress. Now as the Coldstreams loomed out of the darkness,
bayonets fixed, the defenders hit them with all they had.
Guardsmen skidded to a stop and crumpled to the ground
without a sound. Others slammed down hard, yelling out in
their sudden agony. But the rest still came on, gaps in their
khaki ranks now, goaded on by strange illusions. If only I can
make it the next five yards I'm safe ... That corner'll do it ...
Stumbling forward against the machine guns firing from the
ticket office, the black-painted *pissoir*, the outhouses, some of

them fell, faces upturned in agony, hands clawing the air as if they were climbing the rungs of an invisible ladder, fighting off death to the last, while others sprinted on, without even a downward glance at their dead comrades, only to suffer the same fate an instant later.

It was the same on the hill itself. There seemed to be German machine guns everywhere, firing at a rate of 1,000 rounds a minute. The air was ablaze with red, green, and white tracer. Still the Coldstreams pushed on, leaving more and more of their comrades lying dead behind them. Major the Hon. A. P. S. Chichester, who commanded the company that was to clear the top of Longstop, fell mortally wounded. His second-in-command took over. And still the guardsmen kept going, eyes wild and staring, faces lathered in sweat.

Now the Coldstreams were inside the station, running along the rusty rails, firing from the hip as they ran. From the cracked windows, the German snipers continued to fire to the very end, scarlet flame stabbing the darkness as they tried to pick off the Guards' officers. Later the officers would learn to carry the ordinary infantryman's rifle into battle; their useless .38s betrayed their identity. Here and there a bayonet flashed silver, and a German howled piteously as the cruel metal slid into his body. Soon the place would be theirs. Carried away by that crazed unreasoning bloodlust of battle, the Coldstreams thrust home their attack and the Germans—what was left of them—broke and ran.

Sobbing for breath, faces flushed as if they had just run a great race, the young soldiers skidded to a stop and let them run. They had taken the station at last.

But already the shrill whistles and hoarse commands in German further up the tracks indicated that the enemy was preparing an instant counterattack, as was their custom. There was no time for rest. Hastily the guardsmen prepared to defend the wrecked little station. But German resistance on the col and on top of Longstop itself was beginning to peter out. Machine guns were still firing furiously from further away and signal flares were hissing into the sky, summoning

help. Soon, however, all that remained of Colonel Rudolf
Lang's *Grenadiere* was a handful of sullen prisoners, mostly
wounded, and the dead.

Now the Coldstream's officers, those who had survived the
two hours of battle, had time to take stock of their situation.
Instead of the one company with half-a-dozen machine guns
that they had been told by Intelligence was holding Longstop,
there had been a whole battalion of 69th Panzer Grenadier
Regiment, which belonged to General Fischer's veteran 10th
Panzer Division. No wonder they had taken so many casualties.

As war correspondent A. B. Austin of the *Daily Herald,*
who was there, reported: "The Germans seemed to have more
machine guns on the hill than they [the Guards] had imagined.
It wasn't just one slope and then the top. You kept climbing
down into small hollows and then up again. When you had
passed one of the hollows or ravines (or re-entrants, as the
military text-books call them) a German machine-gun nest
you hadn't seen in the shadow would open behind you and you
would have to deal with it before you could go on."[1]

But the young guardsmen weren't interested in Jerry
machine guns and "re-entrants" any more. Standing among
the debris of battle—food-tins, empty shell cases, boxes of
tracer, stray grenades, bits of clothing, corpses, and paper,
everywhere paper—they were impatient to be off again. Here
and there some of the older men—"senior soldiers" they were
called, with tattooed arms and knowing faces—were searching the prisoners, supposedly for information but in reality
ripping off their watches, looting them of their cameras,
fountain pens, pornographic pictures. But the majority simply waited, suddenly exhausted, drained of energy and emotion, as down below the sudden snap-and-crackle of small
arms fire indicated the Germans were counterattacking.
Where were the Yanks? What was keeping the Americans of
the 1st Infantry Division?

Now the first soft drops of rain began to patter down.
Slowly but surely the ground began to turn into mud. The

men shivered in the sudden cold. It was one o'clock on the morning of December 23, 1942, two days before the fourth Christmas of World War Two.

Two hours later it was pouring with rain. The first company of the 1st Battalion of "the Big Red One" came slogging up the hill to relieve the Guards, their raincoats black with rain and their boots and gaiters thick with mud. They were angry, a little afraid—for below heavy fighting had broken out at the railway station once more—and they were very frustrated.

The American battalion commander explained to the Guards that they had not expected to take over an active sector. They thought they were coming up to a defensive position—and now the Krauts were everywhere! Indignantly the battalion commander maintained that his men were not ready to take over under battle conditions.

The survivors of the Coldstream attack, the rain dripping off their helmets, their battledress soaked, watched in dumb weary incomprehension. What was the matter with the Yanks? Why didn't they get into the holes and slit trenches dug by the Jerries before first light arrived and the shit started to fly again?

The Guards' battalion commander made it plain that he had another mission to fulfil once his men had been fed. But the Americans still refused to take over. Then the guards promised tank support and the Americans' argument began to weaken.

The first ugly white of the false dawn was beginning to flush the sky to the east, but still the rain poured down. From below there came the angry snarl of German spandaus and the obscene howl and thump of their mortars. The remnants of the company holding Halte d'el Heri was taking a pasting, the impatient Coldstreams told themselves. Already small dark figures could be glimpsed moving back, firing, stopping, firing, stopping, but all the time moving back, leaving a few still figures in the mud every time they did so. The Guards' commanding officer told his American opposite number it was imperative for him to get his men into position. If they didn't, they might well lose the fruits of this night's victory.

"The trouble with the Big Red One," other GIs used to say, "is that it thinks the U.S. Army consists of the 1st Division— and ten million replacements!" It was too proud, too arrogant, too cocksure. Indeed, before the 1st Division was finished fighting in the Mediterranean, General Bradley would be forced to relieve its commander, Terry Allen, and his deputy, General Roosevelt, because "the 1st Division had become increasingly temperamental, disdainful of both regulations and senior commands."

Now, however, the battalion commander of the 18th Regiment's 1st Battalion decided he would have to knuckle under. His men were out in the open, he couldn't risk an open confrontation with the Britishers (after all, he was currently under British command), and he had been promised tanks. With an ill grace, he gave in and started directing his men to their positions. Salutes were exchanged, a few crude jokes and catcalls between the soldiers, Tommies and Yanks, and the survivors of the Coldstream Guards began to file down the hill to start back to camp and a mug of char. This night they had marched fourteen miles and put in two main attacks. They thought they deserved their char. Moodily the Americans took over in the pelting rain. Longstop Hill was theirs— for a while.

The cooks were frying soya links and canned bacon when the Coldstreams returned. The morning air was pungent with the familiar welcome smell. There was char, too, big metal buckets of it, "real old Sarnt-Major's tea," a deep rich brown, brewed so thick you could stand a spoon upright in it. The soaked, mud-splattered soldiers began to unfasten their brown and white enamel mugs from the back of their small packs in anticipation. On mornings like this, with the rain pelting down and the African sky so gray it looked as if it might never stop again, there was nothing to beat a good "brew-up." Eagerly they buried their red, frozen noses in the delightful warm steam coming up from their mugs. Soon they would lie down in the wet gullies and rest, take off their heavy equipment and ease their weary bones; perhaps they might even dare to change their socks.

That wasn't to be. Suddenly officers and NCOs were yelling orders at the surprised soldiers. They were to move off immediately. Taking hasty gulps of the scalding hot tea, the guardsmen grabbed their weapons. Where was the fire? What had happened?

They were soon to find out. The Yanks had been thrown off the summit of Longstop and in the whole of the Guards Brigade there were no other troops available to help them retake it. Their brigade commander, Brigadier R. A. V. Copland-Griffiths, had reluctantly ordered them back to the attack.

So, numb with exhaustion, the Coldstreams marched back through the pouring rain, another fifteen miles, and at five that night they stumbled into a series of ravines filled with forlorn groups of American soldiers, bogged down vehicles, glistening black rock, and dripping heather. Above them the only members of "the Big Red One" still on Longstop, a pocket of heavy machine-gunners, kept firing away. They would counterattack at dawn, together with the Americans. Like dumb animals, heads bent in resignation, sheep waiting for the slaughter, they slumped in the pouring rain.

Eisenhower reached the front on the morning of Christmas Eve. He and his companions had driven for thirty hours through rain, snow, and sleet, stopping only to talk to soldiers at the sides of the road, visiting groups of GIs of the U.S. 1st Armored Division dug in in pup tents and asking for their comments about the war and the weather. They were unprintable. Now, together with Anderson, Eisenhower and the rest made their way to the headquarters of the British V Corps at Souk-el-Khemis.

But in spite of the weather and the setback at Longstop, General Allfrey, a lanky artilleryman and a man of considerable charm, was still full of confidence. Anderson, his boss—dour, uncommunicative, plagued by administrative difficulties (not the least being that Koeltz of the French wouldn't take orders from him and the anglophobe American corps commander Fredendall would only do so with reluctance)—was not.

As for Eisenhower, he was positively radiating optimism, even after his long bone-shaking journey, and even though he was coming down with flu. He had to. Today he had to prove to Marshall, far away in a hot, sticky Washington, that he was up to the job of getting the British moving and capturing Tunis before the end of the year. The United States, and in particular the U.S. Army, needed a victory after a solid year of defeats.

Anderson told Eisenhower glumly that he had ordered trials of all types of equipment to be used in the present V Corps offensive. Nothing could be moved satisfactorily. "General Mud" was proving too tough for the Allied vehicles. Unlike the Germans, who had quickly modified their own vehicles after their terrible experiences in the mud of Russia in the winter of 1941/42, American and British tank tracks still were too narrow. They either bogged down or threw a track as soon as they hit deep mud.

With this new rain and resultant morass, wheeled vehicles simply could not get closer than 5,000 yards of the forward companies, tracked vehicles no nearer than 3,000 yards. Ammunition was being manhandled two miles or more into the line and the wounded were being brought out the same way by relay teams of stretcher-bearers.

Later Eisenhower would claim in his memoirs[2] that he had realized the offensive had no chance of success and had decided there and then, in that remote Tunisian farmhouse with raindrops streaming down the dirty windows like cold tears, to stop it. But according to the diary of Commander Butcher, Eisenhower's personal aide, he was still advising a despondent Anderson to "keep on the offensive." "Ike agreed with General Anderson and the V Corps General Allfrey that if the bad weather persisted, the attack would have to be methodical shelling of enemy positions with artillery, infantry moving up, tanks for infantry support coming along to break through; when the infantry had reached the limit of the range artillery, move the guns and repeat methodically until Tunis was taken."[3]

It was all very amateurish and unsatisfactory. As the rain pelted down and from the direction of the front came the low threatening rumble of German guns, Anderson offered to resign and go back to England. The French wouldn't serve under him but he needed Koeltz's French infantry; his own losses in the rifle companies were so high. Butcher commented in his diary that Anderson had been "most sporting in his own efforts personally to find a solution, but the fact was the French simply would not go under British command."

Eisenhower assured Anderson that he would sort this problem out, however, and the discussion now drifted to the possibility of giving more responsibility to Fredendall's II Corps in the south. It was decided to detach the 1st Armored Division's CCB from Allfrey's command and send it to Fredendall. The rest of the 1st Armored would follow, so that the II Corps Commander would be in a position to make a spoiling attack on Gabès, Sousse, and Sfax. Those were the towns Rommel would be forced to use for his supplies once he had retired across the border into Tunisia, which he must do soon, when Montgomery seriously took up the pursuit of the *Afrika Korps* with his Eighth Army.

The discussions went on and on, while up on Longstop Britons and Americans died and the rain washed down on those young dead faces with their unseeing eyes. In the end, Allfrey suggested a break for "a spot of food."

The suggestion was accepted with alacrity. But not the food. It was little better than the meal Allfrey had served General Koeltz of the French 19th Corps a couple of days previously. The elderly French Commander had recoiled at the mere sight of his dinner, consisting of bully beef and hard

tack washed down with a mug of water. Even in war, one had
to keep up one's culinary standards. So Koeltz had left in a
hurry, convinced that the V Corps couldn't win the war on
that type of food.

Back in Algiers they did better, much better for themselves.
On December 23, Clark and Murphy had lunch with Admiral
Darlan. The fare provided by "the Little Fellow," as Clark
was now calling Darlan, was splendid. Afterward, when Darlan said, "Tomorrow the Axis press will say I gave this lunch-
eon because a gun was pointed at my head," Clark chuckled
and replied, "If the rest of the luncheons were as good as this, I
would get my gun out every week."

Then it had been Darlan's turn to chuckle.

Later, alone with Murphy in his study, Darlan was less
cheerful. "You know," he said slowly, looking up at the American diplomat from his papers, "there are four plots in existence to assassinate me. Suppose one of those plots is successful. What will you Americans do then?"

Murphy tried to calm his fears as Darlan produced a list of
Frenchmen who might succeed him. Murphy was well aware
that Eisenhower and Clark would be only too glad to see the
end of Admiral Darlan. But he didn't tell the Frenchman
that. Instead he made small talk until finally Darlan changed
the subject and they parted. He would not see Darlan alive
again.[4]

The end was approaching for the little French admiral who
had played both ends of the game for so long. For two months
now, de Gaulle in London had been planning to remove both
Giraud and Darlan; both stood in the way of his quest for
power. Using his representative in Algiers, General d'Astier
de la Vigerie—an aristocrat and supposed royalist—a group
of plotters was formed. From the group a young student was
selected to assassinate Darlan: 22-year-old Bonnier de la
Chapelle, from a well-known Algiers family. He was given a
pistol and told that he would become a national hero if he

killed Darlan. The pretender to the French throne, the Comte
de Paris, would then become King of France and the taint of
Vichy would be removed once and for all.

In reality, de Gaulle knew that Darlan's death would serve
a double purpose. It would discredit the Americans by bringing Darlan's name into the headlines once more, a man who
was both anti-British and an arch collaborator; it would also
leave the way open for de Gaulle to rid himself of Giraud, who
would be easy meat for him once Darlan was removed.[5]

So while the Guards and their American comrades fought
and died on the sodden slopes of Longstop, the killer burst into
Darlan's office. He fired four shots into him before finally
being overpowered by one of the staff officers. Darlan sank to
the floor, mortally wounded.

Far from being treated as a national hero, however, young
Bonnier de la Chapelle found himself arrested and forced to
confess all. Twelve of his accomplices were also arrested, and
one of them admitted that General d'Astier had paid them the
equivalent of $38,000. But before any more details of de
Gaulle's plot could be revealed, General Jean Bergeret, who
was in charge of Darlan's security, had the student shot out of
hand. To this day, no one knows why; perhaps he was part of
the plot too.

Now panic gripped Algiers. Clark clamped an immediate
and total news blackout on North Africa and cabled Marshall
in Washington to plug any possible press leaks there and in
London. Military law was proclaimed. Armed guards appeared on every street corner. A curfew was imposed.

At the hospital where Darlan had been taken, Clark and
Murphy were met by a crowd of excited French officers,
volubly accusing each other of the assassination and throwing
very hostile looks at the two Americans. Forcing a way
through, they were ushered into Darlan's hospital room, but
the admiral was already dead. Clark thought "the Little Fellow" looked calm and peaceful; perhaps death had come as a
release to him after the month and a half he had spent in the
"hot seat." His demise had certainly come as a relief to Clark.

"It was like lancing a troublesome boil," Clark admitted later. "He had served his purpose and his death solved what could have been the very difficult problem of what to do with him in the future."[6]

But there was no time for such considerations now. He had to call Eisenhower at the front, to let him know what had happened.

War correspondent A. B. Austin stood in the mud beside the brigade major, watching the last of the Guards' reserve plodding steadily up toward Longstop, backs bowed against the continuing rain as they vanished into the gray mist of war that ringed the hill. Austin noted that the Brigade Major was looking very tired; he had not had any sleep for nearly thirty-six hours, and he was soaked and hungry. He turned to Austin and said, "It's sad to see one's friends go."

The civilian knew what he meant. They were going to their deaths. Austin could already hear the snarl of the German machine guns up above, followed by the slower pedantic chatter of the British bren and the swift rattle of the American BAR. He knew that some of them would soon be back—wounded, holding their shattered limbs, rolling their eyes and staggering like drunks, stumbling and skidding through the mud. The Coldstreams' commanding officer and adjutant had already been wounded. What was left of the battalion was now commanded by Major Roddy Hill—"magnificent, standing boldly on the ridge, and rallying the troops," as medical officer Lieutenant Grey-Turner described him.

But how many more casualties could they stand, those men of the 2nd Coldstream and their comrades of the 1st Battalion, before they ceased altogether to exist as a fighting force? Austin didn't know. Nor did the brigade major. Above them, the slaughter in the rain continued.

Down in the farmhouse in the valley, the discussions were sti˙ continuing, but at least they were making some progress now. Eisenhower, it had been decided, would take command of the front personally, trying to coordinate the activities of all the French, British, and American troops in Tunisia. General Juin, the French overall commander, had now agreed to work with Anderson, which meant that Koeltz's corps would now consent to take orders from the British. In due course, all American troops scattered between the French and British to the north would be collected and sent to join Fredendall's II Corps.

But there was still the question of the First Army's offensive. In spite of the bad weather and the casualties already being incurred by the infantry on Longstop, the top brass wanted to continue it. Brigadier Currie, an outspoken artilleryman commanding the 9th Armoured Brigade, objected strongly. It should be cancelled forthwith, he asserted. All the tanks sent up to aid the Guards and the Americans at Longstop had bogged down immediately. Anglo-American tanks simply could not cope with the thick red Tunisian goo. Under such conditions, the 6th Armoured Division wouldn't stand a chance.

It was at this stage that Clark in Algiers finally managed to get through to Eisenhower with the news about Admiral Darlan. Eisenhower had been intending to eat Christmas Eve dinner with his men at the front, but now he abruptly changed his plans. He would leave Anderson to make his own decisions about the V Corps offensive: whether it should be continued or stopped. He had to rejoin Clark in Algiers: the whole situation was getting too red-hot for Clark to handle alone.

So, within the hour, Eisenhower had left the farmhouse and was speeding back to Algiers, going all out on the slick dangerous mountain roads, stopping only for "comfort breaks" and living off emergency rations, eaten cold. He arrived in Algiers on the twenty-sixth, just in time for Darlan's funeral.

They all went—Clark, Eisenhower, Murphy, Giraud, the men who had arranged "the Darlan deal." In one way or another, they were all glad that he was dead; the murder, whoever had arranged it, had solved a lot of problems. But they kept their faces suitably solemn throughout the long ceremony in the crowded Roman Catholic church. The only one of them to show any emotion was Giraud—of whom Darlan had sneered that he was fit to command nothing higher than a division. Kneeling at the bier of the man who had repeatedly humiliated and insulted him, the tall soldier bent his head and wept.[7]

On that same day, they brought the Guards and the infantry of "the Big Red One" down from Longstop Hill for good. As the historian of the Coldstreams recorded, "The Americans fought with stubborn courage to the very end."[8] But they had lost 356 men, killed, wounded, or captured, and there was grave danger of their being cut off. The Germans had thrown in a whole infantry regiment to recapture the all-important hill, and a tank battalion of the 10th Panzer Division was on its way to assist the *Grenadiere*. Reluctantly, General Allfrey of V Corps ordered the withdrawal.

Brigadier Copland-Griffiths, the tall, calm, patrician commander of the Guards Brigade, took charge of the withdrawal. He positioned two companies of Grenadier Guards astride the base of the hill to cover the 2nd Battalion as they came out.

They came down the hillside in weary little groups, their khaki uniforms ragged and sodden, their heavy boots made even heavier with mud, gasping with fatigue and strain, faces grim with defeat. None of the usual banter was exchanged between Grenadiers and Coldstreams as they filed through the former's lines. The Coldstreams knew they had been beaten by those other grenadiers, the men from Hamburg against whose fathers they had fought in France in World War One.

Once within the safety of the Grenadiers' positions, the somber roll-call commenced. Names were called out one by one, as what was left of the attack companies assembled in the dripping rain. "Present," they called back, the lucky ones. More often than not there was no response, just a moment's

silence. Their losses were grievous. In addition to their
commanding officer and his adjutant, the 2nd Battalion had
lost three company commanders, three company sergeant-
majors, and eleven platoon sergeants, plus nearly 200 guardsmen. In three short days of its first action in Africa, the 2nd
Battalion Coldstream Guards had lost one quarter of its total
strength.

With Anderson's First Army drawing in its horns, the
whole offensive started to peter out. There were still a few
local actions being fought; a battalion of the Northamptons,
for example, was lost in the fog on the flank of the Battleaxe
Division and was fighting its way back to British lines. But in
spite of the continuing rumble of artillery and the occasional
burst of machine-gun fire in the mountains, the front was
beginning to settle down. The offensive was off; the Germans
had won the race for Tunis.

A miserable Anderson kept a brave face for his troops. In
his Christmas address to them he said: "Good luck to every
man, and as comfortable a Christmas as the depressing rain
will permit. You have done splendidly and fought most gal-
lantly. Keep up your efforts and I know we shall surely win."[9]

But in a private letter to Alan Brooke, Chief of the Imperial
General Staff in London, Anderson said: "I feel deflated and
disappointed, but it is no use getting depressed; it would be too
easy if we all attempted everything and succeeded, and the
Almighty is much too wise to spoil us mortals that way. So
better luck, I hope, next time. And good wishes to you all at
home from myself and all ranks First Army . . . We are
disappointed, but very far from depressed."[10]

It was an unfortunate letter to send just at that moment,
with its news of failure and its defeatist undertones. When
Eisenhower heard about it, he commented that Anderson
"blew hot and then blew cold"; he never knew where he was
with the man. Montgomery, the other senior commander out
in Africa, was shortly afterward heard to declare that Anderson was "a good plain cook" but "unfit to command an army."

Alan Brooke's own reaction back in London is not recorded,

but the British press were loudly critical: the First Army had flopped miserably, they cried, comparing it with Montgomery's successful Eighth Army, now continuing its glorious advance westward against Rommel's much vaunted *Afrika Korps.*

It later became clear, however, that Alan Brooke must have shared Montgomery's opinion. He had to keep Anderson as commander of the First—there would be a shocking scandal if he were sacked now—but the day would soon come when Anderson was deprived of his command in Africa and sent home to take over his old outfit again, UK (Eastern Command).

One year later, harrowed by humiliation and frustration, Anderson would sneak across the Channel to pay a surreptitious visit to Montgomery's fighting troops in France. He got back to England only just in time; Montgomery almost had him arrested for daring to do such a thing. So Anderson had to stay in England, to die a forgotten man, while history passed him by.

It was all up to the Americans now . . .

American troops, equipment, and supplies brought ashore to a North African beachhead during the Allied landing.

GIs disembark at Mers-el-Kebir near Oran, Algeria.

American troops landing at Surcouf and moving inland

American jeeps move inland from Surcouf.

Headed by "Old Glory," American troops set off from Surcouf.

Enthusiastic reception of American troops in Oran

Sentries had to keep back the cheering crowds as American troops entered Algiers.

The first French prisoners taken by the Americans

Left to right: Lt. Gen. Mark Clark, Adm. Sir Andrew Cunningham (British C-in-C, Mediterranean), Lt. Gen. K.A.N. Anderson (Commanding, British 1st Army), and French Adm. Darlan, whose figure was obliterated when this photo was released during the war because of political embarrassment.

Field Marshal Albert Kesselring (left) and Field Marshal Erwin Rommel, the legendary "Desert Fox"

Paratroops in a transport plane enroute from Algiers to Tunisia

Allied troops holding a position facing Mateur, about 25 miles from Tunis

British troops on the road near Medjez-el-Bab

A British guards battalion manning a slit trench before Longstop Hill

A guards battalion going into action at Longstop Hill

After Longstop, Coldstream Guards on the road to Medjez-el-Bab

A 3" mortar manned by Royal West Kents

An American gun crew prepares its mobile 105mm anti-tank gun for action.

Left to right: General Giraud, President Roosevelt, General de Gaulle, and Prime Minister Churchill

An American light tank

Axis prisoners, guarded by American troops, on their way to prison camp

An American tank in Tabourka

What the tanks must have looked like in action. These are conducting a demonstration for a Turkish commission.

A Panzer IV Special, model F-2. It carries one 75mm gun and two machine guns.

A Tiger tank (PzKw VI). It carries one 88mm gun and two machine guns.

A British-built Valentine tank, captured and marked for use in a German Panzer division

A squadron of German Junker 87s (Stukas)

A German Nebelwerfer 6″ multiple rocket launcher

Men of the 8th Field Squadron, Royal Engineers, probing the Thala to Kasserine road with bayonets, in search of mines

Grenadier Guards supported by Bren carriers reconnoitering near Kasserine

An American 37mm anti-tank gun and crew. Barely visible in the background can be seen shell bursts from enemy artillery in the Kasserine Gap.

seven

Back in 1941, during the last spring before America entered the war, there was a certain major general who had taken to driving his private automobile through the lines of the U.S. 4th Infantry Division at well above the posted speed limit. He was known behind his back as "the Green Hornet," on account of his self-designed new tanker's uniform, a startling shade of green.

"The Green Hornet" was not popular with the commanding general of the 4th for constantly exceeding the speed limit, but the commander was reluctant to mention the matter as the offender was the same rank as himself. One day, however, his military police chief, Captain Hunter Drum, reported that "the Green Hornet" had yet again been observed racing through the 4th's lines at Fort Benning "like a bat out of hell." The commanding officer decided that enough was enough. He ordered that the next time his fellow major general went speeding through the lines, he should be arrested.[1]

The very next day "the Green Hornet" was at it again, driving his automobile through the lines of the 4th at top

speed. Drum, himself the son of a general, sprang into action.
He ordered his MPs to give chase, and one young corporal
duly leapt onto his motorbike and zoomed after the offender,
his siren wailing.

The big car went hurtling through Fort Benning, with the
motorbike in hot pursuit, at twice the legal speed. "The Green
Hornet" was taking crazy risks for such an old man—he could
have been the young corporal's grandfather. But gradually
the motorbike gained on him, and the MP eventually passed
him, curving in and breaking so that "the Green Hornet" had
to hit his own brakes too. The big car finally skidded to a halt.

For one long moment the two men just stared at each other:
the embarrassed young corporal and the imperious major
general, the latter now wearing one of the stern faces he
practiced every night in front of his mirror.

At last the corporal stuttered out the words: "General, I am
sorry, but I have to arrest you for speeding in our divisional
area." He swallowed hard, then went on, "General Fredendall
says—"

"Fuck General Fredendall!" snapped Patton—for he it
was—looking the hapless young soldier up and down. "You
and I are both in 2nd Armored territory, and you can go to
hell!"

And with that, General Patton, commander of the 2nd
Armored Division, drove on slowly—after all, he *was* in his
own divisional area now, and he *was* a stickler for rules.
Behind him the young corporal was left standing by the road,
open-mouthed in astonishment.

This little peacetime garrison-town incident demonstrated
the characters of both men: Patton and Fredendall. They
were both getting old, nearing sixty, and had fought with
distinction in World War One. And both were loud, cocky, and
had firm opinions on every subject under the sun. But there
was one difference between them, these two major generals
who would meet again in defeat in the desert nearly three
years later: the one had talent, the other none. Africa would

make Patton's reputation; it would break Fredendall's. Like Anderson, Fredendall was destined to disappear into obscurity—though not quite yet.

Now, however, as Anderson's offensive up north ground to a halt in the mud, Fredendall was ordered by Eisenhower to leave Oran, which he had captured, and take up command of the II Corps once more in the south. The order came at an opportune time for Fredendall. He was sick of Oran's Grand Hotel and the elegant trappings of headquarters life. He wanted to be where the action was—almost.

So Fredendall established his command post some eighty miles behind the front, far up a canyon that could only be entered by a single, fairly impassable road constructed by his engineers. There he had his sappers labor for three whole weeks digging underground shelters in the wooded hillsides against possible air attack, while the staff went around with pistols at their hips and helmets on their heads, as if the Germans might materialize at any moment. "Most observers who saw this command post for the first time," one observer remarked, "were somewhat embarrassed and their comments were usually caustic." Another thought that there was "an excessive emphasis on security and safety."

War correspondent A. B. Austin was unwittingly ironic in his comments on this HQ, eighty miles away from the front. "The American II Corps headquarters," he wrote, "was up a glen in the pinewood ridge just south of Tebessa. Much better hidden, I thought, than similar headquarters in our army. No enemy planes could possibly spot it under these rocks and pines and you could find your way about easily between the different sections . . . White tapes with little labels radiating from a central point on the pine-needled ground showed you where to go." And Austin concluded, without intentional sarcasm, "Officers and men in their woollen caps and windbreaks, like waterproof mackinaws, made the place look like a lumber-camp."[2]

So as 1942 drew to a close, Fredendall had begun to organize his II Corps for battle. At his immediate command was the 1st Armored Division, minus CCB, which was soon to be moved from Anderson's Army. The 1st Armored was commanded by General Orlando "Pinky" Ward, another old general who had fought with Pershing in Mexico and later in France. Bespectacled, reserved, methodical, he had something of the intellectual about him. Naturally Fredendall didn't like him. In fact, he openly detested Ward, who was so quiet in speech contrary to his own brash behavior. And in his own subdued manner, Ward had no time for Fredendall either.

The next outfit to come under his command would be Terry Allen's flamboyant "Big Red One." Another dashing veteran of the Old War, Allen would manage to get along with Fredendall—but only just. It was to be the same with Ryder of the 34th Infantry Division and with Middleton of the 9th Infantry Division, which would join the II Corps as the last of Fredendall's major formations.

Critical of his superiors, Fredendall was outspoken about the defects of his subordinates, ponderous in action, overbearing in attitude and with a tendency to jump to conclusions—probably, more often than not, the wrong ones. So it was not surprising that in the end, when things began to go disastrously wrong for Fredendall, his subordinates turned against him. In his turn, Fredendall railed against them and blamed them for the mess that II Corps was in. Already, as Fredendall started to establish his corps, with instructions from Eisenhower to "provide a strategic flank guard for our main forces in the North [i.e. Anderson]" and later to "undertake offensive action in the direction of Sfax or Gabès in an effort to sever Rommel's line of communications with Tunisia," the seeds of the coming disaster were already being sown by the cocky, loud-mouthed II Corps commander. America's first major battle against the Germans in World War Two would end in shame, disgrace, and defeat—and Major General Lloyd R. Fredendall would bear a great deal of the responsibility for that defeat.

On the last day of 1942, General Eisenhower gave a dinner party in his commandeered villa in Algiers. During the afternoon, although he was suffering from flu and had spent some of the day in bed, he had dictated his thoughts on the campaign in French North Africa so far. "On the whole I think I keep up my optimism very well, although we have suffered some sad disappointments." He realized, of course, that "only the sissy indulges in crying and whimpering," and that the need now was "to get tougher and tougher," to take losses in one's stride and to "keep on everlastingly pounding until the other fellow gives way."[3]

Then for a while Eisenhower forgot duty and celebrated. The gang were already there, plus some "visiting firemen," including Sir Ian Jacob, Churchill's deputy adviser on military matters. Naturally Kay Summersby was the center of attraction. Telek the dog came rushing to meet her, "a barking, jumping, skidding, fat bundle of black fur." He was badly house-trained (the following January, while Marshall was visiting Eisenhower, Telek made water on Ike's bed while the two senior generals watched helplessly), but it didn't matter to Kay. All that mattered was that the gang was together again and this was an occasion for a celebration; after all, it was the last day of the year.

Sir Ian Jacob thought so, too. He felt that he had to make a small speech to cheer Eisenhower up. As he noted in his diary, "He [Eisenhower] has such an exuberant and emotional temperament that he goes up and down very easily, and a small thing like this [i.e. Jacob's speech] might well have a large effect in restoring his self-confidence."

Apparently it did. The drink and the vivacious presence of Kay Summersby helped as well. Eisenhower forgot his worries about the future. He mellowed. Around midnight, after all the kissing and shaking of hands, the slapping of backs and

singing of "Auld Lang Syne," they started playing bridge.
Eisenhower opened the bidding and made seven hearts. It
was a good sign. They continued to play and drink. Finally, at
one-thirty on the morning of January 1, 1943, Eisenhower
wound up the proceedings by making a grand slam vulnerable, which, as Sir Ian noted, "put the seal on his happiness."

Writing in his journal the next morning, a hung-over Harry
Butcher remarked, "I could use . . . some aspirin today." All
the same, it had been a swell evening, and Ike's success at
cards seemed to Commander Butcher to be "a good omen for
the coming year."[4]

A thousand miles away on the other side of Africa, another
commander was ill and despondent that New Year's Eve.
Rommel was suffering from nausea, fainting fits, and dysentery, and his face was covered with desert sores. But then he
had been in Africa for two years now, fighting constantly, and
he had no Kay Summersby or Telek to cheer him out of his
mood of despair. Card-playing he detested as a waste of time,
and he was not particularly fond of drink.

Once he had been a great popular hero. "The Desert Fox,"
the press back home had called him, and hardly a day had
passed without a photo of him appearing in one of Goebbels'
newspapers. Girls and women had sent him adoring fan letters by the score. They had even sold picture postcards of his
hard, tough face with that cleft chin indicating pugnacity and
an iron will-power, as if he were some damned pomaded film
star.

But that had been before the defeat of El Alamein, before
his long retreat westward with what was left of his poor
shattered army. Now Rommel was a pariah, almost abandoned to the desert, starved of supplies and men, while to the
east men and weapons poured into Jürgen von Arnim's command (von Arnim had taken over from General Nehring) to
build up his army for the coming confrontation with the
Anglo-Americans in Tunisia.

On the last day of November, Rommel had flown to see the Führer personally to plead the cause of his army.

Hitler, who received him with *Reichsmarschall* Goering, had attacked him right from the start. Why had he allowed himself to be defeated at Alamein? "You had better material, stronger artillery, more tanks and air superiority," Hitler raged.[5]

"We ran out of fuel, *mein Führer.*"

Goering had laughed cynically. "Yes, but your vehicles fled back along the coast in their hundreds. You had enough petrol for them."

Rommel had kept his temper with difficulty. What did that fat fool know about war? "We had no ammunition, *Herr Reichsmarschall.*"

"All the same, you left shells by the tens of thousands behind at Tobruk and Benghazi," Goering had countered.

Rommel had flushed. "We didn't have enough weapons either!"

Hitler had jumped on him then. "Your men threw them away," he had barked. "Anyone who doesn't have a weapon must croak."

So Rommel had let them have the truth. It was nothing short of a miracle that his army had managed to escape thus far from the British. Unless it was now withdrawn to Italy it would be destroyed—and so would all German and Italian forces in Italy, once the enemy succeeded in setting foot on the Continent of Europe.

That had been too much for Hitler. "Marshal!" he had cried. "I don't want to hear any more of that kind of nonsense from your mouth! North Africa will be defended like Stalingrad is being defended! Eisenhower's invasion army must be destroyed at Italy's door, *not* in the Sicilian living room!"

Rommel had thought it a good idea, but he needed men, planes, tanks, fuel to do it. In the last twenty months he had never received enough supplies to defeat one army—the British Eighth—yet now he was expected to destroy *two* of them.

He opened his mouth to protest, but Hitler had not given him a chance.

"North Africa will be defended," he had snapped. "This is an order, *Herr Feldmarschall.*"

That had been the Führer's last word. Good soldier that he was, Rommel had said nothing more. Angry and frustrated, he had flown straight back to Africa, landing near that stone marker at El Agheila where it had all begun back in early 1941. His *Afrika Korps* had started its life here. From here, only the previous January, he had snatched victory from defeat yet once again. His men had swept into action with the brilliance and elan of the old days; they had thrust all before them, advancing hundreds of miles into Egypt itself, almost to the gates of Alexandria. It had been a great victory.

But victory was just a dream to him now. He was a defeated commander, his army—what was left of it—on the run. Now he knew his beloved *Afrika Korps* would leave their bones in Africa. Hitler would not allow them a Dunkirk-type evacuation; it would be "to the last man and the last round."

Two days ago, Rommel had written his New Year letter to his wife, Lu, back in the Reich, almost as if it were his *Abschiedsbrief* (letter of farewell): "Our fate is gradually working itself out . . . It would need a miracle for us to hold on much longer . . . What is to happen now lies in God's hands . . . We will go on fighting as long as it is at all possible."[6]

Now, as he lay in the truck that served as his home, feeling sick and shaky with the jaundice that had plagued him throughout the past year, Erwin Rommel, the legendary Desert Fox, considered what was to come. Already they had taken one of his best divisions from him—the 21st Panzer—to give to von Arnim. More would follow. Soon it would be the turn of his Italian armor, he knew. Then he who had once been Germany's most celebrated tank commander would be left with a handful of German and Italian infantry to fight to the last or face the ignominy of surrender, a possibility that did not bear thinking about.

Perhaps, in the end, Hitler would save him from that disgrace and fly him out of Africa. After all, everyone knew he was a sick man, who had survived the diseases and privations of the Dark Continent much longer than any of his original staff. They had all been evacuated or invalided back to the Reich long ago. He was the sole survivor.

Yet before he went, Rommel needed a victory. He could not return home to be placed in the "Führer's Reserve," as it was called, a defeated commander.[7] He *couldn't*! If he were, he might never be given another command—like von Manstein, Halder, von Rundstedt, and the rest who had failed the Führer in these last years. But where could he achieve that victory? And how? All the available resources were now going to that damned Prussian von Arnim in Tunisia. What could he still do with his 14,000 Germans and 15,000 Italians?

Slowly Erwin Rommel began to drift into an uneasy sleep this last night of 1942. Now the only sound was that of the sentries crunching stolidly up and down under the harsh silver of the stars, and the singing of the sand—the millions of sand grains contracting in the night cold and rubbing against one another to give out a strange haunting melody.

It was the year of decision. It was 1943.

PART III

THE KASSERINE PASS

*I have never forgotten that harrowing drive: it was
the first—and only—time I ever saw an American
army in rout.*

—Major General Ernest N. Harmon

eight

"Smiling Albert," otherwise Field Marshal Albert Kesselring, arranged the meeting. The big bluff flyer, who always seemed to have a smile on his face—hence the nickname—brought the two rival commanders together on Tuesday, February 9, 1943, on neutral ground of his own choice: the Luftwaffe base at Rennouch, Tunisia. At last he was going to get the two of them, both as temperamental as opera divas, to agree to the new plan of attack.

It was eighteen years since Field Marshal Erwin Rommel had last met Colonel General Jürgen von Arnim. Then as lowly captains they had not liked each other; now as general officers nothing had changed. They still could not stand each other.

The reason was not hard to find. Von Arnim came of a long line of soldiers—his father was a general—whereas Rommel's father had been a lower-middle-class schoolmaster. Von Arnim was the typical stiff-upper-lipped northern aristocrat, who played with his cards close to his chest. Rommel was loud, ebullient, not given to hiding his light under a bushel. Now,

159

after there had been absolutely no contact between the two commanders for nearly two months (von Arnim had arrived in Tunisia in December 1942 to take command), Kesselring had arranged this meeting to dictate *his* terms to the two of them on what should be done next.

All the previous month von Arnim had been battering away at Anderson's First Army in the north. But in early February he had commenced attacking Koeltz's 19th Corps and its attached Americans to the south with considerable success. He had virtually destroyed one of Koeltz's infantry divisions and had inflicted a hard knock on Ryder's 168th Infantry Regiment, taking nearly 1,100 prisoners, more than half of them American.

In the report presented to the conference by the senior Intelligence officer of the 21st Panzer Division, it was clear that the French felt they had been left in the lurch by the Americans. Prisoners claimed that "Americans send us to the front line to fight, while they stay to the rear."[1]

The senior Intelligence man thought that the Americans' morale was good, but they lacked battle experience, he said, and they were badly led. Moreover, they kept "chattering over the radio all the time so that it was easy to follow their progress and their intentions." Both their artillery and tanks kept far back and "more than once had fired upon their own troops." And, it was reported, captured British and French officers alike referred to the Americans contemptuously as "our Italians." It was a point well taken by Rommel who had had to employ Italian soldiers, badly armed and badly led, for two years now.

Rommel could guess what Kesselring was leading up to: an all-out attack on the *Amis*. Although Rommel was soon to be sent home on medical grounds, he was seized by his old enthusiasm. After a fighting retreat of 2,000 miles, what a triumph it would be for his weary *Afrika Korps*—and, naturally, for the field marshal himself—if he could inflict a stinging defeat on those new boys from "the Land of Boundless Possibilities"![2]

Kesselring confirmed Rommel's guess. "We are going to go

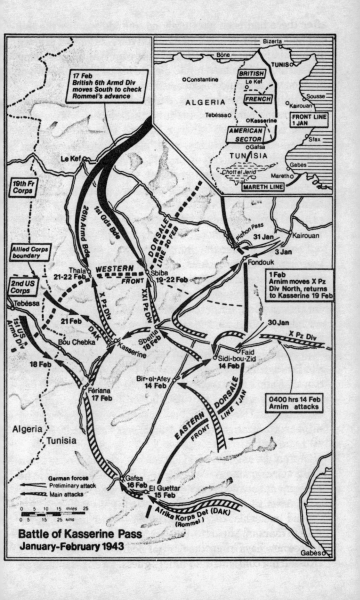

Battle of Kasserine Pass
January–February 1943

all out for the total destruction of the Americans," he said. "They have pulled back most of their troops to Sbeitla and Kasserine ... We must exploit the situation and strike fast."[3]

Swiftly he sketched in his plan. Rommel would attack the Americans to the south, at the oasis town of Gafsa, while von Arnim would do the same to the north at Sbeitla. Once through the mountain passes to the east, the two German armored divisions making the attack, supported by Italian armor, would sweep north, heading for the port of Bone. This bold stroke would remove the threat to the *Afrika Korps'* flank; it might even serve to cut off Anderson's First Army in the north. But above all, it would give the Führer a victory. Kesselring leaned over the desk, that broad, gap-toothed smile of his gone now. *"Meine Herren,"* he said somberly, "after Stalingrad, our nation is badly in need of a triumph."[4]

Three years older than Rommel but still his junior in rank, von Arnim was enthusiastic—but with reservations. There would not be enough fuel for a large-scale operation of the kind Kesselring envisaged. The main thing was to inflict large losses on the French and Americans and force them to withdraw. If Kesselring agreed, he would launch his attack on February 12.

Surprisingly enough, Rommel agreed with the stiff-faced Silesian aristocrat. That would suit him very well, he said; "I can then start my attack on Gafsa two days later, before the enemy can get away." He raised one admonitory forefinger, a characteristic gesture of his, like his schoolmaster father might have done in front of a class of over-eager schoolboys. "What counts isn't any ground we gain, but the damage we inflict on the enemy."

Kesselring, happy that he had achieved at least some agreement between the two commanders, gave in. He accepted the small solution. The conference broke up and "Smiling Albert" now went to work on von Arnim and Rommel separately. He knew that Rommel had hated the long retreat from Egypt. The bold offensive stroke was more his style. What he needed now was "an opportunity to conclude the damaging period of retreats by a successful series of offensives."

Rommel began to share Kesselring's infectious enthusiasm. Perhaps the field marshal's larger solution—an attack right to the coast—was the correct one after all. From all accounts, the *Amis* would prove easy meat after Montgomery's tommies. It could be a great victory.

Then Kesselring sprang his surprise. If Rommel and von Arnim attained the kind of success he envisaged, he would ensure that Rommel would be placed in command of *all* the forces in Tunisia, with the hated von Arnim as his subordinate. After the "nerve-racking" retreat from El Alamein, Kesselring said, Rommel deserved the chance to achieve new glory and fame for himself.

Rommel left, his head buzzing with fresh ideas, full of new enthusiasm. Perhaps this was the opportunity he had been looking for ever since the defeat of El Alamein. A large-scale victory over the Americans might change everything.

But before Rommel and his staff left, Kesselring had a private interview with the doctor, Professor Horster, who had recommended that Rommel should be sent to the Reich for a rest cure. He asked the specialist when he thought his chief should be sent home for his treatment.

The professor, who knew that most of Rommel's illnesses were not organic but of a psychosomatic nature brought on by the strains and stresses of the last two years, considered for a moment. Then he said, "I suggest, Field Marshal, that he depart on about February 20."[5]

Armed with this knowledge, Kesselring hurried away to see von Arnim before he left for his own command. Von Arnim was impatient for his rival to be gone for good so that he might command all Axis forces in North Africa. Kesselring urged him to be patient a little longer. In exactly eleven days, he told von Arnim, Rommel would be flying home for a very long rest cure. Then he, von Arnim, would be running the show.

Kesselring looked at the bleak-faced colonel-general with his trim mustache and chuckled suddenly. "Let's give Rommel this one last chance of glory," he said, "before he gets out of Africa."

Von Arnim brightened up. He actually smiled. "Yes," he agreed. "One last chance of glory . . ."

They shook hands, German style. An hour later Kesselring was in his plane on his way back to Rome. Now it was only five more days to the planned start of the first major attack of the Greater German Army on the U.S. Army in World War Two.[6]

On the evening of the following day, the Supreme Commander of that American Army walked into his office in faraway Algiers to be greeted by a grinning Commander Butcher with his hand outstretched.

"Congratulations!" the former vice-president of the Columbia Broadcasting Service said happily.

Eisenhower looked at his aide in bewilderment. "What for?" he rasped, not taking the proffered hand.

"On being a full general!"

"*What?*" Eisenhower exclaimed. "How did you know?"

Swiftly Butcher explained that he had just received a telephone call from a Captain Barney Fawkes of the submarine mother ship *Maidstone*, anchored out in the bay below. Fawkes had heard on the BBC News that Eisenhower had been promoted to four-star general and had wanted to offer his congratulations.[7]

Now Eisenhower took the hand. He had waited twenty-eight long years for this moment and he had to hear it indirectly through the BBC! "I'm made a full general, Butch, the tops of my profession," he said, a little peeved, pumping Butcher's hand up and down heartily, "and I'm not told officially! Well, maybe it isn't true. How did you say you heard it?"

A smiling Butcher told him again. Just then the phone rang. It was the headquarters message center. The signallers

had received a quick teletype from Mamie Eisenhower back
in the States. For once she was not nagging her long-suffering
husband; instead she had cabled: "Congratulations on your
fourth star!"

At last Eisenhower really believed the news. He called his
staff together—Mickey his orderly, Moaney, Williams, Fos-
ter, his black houseboys—and he promoted them all one grade
on the spot. Then turning to a beaming Butcher he said
happily, "And you can get yourself an aide of your own!"

The only one of his staff that Eisenhower could not promote
that happy evening was "Civilian First Class" (as she called
herself) Kay Summersby. But her turn would come.[8] Now the
gang celebrated. Ike broke out the champagne. General
Hughes got drunk. In Eisenhower's villa they all sat around
the fire, Telek barking excitedly at the noise, toasting the new
four-star general and listening to the phonograph.

Many years later Kay Summersby recorded: "He was very,
very happy that evening. I'll never forget the sheer pleasure
that radiated from him. I remember thinking: There's a man
who has never had much fun in his life."[9]

She was right. Eisenhower's whole life had been the
drudgery of those remote garrison towns, the years waiting
for promotion, the compulsion never to "let one's hair down,"
the endless boredom, the picayune detail of peacetime soldiering in the United States, knowing that life was passing one by,
drifting slowly into middle-age and retirement in Texas,
where the living was cheap and that meager Army pension
might just be stretched from one retirement check to the next.

But that was all forgotten now. Eisenhower, a little drunk
and very happy, enjoyed himself. When Harry Butcher
played his favorite record, "One Dozen Roses," he insisted that
it should be played again and joined in the chorus with his
unmusical voice: *"Gimme one dozen roses, put my heart in
beside them, and send them to the girl I love!"*

That week Butcher recorded in his diary, "Mamie's ears
must have burned!" But Butcher knew that the sentiment was

not addressed to Mamie Eisenhower some 4,000 miles away.
Its recipient, green-eyed and red-haired, was sitting just
across the fireplace from him.

So they sang and drank and enjoyed themselves that
Wednesday night forty years ago, that gang—most of them
long since dead now—while 500 miles away at the front, the
storm was brewing, ready to break soon.

On the morning of February 12, the newly created four-star
general set off for the front to visit his troops. Gone were the
days when he had ridden alone with Kay Summersby at the
wheel of his sedan. Now they set off in a protective convoy,
accompanied by two jeeps filled with armed MPs, as well as a
weapons carrier and a spare sedan. Soon, when they reached
the frontline area, the brass would insist that Eisenhower
should have even more protection. There was something in
the air. Alarming reports were flooding in from British Intelligence that the balloon was about to go up at the front.
German paratroopers and saboteurs had been dropped in
Fredendall's area, and there had been some sniping at American convoys by French and Arab dissidents.

The drive was terrible. Already the famed "Red Ball
Express" system of delivering supplies to the front was in
operation and the truck drivers, black and white, hogged the
center part of the road, going all out, honking their horns,
flashing their lights, in no way impressed by the four stars on
the hood of Eisenhower's car.

Indeed the only person in the little convoy that the hard-
boiled truckers seemed to notice was the red-haired woman
behind the wheel of Eisenhower's sedan. In spite of the fact
that she was dressed in men's slacks and a flying jacket, she
was saluted with wolf calls, whistles, and some very interest-
ing propositions. Eisenhower cursed and fumed, but it made
no impression. Up front, the brass was not very important.
The truckers continued to whistle and make their proposals to
the General's "white meat."

For her part, Kay Summersby was worried more by the

prospect of air attack than possible sexual assault by the rough, unshaven truck drivers. She told Eisenhower seated in the back, "If we're strafed, it's every man for himself. I'm going to stop and run as far away from this car as I can. Don't expect me to hold the door for you!"[10]

"Fine," Eisenhower agreed, but as Kay looked in her rear-view mirror she could see his lips twitching, as if he were trying to stop himself laughing, and she burst out giggling herself. Eisenhower was infected and abruptly they were both laughing uncontrollably until the tears ran down their cheeks.

But Eisenhower was not inclined to laugh twenty-six hours later when he arrived at Fredendall's Command Post hidden in that remote canyon eighty miles behind the front. He didn't like the set-up one bit; nor did he like the fact that Anderson, who had been scheduled to meet him there, was not present.

Finally the British commander was located. He had been trying to convince Fredendall's Intelligence officer that an expected German attack was coming in to the north, not through Gafsa as the American maintained. In the end Anderson gave up, saying, "Well, young man, I can't shake you!" and came over to speak to the Supreme Commander, commenting to Fredendall that he had a "jumpy" staff officer.

Again Anderson repeated his warning of a coming German attack. The messages passing between Africa and Rome, via the *Wehrmacht's* Enigma coding machine, were being decoded almost immediately by the experts at Ultra—the secret establishment in a Victorian manor house at Bletchley in the English home counties—and they all indicated an attack. The question was—*where?* Anderson and Eisenhower's British Chief-of-Intelligence, Brigadier Mockler-Ferryman, thought they knew the answer. The attack would be to the north, they said, with perhaps a feint to the south in the II Corps area.

Eisenhower made a decision. While Anderson returned to his own HQ to prepare for the attack, he would go up front and have a closer look at Fredendall's dispositions.

Kay was now left behind. She was put into the VIP tent—it had a pebble floor instead of the usual "wall-to-wall mud." With the party reduced to Eisenhower and his deputy, General Truscott, and with an American Army sergeant at the wheel of the sedan instead of the Irish woman, they set off again.

What Eisenhower saw was not encouraging. Although Fredendall's Intelligence officer was—in spite of Anderson's warnings—predicting an attack through the passes, little had been done to defend them. No minefields had been laid; no defensive positions had been dug. Fredendall's officers said they had been there only two days and would start their defenses on the morrow.

Eisenhower glared at the complacent officers. "Well, maybe you don't know it," he rasped, "but we've found in this war that once the Nazis have taken a position they organize it for defense within two hours! This includes the scattering of many personnel mines along the front . . . Get your minefields out first thing in the morning!"[11]

By now Eisenhower realized that Fredendall's Corps was spread out all over the place, in what the Britishers called "penny packets." His 1st and 34th Infantry Divisions were completely mixed up with the forward elements of Ward's 1st Armored. And Truscott told him the reason why: Fredendall had not once left his CP to visit the front. All his dispositions had been made on the basis of maps spread out in the operations room in that remote underground HQ.

He continued his tour, visiting Orlando Ward, commander of the 1st Armored. He didn't like Ward's dispositions either, but he didn't interfere, nor did he make any recommendations. In the tradition of the U.S. Army, it was not considered correct for a senior officer to comment on local arrangements made by a subordinate commander. So he contented himself with passing on Anderson's news from Bletchley that an enemy attack was expected in the north on the morrow. There would be a diversionary attack, too, he warned though where that would come was anyone's guess.

Eisenhower left Ward and pushed on to the headquarters of his Combat Command A, located in a tree-lined canyon near Sidi-bou-Zid. Lieutenant Colonel Drake of the 168th Infantry was waiting to be decorated by the Supreme Commander. Putting on his ear-to-ear smile, Eisenhower pinned the Distinguished Service Cross on Drake in the dim light of the blacked-out command post while Truscott and General Mc-Quillan, the CCA commander, looked on. For a while the officers chatted in the tight, stuffy CP. Suddenly the phone rang: it was another message from Anderson. It would be a matter of hours now before the Germans attacked; he had gone to the headquarters of Koeltz's French 19th Corps, just in case the enemy decided to strike there.

Eisenhower bit his bottom lip grimly and went outside for a little fresh air so that he could consider the news. Inside the CP, tension started to mount. The newly decorated hero, Drake, asked McQuillan what would happen if the Germans attempted an encircling movement on his positions: "General, what will we do if the enemy attacks the pass from the east?"

"Old Mac" McQuillan snorted, knowing that Eisenhower might reenter the CP at any moment. "Now don't bring *that* up!" he said.¹²

Outside, all was calm. The front had gone to sleep. Outlined a stark black against the moonlight, Eisenhower could just make out his forward positions. To the left were the heights at Lessouda, and a dozen miles to the right was the vague outline of Djebel Ksaira. Up there Ward's tankers and Ryder's infantry would be settled down in their foxholes now, ready to face another night of bone-chilling cold. Soon it would be midnight —and tomorrow, it struck him suddenly, would be Saturday, February 14, St. Valentine's Day. Slowly he turned and began to walk back to McQuillan's CP, unaware of the bloody valentine already being prepared up there on the heights, ready for delivery at dawn.

At three in the morning, the little convoy set off back to Fredendall's headquarters and a little sleep. The vehicles rolled through Sbeitla. Everywhere the handful of European houses were blacked-out and silent; nothing stirred in the Arabs' miserable hovels either. Suddenly there was a sharp crack. A spurt of bright flame stabbed the darkness. The vehicles braked to an abrupt halt. Eisenhower whipped out his forty-five and started to organize his little force. For the first time in his twenty-eight years in the U.S. Army, Dwight D. Eisenhower had come under fire and was now going to command men in action!

The two drivers took the point, cradling their carbines. Sergeant Barna, the driver, Eisenhower, and Truscott brought up the rear, armed with their pistols. It was a tense thirty minutes, but eventually they cleared the little place without further incident.[13]

Some time later an angry Eisenhower finally arrived back at the underground HQ and told Fredendall "in plain language" of his dissatisfaction with his "defensive arrangements." Then he stalked off to the VIP tent, where Kay Summersby woke up and overheard him telling someone outside he wanted to get a couple of hours' sleep before starting back for Algiers.

"Your driver's in there," the other voice answered. "We'll wake her."

"Jesus Christ," Eisenhower snorted, "don't do that! Let her sleep."

The next thing Kay Summersby knew was that the Supreme Commander was crawling into his sleeping bag in the tent beside her, fully clothed, even wearing a stocking-knit cap pulled down over his ears. Within minutes he was "snoring like a one-man artillery bombardment."[14]

Later, when Kay Summersby arrived back in Algiers, she would be taken aside by Colonel Ernest Lee, known as "Tex" to the rest of the gang because he came from Texas.

"I think you ought to know, Kay," he stuttered, his face scarlet, "there's a lot of gossip about you and the Boss. People are saying that you . . ." He was too embarrassed to continue.

"That we what?" Kay prompted him.

"That you, uh . . . Well, that you sleep together when you go on trips!"

The Irish woman stared at the red-faced colonel and burst out laughing. "We did, Tex! *We did!*" she exclaimed, leaving him even more bewildered and embarrassed than ever.[15]

But that was later. By the time these romantic mysteries and laughing exchanges took place, the villages and passes that Eisenhower had inspected would be in enemy hands; Drake and his command would have vanished, posted missing or dead; and McQuillan's CCA would be virtually shattered.

nine

It was four o'clock on the morning of St. Valentine's Day. Colonel Waters of the 1st Battalion, the 1st Armored Division, rose early as was his wont and climbed straight away to his observation post on top of Djebel Lessouda. He exchanged a few words with the shivering, unshaven GIs of his command, who had spent the night up there on watch duty, and then, focusing his binoculars, peered across at the Faid Pass.

But he couldn't see a thing. A fierce wind had blown up during the night, coming over the mountains all the way from the Sahara. And with it the wind brought flurries of razor-sharp grains of sand that stung his face and obscured his view. He couldn't even hear anything above the roar of the wind. Waters gave up and went back down the hill to his tent.

Just as he reached it, the telephone rang. It was McQuillan's second-in-command.

"What's that shooting?" he rapped.

"What shooting?" Waters queried.

Apparently it had been reported that firing was being heard on the road between Faid and Lessouda. Waters said

he'd check it out. He hung up and tried to get through to the
troops in that area by radio. No answer. He decided to climb
the escarpment again. At first he still couldn't see or hear
anything through the sand storm, but then there came a
sudden break in the keening howl of the wind—and Waters
heard it: the low ominous rumble of artillery fire. The second-
in-command of CCA had not been mistaken. There was some
sort of fire-fight going on down there in the direction of
Lessouda. *Were the Krauts coming?*

They were. Two whole battle groups of the German 10th
Panzer Division were advancing on the positions of McQuillan's CCA, with the massive sixty-ton Tigers of the 501st
Heavy Detachment in the lead already rumbling through the
Faid Pass, driving all before them. The handful of infantry
and the artillerymen that Colonel Waters had dug in up there
were reeling back, abandoning their positions, even their
cannon, in their unreasoning panic. Nothing, it seemed, could
possibly stop those lumbering steel monsters that had appeared so suddenly and frighteningly out of the flying sand.

"Tigers!" The panic-stricken cry was flung from mouth to
mouth. *"The Tigers are coming!"*[1]

Waters, watching the scarlet stabs of flame from up ahead,
was as steadfast now as on that day three months before when
he had first met the "first team." He ordered fifteen of his
Honeys forward, to block and delay the Germans.

It was a futile gesture. The ugly, over-tall Honeys with their
37mm "popguns" were no match for the German tanks with
their 75s and 88mms. One after another the Honeys were
knocked out of action, without being able to make the slightest
impression on the Mark IVs and Tigers, their shells bouncing
off the Germans' thick steel hide only to bury themselves
harmlessly in the hillside.

Suddenly the Messerschmitts arrived, howling in at
ground-level, machine guns chattering, cannon thumping,
snarling in tight turns as they shot up the rear areas. The sand
storm had died down and visibility was improving by the
minute; yet only four solitary American planes appeared to

take up the challenge presented by the numerous yellow-nosed enemy fighters.

As more and more German tanks appeared to both his front and flank, Waters realized his own danger. He started to withdraw his command post—a jeep and a White half-track—further up the slope of the Djebel. Below him he counted more than eighty German vehicles milling about, sixty of them tanks. He was surrounded. But still he did not give into the hysteria that seemed to prevail all around him. He phoned the CCA's CP and told them his position.

"Don't worry about me," he added. "We'll be all right. You get on with the war . . ."[2]

Even as he spoke, the young tank colonel could see some Arabs approaching the stationary German panzers and pointing up at his position—and he didn't need a crystal ball to know what they were telling the Germans.

It was nearly five hours since the German attack had begun. At long last General McQuillan was reacting. He ordered Colonel Hightower, commanding the 2nd Battalion of the 1st Armored Regiment, into the offensive. He was to stop the rot before the panic got out of hand.

Colonel Hightower, who would one day command an army himself, rolled bravely into battle for the very first time. Almost immediately he realized he was outnumbered. He radioed McQuillan that the best he could do was delay the Germans; nothing more.

Now the unequal slogging match commenced. The Shermans rumbled forward into the murk and fog of war, their 75s spitting fire. The Mark IVs and Tigers took up the challenge. The solid AP shot zipped flatly across the desert, a bright, burning white blur, toward the outgunned Americans. Already the German gunners had discovered the fatal weakness of the Sherman. One single shot just glancing off its rear sprocket would turn the thirty-ton American tank into a blazing coffin; its engine was thinly armored and gasoline-burning. No wonder the American tank crews had nicknamed it bitterly "the Ronson"—it burst into flames as easily as a cigarette lighter.

Everywhere the Shermans were rumbling to a stop, taking up the hull-down position and waiting for German tanks to come within range. But the Germans were not doing them that favor. Sherman after Sherman was hit, rocking from side to side with the impact, and almost immediately engulfed in an explosion of smoke and fire as the five-man crew scrabbled their way out and doubled for safety, pursued by the angry red hornets of tracer bullets.

Still Hightower fought on—though not all his men were following his example. One whole reconnaissance company surrendered, over 100 men. And others did the same. They abandoned their vehicles while there was still time and took off their helmets as if in greeting, mumbling the one word of German they all knew: *"Kamerad..."* Their artillery support was crumbling too. The artillerymen were streaming back into the desert, leaving their guns behind, not even pausing to destroy the firing pins in order to render them unusable to the enemy. Carried away by unreasoning panic, they pushed through the positions of the 168th Infantry. *"The Krauts! The Krauts are coming!"* they cried in terror. Here and there an officer would try to stop them, his pistol drawn, his arms outspread as if he were trying to catch his playmates at a childish game of Tag. But there was no holding them. Eyes wild and staring with fear, the fleeing men struggled on.

Watching these chaotic scenes of retreat, Colonel Drake lifted the field telephone to call General McQuillan. "They're running away, General," he announced grimly. "Your men are running away."

McQuillan gasped. "You don't know what you're saying!" He knew instinctively that Drake was telling the truth; his whole command was collapsing in front of him. But still he refused to accept it. "They're only shifting position!"

"Shifting position hell!" Drake cried angrily. "I know panic when I see it!"[3]

He slammed the phone down, and waited. The Krauts

would be attacking him soon . . . The slaughter of the "Ronsons" continued.

Colonel Waters was as realistic and down-to-earth as Colonel Drake. All that morning he had been watching the destruction of his friend Hightower's battalion from his hiding place on the height. Most of his own battalion had suffered a similar fate, and he had lost contact with his supporting infantry from Drake's regiment. He knew it was time to get out, while he still could. At this rate, he told himself, Combat Command A was not going to exist much longer.

He scribbled a quick note to McQuillan, telling him he was bringing out what was left of his battalion as soon as it was dark. One of his men volunteered to take it through the German lines to Sidi-bou-Zid, and he slipped away like an old scout in Indian country. An hour later the same soldier reappeared, gasping for breath, his shirt red and wet with blood. He had been shot by one of Waters' trigger-happy survivors just after starting out on his mission. Apologizing for his failure he sank down on his knees, while Waters gave him a shot of pain-killing morphia and made him as comfortable as possible.

On the plain down below, littered with the burning tanks of Hightower's shattered battalion, the battle was beginning to quiet down. The Germans were sending out infantry patrols, as their tanks rumbled westward, searching for American survivors—yet again they were being helped by the Arabs, out for loot and German favor. Somehow Waters knew that time had run out for the 1st Battalion.

Hightower, down on the plain, was fighting his last battle. His tank—manned by himself, Sergeant Clarence Coley, and three other men—had been struck several times already by German shells, fortunately with no casualties. But their ammunition was running out. Indeed, when the end inevitably came, they had exactly three shells left.

Then the Sherman staggered as if it had just run into a

brick wall. Abruptly the inside of the turret glowed a frightening pink. There was the acrid smell of metal burning. Petrified, Hightower and Sergeant Coley watched as the armor-piercing shell whirled around the inside of the turret, clattering madly, like the noise a kid makes running an iron bar along a length of rails. If the shell hit something solid, they knew, it would disintegrate, sending steel splinters flying everywhere. They would be flayed alive. Suddenly the shell stood on its end, revolving like a spinning top, smoke and flame pouring out.

Hightower had had enough. "Let's get the hell out of here!" he cried, and bailed out.[4]

Coley tried to do the same, but he couldn't raise his escape hatch. Now the Sherman was beginning to burn. Somewhere tracer bullets were exploding. There was the stench of escaping oil. It wouldn't be long before the whole damn tank went up in flames. Desperately, the sweat streaming down his contorted face, Coley tried to thrust open the hatch. Three times he tried. He gave up, nerves jangling. Then he had an idea. He dropped into the driver's compartment, wriggled to his escape hatch and dived head-first into the sand. He was out! Scrambling to his feet, he began to run . . .

Just in time. Behind him the Sherman exploded and he was nearly knocked from his feet by the hot blast, which tore the very air from his lungs and left him gasping and choking for breath like an asthmatic old man.

Half an hour later Hightower and his crew crawled back to headquarters, having hitched a ride on a halftrack laden with wounded. There he found that he had exactly seven tanks left from his original fifty-one. To all intents and purposes, his battalion had been wiped out.

Up on the hill, completely alone now in the late afternoon, Waters heard footsteps among the rocks. He thought it might be his driver, whom he had sent to retrieve a radio from the halftrack. He rose from where he had been hiding this last hour or more.

Facing him were seven men in the dusty khaki and peaked caps of the German Army, with two Arab guides. Slowly Waters raised his hands. It was all over. Now would start the long journey back to Tunis, from there to Italy, to Poland, and finally to Germany itself. Lieutenant Colonel John Waters was "in the bag," like so many of his comrades of the 1st Armored Division. But Waters was not just anybody. He was George Patton's son-in-law.

Soon his father-in-law would restore the fortunes of the sadly battered II Corps; it would be the first step on his road to fame. But he would never forget his son-in-law languishing in a German prisoner-of-war camp. One day Patton would abuse his power, risking the lives of the men under his command, to rescue Waters—without Eisenhower's permission. This failed rescue would be the beginning of the end for "Blood and Guts" Patton.

In Africa this terrible day, many things were ending—and starting.

Now it was the turn of Drake's infantry of the 168th. Young Major Robert R. Moore, commanding the 2nd Battalion of the 168th, right up front at Lessouda, knew by mid-afternoon that he and his 600-odd men were cut off. But what was he to do? His regimental commander, Drake, a man he feared more than the Germans, had impressed upon him that there was to be no withdrawal. In fact he had told Moore once that any soldier who left his position without orders should be shot. And he had added, too, that the men must learn to hate the Germans. "I will notify you," Drake had snapped crisply, "when I want prisoners taken."[5]

So without orders from Drake Moore knew he could not withdraw, even though he had seen what was left of CCA's armor scuttling to the rear, leaving him up here all alone.

At dusk a light plane zoomed in low over the Lessouda position, and a message came winging its way down to the waiting officers. It was from no less a person than the commanding general of the 1st Armored.

It read: *"Tank destroyers and infantry will occupy positions at 2200 tonight to cover your withdrawal. You are to withdraw to position . . . where guides will meet you. Bring everything you can. Signed-Ward."*[6]

Moore hesitated no longer. He called his company commanders together and told them how they were going to pull out.[7] They would move cross-country parallel to the Sbeitla road. They would walk in an extended column, boldly and making no attempt at concealment. In this manner Moore hoped that, in the darkness, the Germans to their rear would take them for their own troops. All wounded and prisoners would be taken with them. If the prisoners made one wrong move, they would be bayoneted.

And so, when the time came, they set off. They encountered a German artillery position almost at once. A German called out something. Moore, who was at point, remained silent and kept on walking. The artilleryman shook his head and then went back into his hole. Moore wiped the sweat off his face. It was working!

They had moved a mile over that barren countryside when Moore heard voices to his front. He strained his eyes in the darkness and could just make out somebody walking toward him casually. He heaved a sigh of relief. Of course: it would be one of the guides sent by Ward.

Moore was wrong. At thirty yards away, the lone man stopped and called out a question—in German.

Moore tried the trick he had used on the artilleryman; he said nothing and kept on advancing. Now there was no sound save that of the night wind and the steady soft trudge of many feet.

The German called out again.

Every nerve in his body was shrieking at him to run for it, hide, take cover—but Moore just kept tramping steadily on, his silent column of men in his wake. They passed the lone German. They were going to do it . . .

Abruptly the stillness was broken by the high-speed hysterical hiss of an MG42. They had been spotted! Moore cupped his hands around his mouth and yelled frantically, *"Scatter! Run like hell!"*

As tracer hissed toward the men of the 2nd Battalion, German burp guns opened fire on them. Flares hissed into the sky to erupt in incandescent silver light. Orders and counter-orders were shouted. Angry cries rose on all sides.

Then they were running, all six hundred of them, fear lending speed to their flying feet, scattering into groups of two or three, disappearing into the desert night.

Moore pelted on and on until finally he could run no more. He flung himself into the sand, gasping for breath, lathered with sweat. Behind him, German mortars had joined in the one-sided battle. Everywhere there was the obscene howl of mortar bombs and the thick chesty thump of missiles exploding.

For what seemed an age, Moore lay there listening. Gradually, however, the snap and crackle of rifle fire began to die away, until it stopped altogether. He got to his feet and cautiously started searching for survivors. In all, he found less than twenty. Grimly they resumed their long march westward across the desert, without either food or drink.

Thirty-six hours later Moore was challenged again—but in English this time.

"Are you that lost infantry bunch?"

"Oh boy," gasped Moore. "Am I glad to hear your voice."

They had made it. They had reached the safety of an American unit.

For some reason, Moore was still clutching his sleeping bag when they found him; he had hung onto it all the way from Djebel Lessouda. "The Krauts could have my tin hat," he joked, "but I wasn't going to give them my English fleabag—no sir!"

But Moore's elation soon dissipated. He discovered that fewer than 300 of his soldiers had managed to reach safety that night. He had lost half his battalion.

Among the men he had lost was the battalion chaplain, Captain Gene Daniels. Daniels had volunteered to stay behind

and go into captivity because he refused to leave two badly
wounded German soldiers. "They need my help," Daniels had
said quietly; "I shall stay with them."[8] His act of selflessness
would cost him two long years behind the wire.

Some hours later, utterly exhausted and yet unable to sleep,
Moore was still waiting for more survivors to turn up when he
bumped into Lieutenant Colonel Gerald Line, the 168th
Infantry's executive officer. He too had managed to escape the
débâcle at the front and had walked for nearly two days across
the desert, without food or water—without even company; he
had done it alone. Like Moore, Line was exhausted, but he
couldn't sleep either. He told Moore sadly that, so far as he
knew, he was the only member of Colonel Drake's headquarters to have escaped. At Ward's headquarters, Colonel Drake
and the rest of the regiment were deemed lost. Forever.

Drake had sent a last message to General McQuillan, ac-
knowledging his permission to withdraw. And he'd added a
postscript to the message, stating without bitterness: *"Besieged. Good strength. Good Morale."*[9]

Now he set off for the rear, he and more than 1,000 of his
men. Their plan was to try to fool the Germans by removing
their helmets and wearing overseas caps instead; in the poor
light they just might be taken for German soldiers.

They hadn't gone very far when Drake realized he was
leading his men through a German tank park. A Mark IV
rumbled toward them, and a man standing in the turret saw
them and called out to them. But—like Moore—Drake just
ignored the challenge and kept going. The tank rumbled
away. Then they were crossing a patch of open ground as a
six-wheeled German scout car drove toward them. This time
the Americans didn't wait for a challenge; someone tossed a
grenade into the open turret. The scout car immediately
caught fire, but, surprisingly enough, the other Germans in
the vicinity paid it no attention whatsoever. So Drake and his
men marched on . . .

Their luck could not hold, however. At first light, the enemy finally woke up to the fact that a long column of American soldiers was passing through their lines. A convoy of trucks full of infantry drove up, the Germans leapt out and, at a range of less than one thousand yards, opened fire with their machine guns.

The Americans panicked. Officers bellowed orders. Noncoms shrilled their whistles. But several hundred of Drake's men ran straight toward the Germans to surrender or threw away their weapons and cowered in the dirt as best they could, dodging the bullets that hissed over their heads.

By sheer strength of personality Drake somehow managed to retain control of a few hundred of them. He formed them into a circle, as if they were back in the days of wagon trains and Redskins. But these Redskins drove to the attack not on ponies but in Mark IV tanks.

A German scout car burst through the circle; they couldn't stop it, armed as they were only with their Garands and BARs. The commander waved a huge white flag at them—he wanted them to surrender. Angrily Drake yelled at his men to get rid of the damn thing. *He* wasn't going to give up like that!

But it was too late. German tanks had followed the scout car into the circle of GIs and started to break them up into little scattered groups, threatening them with those long overhanging guns of theirs, which twitched from side to side as if sniffing out victims.

One tank trundled to a halt just yards from Drake, and the officer popped his head out of the turret, pointing a rifle at him.

"Colonel—you surrender!" he demanded.

"You go to hell!" Drake cried. He turned his back on the tank, folding his arms across his chest, waiting for the impact of that first bullet . . .

Nothing happened. The tank simply swerved away, brushing by Drake's elbow. But even so, Drake knew the end was near. The Germans were swarming all over the place, disarming his men and going through their pockets, yelling in triumph when they found the highly prized American cigarettes or bars of chocolate. There was nothing Drake could do now. Sadly, he walked over to where some of his men lay wounded, faces white and contorted with pain. Two Germans armed with rifles followed him.

A little later, a car drew up beside Drake and a German officer invited him to get in. Reluctantly Drake did as he was bid and was driven to German headquarters. There he found himself being saluted by a senior officer—a general, perhaps; Drake didn't know—who said: "I want to compliment you on your command for the splendid fight they put up. It was a hopeless thing from the start, but they fought like real soldiers."[10]

Drake's reply is not recorded, but those few kind words from the enemy must have served to ease his pain—at least for a moment—over the loss of his regiment. He would have plenty of time later to consider what had gone wrong that night and how he might have managed things better. For Drake, too, was about to undertake that enforced journey north to Germany. He would not see freedom again before April 1945.

As that bloody St. Valentine's Day of 1943 finally drew to a close, it was clear that the first day of the Battle of Kasserine Pass—as it later became known—had seen a great victory for the Germans. In this, their first engagement with the U.S. II Corps, the Germans had triumphed.

The Americans had suffered appalling losses, as General McQuillan was finding out that night. He was totting up the losses suffered both by his own command and by Colonel Drake's 168th Infantry. Just two days ago, when Eisenhower had visited McQuillan's headquarters to present Drake with his medal, the 168th had had a strength of 189 officers and 3,728 men. Now, even though one battalion had not engaged in operations and was still virtually intact, only 50 officers and 1,000 soldiers remained. And McQuillan's own losses were almost as bad. Some 52 of his officers and 1,526 of his men were still unaccounted for, including at least three colonels listed as "missing, presumed dead."[11]

But the full extent of the German victory only became clear as McQuillan's reconnaissance planes swept low over German positions that night, dropping their blood-red flares to illuminate the scene below.

Stretched between the Faid Pass and the crossroads leading to Sbeitla lay 44 tanks, 59 halftracks, 26 artillery pieces and at least 22 trucks—all American, all abandoned by their panic-stricken crews, some of the equipment still burning.

The American Army in Europe would never experience anything like it again, until the day Eisenhower received his fifth star and the Germans came storming down from the snowbound heights of the Ardennes to begin the Battle of the Bulge.

But the Battle of Kasserine Pass had only just begun. There was worse to come—much worse . . .

ten

They called him "Gentleman Jim." But Colonel Jim Alger's easygoing manner belied a deep sense of purpose and confidence. This morning Alger was taking his armored battalion into action for the first time, yet anyone watching him as he made his preparations, with the blood-red ball of the sun tilted on the horizon, would have thought he was about to go out on a day of maneuvers, not to do battle.

Ward personally had worked out the plan. With Alger's armored battalion in the lead, Colonel Stack in command of his reserve, Combat Command C, would attack the Germans dug in at Lessouda and throw them back. Ward, back at the 1st Armored's CP, felt that Stack and Alger would have numerical superiority. Intelligence reported that the enemy had 40 tanks at Lessouda, while Stack had Alger's 54 tanks, plus tank destroyers, artillery, engineers and most of his 6th Armored Infantry Regiment.

Poor hard-pressed Orlando Ward would soon discover his error. There were nearly 100 German tanks just waiting for Alger's Shermans to walk into the trap and be destroyed.

While Stack hurried his force for the counterattack to the front, Alger was briefed by Hightower, the senior survivor of the St. Valentine's Day débâcle, and CCA's second-in-command. The two of them explained the terrain to the diffident colonel, the best approach tracks, the way the German tankers fought. Then they shook hands and the second-in-command snapped officiously, "Seek the enemy armor and destroy it!"[1]

"Yessir," Alger answered and saluted—in the very same instant that the Stukas dived out of the sky. Howling down full throttle, sirens wailing, engines racing, they seemed destined to slam into the ground. But, at the very last moment, their pilots pulled the evil-looking gull-winged planes out of their tremendous dive, pressed back against their seats by the G-force, eyes bulging out of their sockets like those of a madman, threatening to black out at any moment. Ugly black eggs, bombs, began to tumble in profusion from the dive-bombers' blue bellies.

Down below, Alger's command disintegrated. Shermans careened across the desert seeking cover as the bombs exploded on all sides, sending up angry eruptions of flying sand and pebbles. Infantry abandoned their halftracks and doubled away to the nearest holes, leaving the vehicles with their engines still running.

Again and again the Stukas fell out of the dawn sky. By now the whole area was pockmarked with great steaming brown holes. Here and there a vehicle stood wrecked and burning, while Alger's men and tanks ran ever further away to escape that eerie banshee keening and the deadly bombs. And then finally the German planes were gone, winging their way back east, leaving Alger to collect his badly shaken command and prepare for the great counterattack. He was off to a bad start.

Two hours later the attack commenced. It was done with great precision, as if this were some stateside maneuver and not an operation of war. Alger's battalion was in the lead, his three companies of tanks rattling forward in parallel columns. To each flank, as the armored textbook back home prescribed, there were White halftracks, mounting 75mm cannon; they would act as tank destroyers. Behind them came two batteries of self-propelled artillery, side by side, followed by Colonel Stack's infantry, riding in "deuce-and-halves," the standard two-and-a-half-ton trucks, and more halftracks.

It was a splendid sight. Viewing the attack from a height through his field glasses, Colonel Stack was proud of his command. They were advancing strictly according to the rules, keeping their distances, each vehicle in its place, ready for anything. They looked for all the world like some nineteenth-century military print depicting one of Napoleon's battles.

For thirteen miles, making no attempt at reconnaissance, this armored steamroller advanced in a dead straight line across open country, clearly visible to the watching and waiting Germans of the 10th and 21st Panzer divisions. They let them come on, wondering at these naive *Amis* who fought their battles according to the book.

Now the perfect formation started to break up a little, as Alger's leading tanks ran into a series of irregular irrigation ditches and were forced to find gullies where they could cross. Behind them the great parade still continued. But not for much longer.

Now the Germans began to react. Dive-bombers swept out of the sky to attack the leading companies, and from the heights German artillery started to fire. The desert floor erupted, while American tanks swerved and skidded to left and right to avoid the shell bursts.

Stack, still watching from the rear, was unmoved. His own artillery took up the challenge now. The artillerymen unlimbered their howitzers and prepared to commence the counter-fire. Everything was going exactly as the textbook prescribed.

But Alger wasn't feeling so confident now. Disturbing reports were flooding in from his companies to the effect that German tanks were concealed on both his flanks. Unknown to the young colonel, the Germans were letting him ride right into a classic trap. As soon as he and his tanks were settled neatly into it, they would attack from two sides and cut him off from his supporting infantry.

Alger took up the challenge personally. As fifteen Mark IVs crawled out of their hiding place toward his battalion, trailing huge wakes of sand behind them, he ordered a company to follow him. With his aerials flicking like silver whips, he led the attack. Now the cannon began to boom, while blurs of armor-piercing shells hissed back and forth. Machine guns chattered. Suddenly all was flying sand, smoke, confusion—and sudden death. The slaughter of Jim Alger's battalion had commenced.

Another fourteen German tanks had emerged from the smoke of battle on Alger's left flank. He reacted at once. Leaving the company to tackle the Germans on his right flank, he called up his reserve company and raced to meet them. Again he led the attack personally.

Now Stack's infantry were paying the butcher's bill, too. German fighters came sweeping in low across the plain, machine guns chattering frantically. Almost at once panic set in as the men abandoned their vehicles and raced for cover, slugs stitching an untidy blue-sparked pattern at their flying heels.

From his vantage point on the heights, a suddenly deflated Colonel Stack could see exactly what was happening. He had sent his command straight into a trap. The Germans were converging on his armor and stalled infantry from both sides. If he didn't pull them out soon, they would be wiped out. He called Alger and asked him anxiously how things were going.

Alger remained cool to the very end, although his tanks were burning all around him. He replied in that polite easy manner of his, "Still pretty busy."[2]

It was the last that Stack was to hear from "Gentleman Jim." Time and time again, as the filthy smoke of burning tanks spread across the battlefield, Stack tried to contact Alger—but in vain. Alger's tank had been hit and destroyed. His radio operator had been killed, his crew and himself

captured. Like Waters and Drake and half a dozen other
colonels, Jim Alger was heading for the cage. His first action
in World War Two had been his last.

At six o'clock that terrible February 15, Stack gave up. He
ordered his infantry and artillery to retreat. They did so
gratefully and relatively unscathed. Alger's men were not so
lucky. They lost 15 officers and 298 men that afternoon and
left 50 shattered Shermans on the battlefield. Fredendall's II
Corps had been defeated once again.

From this day onward, the 1st U.S. Armored Division
would be stigmatized in the secret files of Anderson's First
Army as "not combat-worthy."[3] In two days it had lost 98
tanks, 57 halftracks and 29 artillery pieces. Its only effective
unit was Combat Command B, still under Anderson's command. In essence General Orlando Ward, quiet in speech and
manner, was a commander without a command; and even as
this day ended, his loud-mouthed superior, Fredendall, was
calling Truscott, Eisenhower's deputy, to report the 1st
Armored's losses and hinting that "Pinky" Ward should be
removed.

And indeed Ward's days were numbered—though so were
Fredendall's. Fredendall went first, returned to the States by
an administrative decree. Ward's return would be more dramatic. Patton, Fredendall's successor, would order Ward to
attack a hill. "Don't give me any excuses," he would bark at
Ward. "I want you to get up there and lead the attack personally. Don't come back until you've got it."[4]

Ward would lead the attack personally. It would fail and
Ward would be brought back on a stretcher, his eye shot out.
That would be the end of Ward's activities in North Africa.

Oberleutnant Heinz Schmidt—young, dashing, intelligent—
had been with the *Afrika Korps* right from the start. For
months he had been the Desert Fox's personal aide. Now at
last he had been returned to regimental duties, assigned to his
old unit Special Group 288, commanded by Colonel Menton,

an old comrade of Rommel's from World War One and one of
the few men in the *Afrika Korps* who dared to call the Field
Marshal by his given name and address him as "thou."

The Special Group had been trained for duties in Iran, but
nothing had come of it. Instead they had supplied the
reconnaissance for the 90th Light Division for most of the
desert campaign. Now Menton's command, with Schmidt in
the lead, were going to do the same for Rommel. At last the
Desert Fox was going to take a hand in operations against the
Amis. Within hours he would be coming up to the front
himself to plan his next move; by that time the oasis of Gafsa,
which barred the route westward, had to be captured for his
personal inspection.

As darkness descended upon the battlefield on the evening
of February 15, Schmidt's vehicles crept toward the oasis.
Schmidt had been briefed that the oasis was held by American paratroopers and the British of the Derbyshire Yeo-
manry. Cautiously they worked their way through the minefields laid by the Americans; they had been planted pretty
obviously in the road and the ditches on both sides of it, but the
light was failing and they had to be cautious. Yet all the same
Schmidt and his men were "excited at the thought of meeting
Americans on the battlefield for the first time." In their time
the men of Menton's Special Group had fought British,
French, Indian, Australian, South African, and New Zealand
troops. Tonight, as they neared the silent black oasis, they
were going to have their first crack at the *Amis*.

But it wasn't to be. Unknown to the Germans, Anderson
had ordered the oasis to be evacuated; the American II Corps
was pulling in its horns. So Schmidt and his men entered the
oasis to the cheers of the remaining Arabs who hailed them as
liberators, and they spent the night looting what little of the
splendid abandoned American rations was left after those
same Arabs had had their pick of them.

A few hours later Rommel himself appeared. The evocative
sight of the road to the oasis and beyond packed with wrecked
and abandoned American equipment stirred the old feelings

inside his sick body. It was like the great days when the Tommies had been fleeing toward Egypt leaving the roads behind them choked with booty. En route the Arabs cheered him, too, and Rommel smiled back, waving his celebrated fly whisk at them, not caring that they were openly looting the wrecked U.S. trucks.

He rolled into the oasis itself. The Americans in their panic the previous evening had blown up their ammunition dump, indifferent to the fate of the Arabs. So far 34 corpses of men, women, and children had been recovered from the wreckage of their huts; another 80 Arabs were still missing. Still that did not stop them milling around the field marshal's car, celebrating their liberation by the Germans with "wild whoops of delight," according to Rommel's diary.[5]

Over and over again the ragged, dirty throng shouted the same two names: *"Hitler! . . . Hitler! . . ."* and *"Rommel! . . . ROMMEL! . . ."*

It was a heady reception. In fact it was just like the old days when he had been welcomed everywhere by cheering Italians and Arabs as his ever-victorious *Afrika Korps* rolled toward Egypt and final victory. Could he not repeat those old victories? Had not his motto been always that audacious *"Exploit! Exploit! Exploit!"* Well, here was a situation to exploit. Perhaps Kesselring had been right after all. Why content oneself with the smaller solution, which had already been achieved? The Americans had retreated as von Arnim had wanted. Wasn't there a good chance, after all, that they would be able to drive to Bône on the north coast and rip a big hole in the rear of the Anglo-Americans? Why not try?

Carried away by his new enthusiasm, his varied illnesses and pains forgotten now, Rommel telephoned von Arnim immediately and outlined his new plan. He intended to push on to the next village with a reinforced assault group. There, at Feriana, he would have two alternatives—because the road forked. He could strike north to Tebessa in Algeria, or northeast through Thelepte to a place called Kasserine, where he could join up with the panzers driving from Sbeitla.

For the first time, the name of Kasserine, the obscure hamlet that would soon be frontpage news throughout the world, had been mentioned.

Thinking he had von Arnim's support for his new plan, Rommel drove over to where Colonel Menton was camped. The two old comrades, both Swabians by birth, got down to business immediately, talking in that thick local dialect of Swabia, which other Germans, especially the northerners, find so quaint and amusing.[6] Rommel had an urgent and new assignment. He wanted Menton to send a heavy reconnaissance force, supported by tank destroyers, toward Feriana. If possible, Menton was to push through the village with the rest of his regiment, while the reconnaissance would probe the area ahead so that he, Rommel, could decide which route was better suited for his bold new plan.

Ten minutes later *Oberleutnant* Schmidt was on his way again. The road to Kasserine and Rommel's last battle lay open.

That same evening, as young Schmidt set out on his adventure into enemy territory, General Truscott was attempting to catch up on some badly needed sleep. All day he had been throwing in unit after unit—cooks, military policemen, anything and everything he could find—to bolster up Fredendall's sagging II Corps front, while the bad news came flooding in virtually hourly.

But just as he managed to doze off, someone arrived to wake him. Fredendall was on the phone yet again. This time he reported that Anderson had authorized him to withdraw. German tanks had entered Sbeitla and Ward's CP was under direct attack. He had ordered infantry from "the Big Red One" and Colonel Moore's engineers, plus some tank destroyers, to hold the line while he withdrew what was left of Ward's 1st Armored to safety. Colonel Stark of the 26th Infantry Regiment, the 1st Infantry Division, was to hold the line, together with Colonel Moore, for at least twelve hours. Then if he were forced to pull back, he was to do so to the pass at Kasserine—which, at all costs, he must hold.

Truscott absorbed Fredendall's news and then passed over his information. Anderson was sending two brigades to Fredendall's assistance. The Guards with their old comrades from Longstop, the 18th Infantry (also from the 1st Division), would secure the undefended pass at Sbiba, the one Anderson thought most likely to be attacked by the Germans. Another brigade, Brigadier Dunphie's 26th Armoured Brigade, was coming down to take up positions in the general area of Kasserine.

For once Fredendall, the anglophobe, did not object. Any reserves, even if they were British, were welcome this night, until the American forces released from Patton's army in Morocco came up to aid him.

Finally Truscott told Fredendall his latest piece of information: he was being sent back to ready the 3rd Infantry Division for the attack on Sicily. Now there was to be a new overall commander of all the forces in Tunisia, including Montgomery's, a man whom Truscott would later call "outstanding among Allied commanders."

Fredendall asked if he were a "Britisher."

Yes, Truscott told him. He was Field Marshal Alexander—and he was already operational.[7] A fresh wind of action and determination had already begun to blow in Tunisia.

Alexander (no one had ever been known to call him by his given name, Harold; even his wife called him Alex) had always lived up to that heroic name. All his life he had sought—and found—adventure, fighting his way through one heroic episode after another. He had fought on three continents and been wounded twice; he had commanded men in battle of all nationalities and colors—even *Germans!* (After World War One he had commanded a German regiment fighting the Bolsheviks in the Baltic states.) In 1937 he had been the youngest general in the whole of the British Army.

He had been the last British soldier off the beach at Dunkirk.
Sent to Burma to retrieve the hopeless situation there in 1942,
he had somehow managed to achieve the impossible; Churchill later said of him, "If we could not send an army, we could
at any rate send a man." For the last six months he had been
Montgomery's chief in Cairo, where he had done as much as
any man alive to ensure that the British won their first real
victory of World War Two at the Battle of El Alamein.

Sportsman, painter, dandy, Alexander liked to lead from
the front, just as he had done when commanding the Irish
Guards in the trenches back in the Old War. Unruffled in
defeat, modest in success, he had been called "the last of the
gentleman-generals."

Now Alexander was coming to command Americans for
the first time, right in the middle of their worst crisis of the
whole war so far. Here he was in Tunisia, ready to give orders
to American commanders who were all older than he was and
to tell them and their men some very unpleasant home truths
about their abilities as officers and soldiers. He would tell
them that their soldiers were "ignorant, ill-trained, and
rather at a loss, consequently not too happy." To his face he
told Patton that he found American soldiers "mentally and
physically soft and very green." As for their commanders, in
particular Fredendall, he would tell Eisenhower, when
pressed: "Surely you must have better men than *that*?"[8]

But Alexander began with a critical look at his fellow
Briton, Anderson and his First Army. Later he would report,
"Frankly I am shocked at the whole situation as I found it.
Although Anderson should have been quicker to realize true
state of affairs and to have started what I am doing now, he
was only put in command of the whole front on 24th January.
Real fault has been lack of direction from above from very
beginning. Am doubtful if Anderson is big enough for job,
although he has some good qualities . . . Hate to disappoint
you, but final victory in North Africa is not just around the
corner."[9]

Anderson with his awkward manner and his sheepish

appearance, dressed in Old War breeches and puttees, did not impress Alexander, ever the spruce soldier. He was shocked by the way Anderson had allowed the confusion of nationalities at the front and by how British and American units had been broken into little groups to support the French of Koeltz's Corps. On his very first day, encountering an officer of the 8th Argylls and learning that he was returning from a mission with half his battalion, Alexander snapped bitterly, "Wonderful! A first-hand example of what I supposed, splitting battalions into penny packets!"

But as February 16 gave way to February 17 and Rommel's men raced for those vital passes, Alexander had more important things to do than censure his senior officers, British or American. The first and most important thing was to get the back-up force down from the north to support Fredendall's sagging II Corps before it was too late.

More than ten thousand British soldiers were hurrying southward through the night. Coldstream and Grenadier Guards, Riflemen, soldiers of the old traditional regiments of the British Army; Lothians and Leicesters of the territorials; men of the Army's newest formation, the Reconnaissance Corps—all of them were desperately trying to reach their positions before Rommel struck. Soon they would be greeted by a special message from the new army commander, Alexander. It was blunt to the point of brutality: *"The position must be held at all costs!"*

But unknown to Alexander, his men had already lost the race to reach their stop-lines before Rommel. For nearly thirty hours now, *Oberleutnant* Heinz Schmidt had been working his way down side tracks and minor roads, worming in and out of scattered groups of retreating *Amis*. They had passed an airfield with 60 abandoned U.S. aircraft on it. They had captured six American halftracks, again abandoned as their drivers fled at the first sight of these men of the *Afrika Korps*. They had been sniped at once from an Arab village, but *Oberleutnant* Schmidt's men had soon put a stop to that. In the usual pitiless manner of the German armored corps, they had swept into the place with all weapons blazing, not caring whether they hit the miserable ragged civilians or not. It was a technique the Americans would only learn toward the end of the war, when Patton's Third Army shelled and machine-gunned every German village they entered, whether defended or not, leaving behind what Patton cynically called "The Patton War Memorial."

The sniping had stopped at once. Arabs had come racing out, "waving and shouting in the false jubilation which these people always accorded any apparently victorious troops," as Schmidt recorded later.[10] Indeed, the local sheik even tried to kiss Schmidt's hand, and when the handsome young German pulled back in disgust, the old man grovelled on his knees and kissed his boots instead!

But that was all behind them now. The road was dropping steadily as the little convoy began to come down from the hills. Ahead of them, the countryside was dominated by a single recognizable feature: the Kasserine Pass.

Suddenly they were being attacked. American shells began to gouge up stones and earth on both sides of the road. They had been spotted! *"Tempo! Dalli! Dalli!"* Schmidt yelled. His vehicles charged forward, racing through the black mushrooms of smoke and flying metal. They were careening round a bend, fist-sized pieces of gleaming steel howling off the rocks to their right, when the lead driver hit his brakes hard. Before him there was an open wadi. It would be suicidal to attempt to cross it; they'd be sitting ducks for the Americans. Schmidt agreed. He ordered his men out of the vehicles. They would scale the heights above the *Amis*.

So, hand over hand, the Germans began to heave themselves up the steep rock face, using every boulder and fold in the rock as cover against the American shells. Schmidt, in the lead, put his head above the crest. An angry burst of machine-gun fire struck up a flurry of hurrying blue sparks to his front. He dropped back hurriedly. There was a machine-gun team just thirty yards away! Apparently some of the Americans hadn't fled after all. He paused for a swig of water, wondering how he was going to get over that damned crest.

Just then Schmidt's radio operator, red-faced and panting, came crawling up, burdened by the heavy set. Immediately Schmidt made use of the exhausted soldier. He called one of his section leaders, Lieutenant Becker, and ordered him to bring flanking fire on the lone *Amis*.

Five minutes later there was that familiar high-pitched hysterical hiss of a German MG42. The *Amis* stopped firing almost immediately and fled. Schmidt did not wait for a second invitation. *"Los!"* he commanded and swung himself over the crest, followed by his troopers. They had obtained their objective, the heights. And there down below them was the Kasserine valley, ten broad miles of it, filled with *Ami* vehicles rumbling up and down in a steady stream, happily unaware that Rommel's *Afrika Korps* was in position already above them.

"There we were," Schmidt recorded later, "looking down on the whole hinterland of the American front as though we were spectators at the maneuvers of a midget army. How small the men and trucks and guns seemed there below, and how innocuous!"[11]

But the innocuous midget army would soon be testing Schmidt's men to the limit. Already Colonel Menton's messengers were scurrying around down below, delivering his orders to the lead units: *"Attack Kasserine Pass! 1st Battalion left of the road, 2nd Battalion to the right of the road . . . ATTACK!"*

eleven

Rommel was resting in his operations truck after a heavy lunch with a local sheik—they'd had *couscous*: semolina laden with bits of mutton smothered in a burning hot sauce—and he was fuming. The whole American front was crumbling; Menton was already on the Pass; Arab spies reported that even further back at Tebessa in Algeria the Americans were blowing up their fuel dumps. Yet the full-scale thrust he had envisaged was not taking place. Von Arnim seemed to be sitting on his thumbs, letting the *Amis* escape instead of exploiting this tremendous opportunity. Every single objective along the road to Kasserine had been taken. It would be child's play for a commander to send the three panzer divisions at von Arnim's disposal down that road and knock Eisenhower's soldiers right back into Algeria.

Suddenly Rommel's patience snapped, and, according to his diary, he decided to "stake everything on one big gamble by throwing all we've got at Tebessa."[1] As he told his staff, he had "never before staked the lot on one throw of the dice. Even in his most daring operations, he had always kept something

in reserve to master any sudden twist of fortune." Now he was
prepared to accept the supreme gamble. Win all, or lose all!

Without resorting to the normal military channels as tradition and custom required, Rommel radioed his proposals
directly to Rome. *"If you agree, I request the 10th and 21st
Panzer divisions be placed under my command and moved
rapidly to assembly area Thelepte—Feriana. Rommel."*[2]

Two hours later a delighted Kesselring, who had wanted
the Desert Fox to take this course right from the start, answered with a provisional go-ahead. He cabled both commanders, Rommel and von Arnim, who was dragging his
feet: *"I consider it essential to continue the attack toward
Tebessa and northward by concentrating all available forces on
the left wing and exploiting our recent successes with a blow that
can still have vast consequences. . . . This is for your preliminary information. I shall speak in this sense to the Duce
today."*[3]

Rommel was over the moon. But there was more to come. A
little later Kesselring cabled again. Rommel was to be put in
command of all mobile forces of his own *Afrika Korps* plus the
10th and 21st Panzer Divisions. It meant that Rommel, and
not von Arnim, his hated rival, was now in charge.

Rommel immediately issued orders for an all-out attack on
Kasserine the following dawn. That evening, an aide noted,[4]
he ordered a bottle of champagne and declared, "I feel like an
old cavalry horse that has suddenly heard the bugles sound
again!"

Oberleutnant Schmidt and his men—and the handful of
American prisoners they had taken—were hiding among the
rocks while the drone of tank engines and rusty clatter of
tracks grew ever closer. It was raining hard and visibility was
bad, but suddenly they saw it: an American Sherman with its
hatch open.

The tank commander was staring around in obvious bewilderment. "What's this barricade doing here?" he shouted—

meaning the American trucks that Schmidt's men had wrecked on their probing reconnaissance.

Huddling back among the shadows, Schmidt's men stuck their pistols into the ribs of their frightened prisoners to keep them silent. The Sherman stopped. But they hadn't been spotted—the tank crew were clambering out to clear away the wreckage.

Suddenly the silence was broken by the rattle of a machine gun. Tracer zipped through the rainy darkness toward the Sherman. Schmidt cursed: he had forgotten to tell his machine-gunner further down the wadi not to open fire.

But the Sherman's commander reacted unexpectedly. He ducked back inside his turret "like a rabbit at a bolt-hole" and the tank immediately began to reverse, firing wildly to either side. Schmidt and his party scrambled for the cover of a nearby bridge just as five American Shermans rumbled over their heads.

So the *Amis* were retreating. But what would happen next, wondered Schmidt, waiting tensely under the bridge. The American infantry were dug in only a few hundred yards away. Would they rush forward and take him prisoner, just as he had taken these Americans now eyeing him so intently?

One of his prisoners, a lieutenant from Brooklyn, turned to Schmidt and offered him a cigarette, asking, "Well, what's happening, bud?"

Schmidt shrugged, putting a brave face on it. "Wait," he said tersely.[5]

And so they went on waiting, listening to the drone of tank engines rumbling around their hiding place in the wet smelly tunnel, Germans and Americans alike wondering who would be the prisoner tomorrow.

An hour went by and still the American infantry had not come forward. Then suddenly shells began to fall all around their hiding place. Above them the bridge shuddered and shook; a thin rain of cement dust started to fall. Did this mean the *Amis* were coming to take them? They clutched their weapons anxiously, hands slippery with sweat. Schmidt told himself that he would like to see the lieutenant's Brooklyn some day—but not as a prisoner. His one ambition right now was to survive and qualify to become a farmer in Natal where he had been born.

But Schmidt was not fated to become an American prisoner-of-war just yet. He didn't know it, but his abortive probing attack at the Pass had had its effect. The Americans down there were nervous, peering into the darkness fearfully, some of them already abandoning their positions and heading for the rear, throwing away their weapons as soon as they were out of sight of their officers.

As the drone of the Shermans' engines died away in the distance, the lieutenant from Brooklyn suddenly grinned at Schmidt. He knew now that he was heading for a German POW camp. He stretched out his hand. "Have some gum, chum?" he offered.

For the first time in his life Schmidt tasted chewing gum, as he returned to Menton's headquarters to receive his new orders. They were simple, and the same as before. *"Attack!"*

Now, as Rommel's men prepared for the attack the next day, February 19—it would be one of the most crucial days in his career—the Americans holding the Kasserine Pass were making equally frantic preparations.

Shaped like a crude capital X, the pass was one mile broad at its narrowest point and flanked by the Hatab River and by heights that reached to 1,000 feet in places. It was not an impregnable position, but any defender could exact an exorbitant price from an attacker. By mining the valley floor, the defender could force the attacker to stick to the road, where he could not escape observation. And this is precisely what Colonel Moore had done.

Fredendall had asked for and received *all* the mines in American stocks in North Africa, and Moore's engineers had spent the entire day planting them along the routes the German attackers would have to take. The GIs at Kasserine Pass were now dug in behind a triple belt of anti-tank and anti-personnel mines.

Moore was currently in charge of nearly 2,000 infantry and engineers at the pass, but there was only one man in that whole force who had been under fire before—a young captain. Moreover, that day's skirmish with Schmidt's men had made the Americans jittery and apprehensive. Many of them had already quit their positions and attempted to escape to the rear. Moore had managed to round up some of them, forcing them back to their foxholes at pistol point, but now more and more of them were slipping away unnoticed in the darkness.

As German signal flares began to shoot into the dark rainy sky, tension in American ranks was rising by the minute. Discipline was rapidly breaking down—and, as Moore later admitted, fear and poor control by officers and noncoms were the root-cause. The defenders of the pass were in dire need of an experienced combat officer if they were not to break altogether.

Fredendall had already chosen the man: Colonel Stark, commander of "the Big Red One's" 26th Infantry. Stark had fought in CCA's recent action, and was reputed to be tough—after all, he was a regimental commander in "the Big Red One"!

In that typical slangy manner of speech of his which caused so many of his orders to be misunderstood, Fredendall called Stark that night and said, "I want you to go to Kasserine right away, and pull a Stonewall Jackson. Take over up there."[6]

Stark was flabbergasted. "You mean *tonight*, General?"

"Yes—immediately. Stop in at my CP on your way up."

Stark put down the phone, cursing. Hurriedly he snatched up his bedroom and equipment, summoned his staff and set off through the rainy darkness to meet Fredendall.

Up front, more and more soldiers were deserting their posts. They had never been in combat before, but they could sense what was to come. Fear was in the very air.

Stark was not the only one making his way toward the rapidly crumbling front that night. The British were, too. North of Kasserine, the trucks of the Guards Brigade were grinding their way up the steep narrow roads to Sbiba, where they were going to fight alongside the 18th Infantry—the same division they had fought with at Longstop two months ago. But the British were making slow progress, for they were having to fight a counterflow of fleeing American vehicles.

Captain Nicolson, an Intelligence officer with the Guards, later recalled[7] seeing an American truck crammed with infantrymen flashing past, the GIs leaning out and shrieking: "He's right behind us!" And there was no need to specify who "he" was.

The leading troops of the 56th Reconnaissance Regiment had a similar experience when they were coming up as the spearhead of Brigadier Dunphie's 26th Armoured Brigade behind Kasserine. As one of their sergeants recorded later, "The road was a chaos of retreating Americans and their transport—though not enough transport to carry many of the GIs who . . . were all in."[8]

Delayed by the westward stream of American men and vehicles, the British convoys began to slow down and bunch on the open roads—presenting the perfect target for enemy planes. Surprisingly, no German fighters appeared, but as the Recce men waited in their armored cars and halftracks for the lead troop to clear a way through the hordes of retreating Americans, they could hear the ominous rumble of gunfire coming from up ahead. And they knew what that meant: in spite of the cover of night, the Germans were ranging in.

The moment of the great attack was growing ever closer.

"It was one hell of a long night," ex-PFC Grimes recalled long afterward; he had been part of the infantry already up at the front. "Everybody was jumpy and nervous. Some engineers came up and brought us mines to dig in. We'd never even *seen* a mine before and had no idea how to dig them in and place them in a pattern. But the engineers were not stopping. They were too scared. They took off and let us get on with it, digging them in the best we could in the mud. They never went off later."[9]

Grimes went on to describe how the tension continued to increase throughout the night. Jittery patrols shot each other up in the darkness. The men in muddy foxholes scared each other with stories of the invincible German Tiger. They heard imaginary tanks approaching . . .

By the end of that night, many of the men had already "bugged out"; and as Grimes said, "If it had stayed dark any longer we'd have lost the whole goddam company!"

As a reluctant dawn brought an end to the darkness that morning of Friday, February 19, at least the rain had ceased, carried away on the cold wind that was now blowing through the pass. It was seven o'clock.

All along Rommel's front, his armor was tensed in readiness: one group would attack the Guards and the 18th Infantry at the Sbiba Pass; the other group would attack Stark's force, with Dunphie's 26th Brigade in reserve at Kasserine. The stage was set; the drama could commence. For the first time in World War Two, the German Army would be fighting a major American force—and no less a person than Field Marshal Erwin Rommel himself would be leading that attack on poor bumbling Fredendall's II Corps.

The first to be hit, though, were not the men at Kasserine, raw and inexperienced as they were, but the comparative veterans of the Guards Brigade and the 18th U.S. Infantry. At 0900 hours precisely, the Germans attacked. The British and Americans retired gradually and completely under control, leading Rommel's tankers right into the belts of mines.

By noon the Germans had halted and, together with their Arab guides, were trying to discover some way of outflanking the British minefields, which were well covered by the Anglo-American artillery on the heights beyond.

Rommel drove up through the rain, the road deep with slime. He was not at all pleased with Colonel Hildebrandt, commanding the 21st Panzer Division. It had taken the armored commander four hours to cover fifteen miles against hardly any opposition. He thought the Colonel "dawdling" and "inefficient" and ordered him to push on to the east, out of range of the artillery, and then northward against the Americans of the 1st Infantry Division. In pouring rain, Hildebrandt did as he was ordered. Twenty-five Mark IVs and some truck-borne infantry set off east.

Now the British took up the challenge. A troop of Valentine tanks from the 16th/5th Lancers rumbled out of their hiding places to deter the Germans, advancing in the best cavalry tradition, although they were hopelessly outgunned and outranged. One after another the British tanks were picked off by the Germans while they were still out of range. Eventually the remaining Lancers withdrew, leaving the Germans in possession of the field.

Hildebrandt now rushed up several batteries of light field howitzers, while the infantry started to dig in and the Mark IVs probed forward toward the Americans. Almost immediately the German gunners started to shell the enemy artillery positions.

The American reply shook them. Up there on the ridge, the gunners of the 151st Field Artillery Battalion had an excellent field of vision; they sent a hail of steel and high explosive down on the German gunners. Now it was Rommel's Mark IVs that were taking all the punishment. Panzers were shuddering to a stop everywhere, shattered tracks unfurling behind them like broken limbs, thick white smoke pouring from ruptured engines, as tracer ammunition started to explode and zig-zag crazily into the rain-heavy sky.

It was too much. The dozen surviving Mark IVs turned and scuttled back to safety, leaving the burning field to the dead— and to the British engineers, already crawling out from their positions to ensure that the disabled Mark IVs left behind would never run again.

The first attack made by Rommel's men this Friday had failed. Angrily he drove off, convinced that the fault was

Hildebrandt's. But, he told himself, if he were going to break through this day at all, it would be at Kasserine—*and break through he would!*

To Schmidt's right, infantry and engineers were on their knees in the mud, uniforms soaked black with the pouring rain, probing and stabbing with their bayonets. They looked for all the world as if they were cutting asparagus, he thought, rather than looking for the deadly mines lying beneath the surface of the mud and holding up the attack on the *Ami* positions beyond.

He watched for a while as they scraped around the mines they had discovered, thick fingers suddenly sensitive and delicate, probing around in the mud for the round metal shape and the cross-pieces of the spider before unscrewing the detonator. They worked in complete silence, sweat dripping from their intent faces, for they knew the *Amis* might have booby-trapped the mines, attacking matchbox fuses underneath them which would release a charge and explode the whole devilish contraption if they weren't handled carefully, or linking one mine to another by a cunning, almost invisible, trip-wire.

Then Schmidt dismissed the *Pioneere*. He raised his binoculars and surveyed the road that wound through the Pass. As he watched, a Sherman tank slid into view; it was flying a white flag. But he decided it wasn't surrendering, just coming to collect the morning's casualties. He swung his binoculars round, focusing them impatiently. Where were the *Amis'* main positions? He knew they were up there somewhere, hiding in the folds of the sodden ground, just waiting for Menton's Special Group to attack . . .

Then Schmidt lowered his binoculars and rubbed his unshaven chin thoughtfully, a sudden grin on his young face. This afternoon the *Amis* were in for a surprise. As soon as the engineers had cleared the mines, the new secret weapons would rumble up. He knew for sure that they and the

Stukas—"Hitler's flying artillery" as the dive-bombers had once been called—would soon clear away the *Amis*. Then the road through the vital Pass would be theirs.

Impatiently he waited as the engineers slowly advanced, prodding and probing, faces greased with sweat. It would not be long now before the *Nebelwerfer*, the new wonder weapon, went into action in North Africa for the very first time.

Two miles away, Colonel Stark was standing beside the odd-looking figure of a tall gaunt man wearing a pleated woolen skirt, both of them surveying the stalled Germans' positions.

Stark's companion was Brigadier McNabb, just as Scottish and as dour as his superior, General Anderson. McNabb had been asked to come up and have a look at the situation at Kasserine by a worried Brigadier Dunphie of the 26th Armoured Brigade. So here he was, kilt flapping damply around knees that were blue with cold, taking in the scene and knowing that as Anderson's chief-of-staff he now faced an important decision. Should he release Dunphie's 26th Brigade to aid Stark or not? For the Brigade was Anderson's last reserve.

It seemed to him, he later reported, that Stark had enough troops to be able to cope with the situation, though he admitted that the American colonel—commanding a mixed formation of doubtful value, most of the men unknown to him—did appear to "lack a good grip on things."[10] But he felt he couldn't release Dunphie's armor to him just in case the Germans broke through the Guards.

So Stark would have to make do with what he had. As a concession, McNabb did allow Dunphie to send forward a small detachment of infantry, tanks (ten in all), a few anti-tank guns and a battery of artillery commanded by Lieutenant Colonel Gore. For the twelve short hours of its existence, before it was wiped out, this little British unit would be known as "the Gore Force."

With that McNabb went, his soaked kilt swinging as he tramped off toward his waiting staff car, thrusting his shep-

rd's crook into the mud, leaving Colonel Stark to face the
ght at Kasserine Pass.

e hour later, the Germans' new wonder weapon snapped
to action. With a banshee howl the first six-barrelled, elec-
ically operated mortar opened fire. The rockets tore into the
rkening sky, white smoke spurting behind them in a thick
ail as they came racing toward their targets: the petrified
gineers and infantry had never heard anything like it
fore.

Now Schmidt gave the infantry signal for advance, jerking
s clenched fist up and down rapidly three times, while the
ortars howled and Stukas came hurtling out of the sky in
at death-defying dive of theirs. The infantry surged for-
ard. This night they'd take that damned pass or—die in the
tempt!

Vhat happened during the night of 19-20 February," states
e official U.S. history of the campaign in North Africa,
annot be clearly reconstructed from the record."[11]

But one thing *is* clear: Stark's men of "the Big Red One"
oke. Company A of the 26th Infantry was surrounded first,
d its commander was captured—though he escaped later.
hen, as the official history puts it delicately, "the other com-
nies went out of battalion control. Stragglers reported the
tuation after daylight." In essence Stark's battalion had
nished.

Schmidt was in the lead that night. As he and his men
shed forward to the attack, screaming in their fury, carried
vay by the mad blood-lust of battle, the Americans broke
d fled.

American tanks rumbled forward but the sight of
chmidt's men was too much even for those thirty-ton mon-
ers. They turned tail and scuttled back toward the Pass. In
eir frenzied haste, two of them got stuck in a wadi; as
chmidt's men raced up, "their crews abandoned them and
ed."

The way ahead had been opened for Rommel. Leavin Moore's engineers dug in on the other side of the Hatab Rive tying them down with heavy patrol activity, Rommel gan bled all. Hurrying up front to see for himself what was goin on, he found General von Broich commanding the stalled 10t Panzer. He asked why. Awkwardly von Broich explaine that he was waiting for motorized infantry to come up to cove his advance.

Rommel lost his temper. "Go and fetch the motorcycle ba talion yourself," he snapped, "and *you* are to lead it into actio too!"[12]

His harshness had the required effect. The 10th Panze slowly began to advance into the Pass without any infantry cover them, even though scattered groups of Americans sti held the heights on both sides. Supported only by those terr ble electric mortars lobbing 80-pound rocket-bombs up to distance of four miles, screaming in ear-splitting element fury, the Mark IVs rumbled forward.

Things now started to go disastrously wrong for th defenders. Colonel Moore's CP was overrun, and all commu ication between the engineers and Colonel Stark was los Several of the engineers' companies broke and ran. The a tached French gunners with their ancient *soixante-quinze* ran out of ammunition and, pausing only to destroy the firin pins of their vintage cannon, they abandoned them and fle after the rest. All the traffic was westward. Frightened me and their commanders scrambled and fought to get awa before they were overtaken by the armored monsters pursu ing them down the Pass. But amid all that confusion, a sma force of ten tanks and a company of the Rifle Brigade wer advancing to meet the enemy. Like the 17th/21st Lancer covering their rear, the Riflemen—"Green Jackets" as the were called—had fought the Americans in the Revolutionar War; indeed, much of their early training had been based o what they had learned from their American opponents those days. Now, while the last of Stark's reserves were cut o by the advancing Germans, they were going to die for thei one-time enemies. This was going to be the Gore Force's finest hour—but the price they would be forced to pay was cruel.

Lieutenant Colonel Gore took up his position with his left flank against the mountainside on the northern corner of the Pass. Here he dug in his anti-tank guns and covered them with his "Green Jackets." Now he sent forward his armor—slow, old-fashioned Valentines of the Lothian Horse, all ten of them, supported by a handful of American tank-destroyers. Under their commander, Major Beilby, they sallied forth to stop a whole German panzer division.

The defenders were crumbling fast. Mixed elements of the 1st Armored and the 1st Infantry holding the northwestern entrance of the pass were cut off. The drivers of their half-tracks down below in the wadis took off, leaving the armored infantry to fend for themselves. Colonel Moore and his second-in-command of the 19th Engineers were slogging to the rear and on their own. Soon they would appear at Stark's head-quarters to report: "The 19th Engineers no longer exist."

The German advance was inexorable, unstoppable. Supported by those terrifying "moaning minnies" (as Allied troops soon learnt to call the *Nebelwerfer*) thundering to their rear, the first tanks lumbered forward into the pass, trailing panzer grenadiers in the combined tank-and-infantry formation known as a "grape."

Even as the Lothians spotted the first Mark IV trundling toward them, Fredendall was meeting the commander of his last reserve—Brigadier General Robinett.

Robinett, commanding the 1st Armored's CCB, had been attached to Anderson's First Army since December. Now he had been released to Fredendall with his combat command as the Corps Commander's last reserve. Hurrying on ahead of his men, through crowds of excited Arabs who were thronging forward in expectation of rich pickings—they seemed to sense already that the Americans were retreating—he met Fredendall by the roadside.

Fredendall told the big bluff officer, who had already had

considerable fighting experience with the British, that
Stark's command was collapsing.[13] Except for "the Gore
Force," he said, there was little to prevent the Germans
advancing through the pass toward the village of Thala. The
British 26th Brigade would have to hold on there the best they
could, declared the Corps Commander, while Robinett led his
men to the southwest. There they should block the road to
Tebessa, throw the enemy back out of the valley "and restore
our position . . . in the Kasserine Pass."

Robinett thought it was a tall order, but he didn't voice his
opinion to Fredendall.

Just before jumping into his jeep and driving away, Fredendall clapped Robinett on the shoulder. "If you get away
with this one, Robby," he said, in his characteristically unrealistic, over-expansive manner, "I'll make you a field marshal! . . . Good luck!"[14]

But Robinett never made field marshal. Within a week his
foot would be nearly severed by a German shell and he would
be evacuated back home to the States, his combat days finished for good.

Major Beilby of "the Gore Force" had already been wounded,
but he was still running from tank to tank shouting encouragement to his hard-pressed Lothians, while up above them
the Stukas circled angrily, trying to find a gap in the clouds so
that they could dive-bomb those stubborn Englishmen who
were holding up the advance of a whole division.

By now even the Lothians were beginning to retreat. Bound
by bound, pausing at regular intervals to assume the hull-
down positions and slam AP shells into the pursuing Mark
IVs, they left behind them yet more outgunned Valentines
and burning American halftracks.

The Germans pressed them hard. Just a mile to the rear,
Rommel urged them on, animated by that old fury and
excitement, cursing them, cajoling them, as more and more of
his troops rolled forward to push those stupid obstinate Tommies out of the vital Pass. They had to break through today—
they *had* to!

Six of Rommel's heavy self-propelled guns were rolling into the pass, the Lothians' shells bouncing off their thick hide. Bielby, walking up and down with German shells exploding all around him, commanded his remaining tankers to withdraw; then he clambered up onto the turret of his own tank, bleeding badly. The end wasn't far off for the 2nd Lothians.

Colonel Stark had to abandon his CP. All afternoon, while Gore held the pass, his own infantry had come straggling back in disorder. Somehow or other he had managed to reform them and send them back to the line. But there was no holding them now, and the snap-and-crackle of small-arms fire close by indicated that his command post would soon be overrun. Now it was his turn to "bug out."

With his headquarters staff he began to walk back to Thala. Stragglers appeared everywhere, white-faced and wide-eyed. In panic-stricken gasps, they told their colonel that the Germans were only 200 yards behind them.

Stark did not believe them. He slogged on steadily, followed by the exhausted stragglers. Apart from those of his men still cut off on the heights, Stark's party were the only Americans left alive out of the original force of Moore's Engineers, Ward's Combat Command Reserve, and his own 26th Infantry. Within the short space of thirty-six hours his whole force had simply wasted away. For what? Already the jubilant tankers of the 10th German Panzer Division were dealing the death blow to "the Gore Force," the last defenders of the Pass.

One by one the Valentines were picked off as they started to withdraw down the wadi. They hadn't a chance against the German self-propelled guns. Major Beilby's tank received a direct hit. It burst into flames, a neat gleaming silver hole skewered in its side. Beilby didn't get out.

Now Colonel Gore ordered his gunners to fire over open sights and started pulling back what were left of his "Green Jackets." Six American Grants of the 1st Armored came rolling up to cover their withdrawal. Four were set ablaze by German gunfire. In the gaudy light of the fiercely burning

Grants, the Germans now concentrated on knocking out Gore's six-pounder anti-tank cannon. The gunners fought to the last, as the infantry doubled from position to position, sacrificing themselves to save the Americans, just as the three remaining Lothian tanks were doing further ahead.

The Arabs were already stealing out of the shadows into that ruddy glare to strip the bodies of the dead as the last but one six-pounder was knocked out and with it the remaining three Lothian Valentines. The Pass was open.

The Germans charged forward. The only obstacle now barring their way into Algeria, and delaying the great triumph that Rommel had prayed for, was Dunphie's feeble 26th Brigade on the road to Thala.

By nightfall on February 20, the road through the Kasserine Pass was wide open. The Germans were surging forward, their tanks and crowded convoys of packed infantry in trucks rolling past the burning wrecks of the Lothians' tanks and the stripped naked corpses of the gunners, already beginning to stiffen in the night cold.

Obscure, humble men, they had gone to their death willingly enough. There would be no medals or honors for them, though they richly deserved them, those unknown young men who had saved the day for General Fredendall and his II Corps.

The fighting went on for a further four days. More than once it was touch and go. But "the Gore Force's" valiant defense of the Pass had given Fredendall the precious gift of time, enough time for him to prepare his second line of defense—which would finally stop Rommel's drive.

In the end the Battle of Kasserine Pass would be acclaimed as an Allied victory (which it wasn't). Fredendall would go home to America honored and acclaimed, "kicked upstairs" to the rank of lieutenant general, and given a hero's welcome.[15] But those young British soldiers would remain in Africa for ever, dead before their time. Like many of Fredendall's own men, they died before they had begun to live, their memories treasured only by a handful of friends and relatives back home.

twelve

The gravel-voiced, barrel-chested armored commander fought valiantly to awaken, but it was of no avail. He had been on the road now for more than twenty-four hours, all the way from Morocco to Algiers and from thence to here, Constantine. Sleep simply would not allow him to escape from its clutches. Thus it was that Eisenhower, the Supreme Commander, and his aide, Commander Butcher, dressed and kitted out the old warrior. As General Ernest Harmon, temporarily relieved of his command over Patton's 2nd Armored Division, would relate many years later: "I have enjoyed telling my grandchildren that a future President of the United States once laced up their groggy grandfather's combat boots."[1]

When Harmon had arrived at Eisenhower's headquarters in Algiers the day before, Eisenhower's "encouraging and magnetic grin" had not been much in evidence. The news from the front that day was bad, very bad. Word had just reached him that the American forces at the Kasserine Pass had been overrun; it was supposed that Rommel would now strike for Tebessa. What's more, Fredendall had just telephoned Ike to tell him that Ward was no good; he had demanded his immediate replacement.

But Eisenhower had demurred. He had been informed by Alexander that Fredendall was "dithery," and it was pretty clear that the II Corps commander had lost the confidence of the men under his command due to his handling of the battle since February 14. Now Eisenhower had a proposition for Harmon: he was to take over command either of the 1st Armored from Ward, or of the II Corps from Fredendall.

Harmon had been astonished, blurting out: "Well, make up your mind, Ike—I can't do both!"[2]

The sorely tried Supreme Commander had to agree. "But," he admitted, "right now I don't know what is to be done down there. Your first job is to do the best you can do to help Fredendall restore the situation. Then you will report direct to me whether you should relieve Ward or Fredendall."

That had been yesterday, February 20. Kay Summersby had driven Harmon and Ike all the way to Constantine, and he had fallen asleep while Ike had briefed him, even though German planes were attacking. Later Eisenhower wrote him a letter complimenting him on his calmness.

So now Harmon was continuing alone to the front, save for one aide, Captain Rooney, setting out for Tebessa.

"I have never forgotten that harrowing drive: it was the first—and only—time I ever saw an American army in rout," Harmon recalled, many years later.[3] "Jeeps, trucks, wheeled vehicles of every imaginable sort streamed up the road toward us, sometimes jammed two and even three abreast. It was obvious there was only one thing in the minds of the panic-stricken drivers—to get away from the front, to escape to some place where there was no shooting."

Two or three times Harmon's jeep was forced off the road by these panicked drivers. Thinking he and Rooney might be killed if this went on, Harmon suggested they should pull off the road and wait.

But Rooney was adamant. "No, we must keep on, General!" he kept repeating through clenched teeth, hanging onto the wheel of the jeep as if his very life depended upon it.

Finally they reached Tebessa. The town was almost deserted, but they managed to discover a lone sentry and asked for Fredendall's CP. He directed them to Fredendall's strange underground headquarters and they found him sitting in a chair near the stove. Fredendall's first words shocked Harmon. "We've been waiting for you to arrive," he said. "Shall we move the command post?"

"No sir," Harmon replied in his firmest voice, cast as usual deep in his boots. "We will let it stay here."

"That settles it," the corps commander said, as if Harmon were his superior officer. "We'll keep the command post here." He then handed a bemused Harmon a typewritten sheet. It ordered him to take battlefield command of not only the 1st U.S. Infantry Division, but also the British 6th Armoured Division, over which Fredendall had no authority. Fredendall finished by explaining that he was expecting the Germans, as he expressed it in his customary colorful language, to give him their "Sunday punch." Thereupon he retired to bed, leaving the newcomer in complete charge, with the II Corps' front apparently collapsing all around him. It was not an enviable position for a man to be in, especially one who had not heard a shot fired in anger since World War One, save for the little fracas in Morocco in November three months before.

By now the command structure in the II Corps area was a complete mess. Not only had Fredendall delegated his authority over two of his divisions to Harmon, but he had also empowered another newcomer—Dunphie—to place Robinett's CCB under his command, using what was left of Colonel Stark's communications system to link the CCB with the 26th Armoured. "For the co-ordination of this attack [the expected German one] Robinett comes under your command," Fredendall told the Britisher.[4] This meant that Dunphie was supposed to lead not only his own brigade, but also Robinett's CCB, separated from him by a broad valley. But there was worse to come. Someone (probably Anderson) had inserted another link in the chain of command: a certain Brigadier

Nicholson, second-in-command of the British 6th Armoured Division.

A gray-haired elderly officer, soft of voice and gentle in manner, Nicholson was to be given command of something called "the Nickforce" (the British loved these personal battlegroups, to which they gave their own commanding officer's name in the tradition of the old nineteenth-century colonial wars). This was to be composed of a raw, untrained battalion of the 2nd/5th Leicestershire Regiment, with to their front what was left of the 2nd Lothians and the 17th/21st Lancers, "the Death or Glory boys." It would be the job of this special force to take the first attack on the defenses at Thala.

Thus it was with this hodge-podge of commanders and units, with the corps commander sleeping soundly to the rear—and, if we are to believe Harmon, helping himself generously to the whiskey as well—that the Allied front on that morning of February 21 waited for Rommel's final attack. Today, if he broke through, there would be nothing to stop him racing for the sea. Every single unit that Alexander could commit to the battle had been thrown in; the reserves coming from the west were many hundreds of miles away.

It was a Sunday, but it was not the ringing of church bells that awakened the tense waiting Americans and Britons, rather the hollow boom of German guns, their echo reverberating around the surrounding hills, summoning them to worship at the temple of the God of War.

A. B. Austin, the war correspondent for the *Daily Herald*, was at Thala that Sunday when it started. He described the hostile countryside thus: "a bleak valley" with "a brown dirt road snaking through it." The morning was still cold and dull, but already the new commander Brigadier Nicholson was up and about after a long journey here during the night. He stopped his scout car and exchanged a few words with the civilian. His floppy black beret flapping in the strong wind, he indicated the small, dark figures spread out to the east and told Austin they might be Arabs—and then again they might be "Jerry."

Just at that moment the headquarters radio set started to crackle urgently. An operator raised his head from his set and shouted to Nicholson: "Enemy infantry and two vehicles advancing up road, sir!"[5]

Nicholson was still absorbing this information when there came the long *b-r-r-r* of one of his forward tanks firing its machine gun. Perhaps the tank had taken the German infantry under fire.

Again the radio crackled. "Message from the gunners' OP—they can see three groups of German tanks, sir!" the wireless operator yelled above the increasing noise.

Nicholson made his decision. He nodded courteously to Austin and sped away toward the sound of the firing. Austin had been in North Africa now long enough to know what was coming. *This was it!* He decided there and then that "this was no place for soft-skinned vehicles." He and his escort turned the other way and drove full-out to the rear. The battle was about to begin.

But it did not develop so swiftly as a somewhat nervous Austin thought it would. Rommel's 10th Panzer Division was taking his time. Earlier on, Rommel himself had made an appearance among his troops, and as one observer recorded in a letter to Rommel's wife, "You should have seen their eyes light up as he suddenly appeared, just like the old days, among the very foremost infantry and tanks, in the midst of their attack and we had to hit the dirt just like the riflemen when the enemy's artillery opened up! What other commander is there who can call on such respect?"[6]

But once Rommel had turned and driven back to the Pass at Kasserine, his leather coat covered with mud, his face drawn with fatigue, all elan and fire seemed to go from the 10th Panzer Division. Now under the command of General von Broich, they took their time over the preparations.

For five long hours they were watched by the British, hidden behind a ridge, who had already worked out that a whole division was assembling to their front. Now, just before four o'clock, when back in England they would be preparing tea and settling down to listen to the BBC Home Service for the rest of that foggy February evening, the German tanks formed a line. It was done with almost pedantic deliberation, "in a manner that was beautiful to watch, but very frightening," as one of the watching Lothians recalled later.[7]

There was a clatter of tracks and a rumble of tank engines, each one 400hp. Clouds of blue smoke rose into the afternoon air. Sand spurted up from their wakes as they started to waddle forward, a mass of 30 heavy tanks, 20 self-propelled guns, and 35 halftracks filled with infantry. The 10th Panzer Division was at last coming into the attack.

The Lothians on the left of the dirt road and the Lancers on the right prepared to take the shock. They had been summoned here in process of changing their antiquated Valentines and Crusaders for brand-new Shermans—but those Shermans had gone instead to Ward's 1st Armored. So they were facing the armored might of the 10th with their old, slow, thin-skinned tanks, armed with that hopeless two-pounder "popgun" which had been out of date back in 1939.

The awesome line of armor rolled toward the waiting British, soldiers on foot prodding the ground with bayonets, searching for anti-tank mines. With a great ear-splitting snarl, the first long 75mm German cannon crashed into action. Scarlet flame stabbed the gray air. That single shot seemed to act as a signal for the rest of the attack formation. Suddenly the whole armada opened fire. In an instant the air was full of glowing white streaks, as the AP shells hurtled toward the British tankers scuttling about on the ridges to both sides of the road.

Colonel Hamilton-Russell, commanding "the Death or Glory boys," had his tank hit almost immediately. Dazed, his head ringing with the impact of that great, booming blow on his Valentine, he stumbled to the nearest Lancers' tank and took it over. Before this day would be over he would have a further two tanks "shot from under him," in the parlance of the old horse cavalry.

Now as the Lothians and Lancers withdrew under the sheer pressure of this armored monster, they began to make smoke. Little bombs burst from the dischargers attached to their turrets and exploded in blinding white smoke clouds to their front, as their Valentines and Crusaders slipped from fold to fold, their popguns outranged, using every bit of cover for concealment and hoping that they could remain hidden long enough for the Mark IVs to come within firing range.

A terrible hour passed. By this time the Lancers had been reduced to twelve tanks. The 2nd Lothians fared little better. Both regiments had left the road and ridges behind them littered with burning and shattered tanks, their crew-men mown down by enemy machine guns as they tried to make their frantic escape, sprawled out like bundles of abandoned rags. Huge mushrooms of black smoke streamed into the darkening sky and, through the haze of war, cherry-red flames burned steadily. Soon it was clear that those raw infantrymen of the 2nd/5th Leicesters, virtually straight off the boat at Algiers, would have to tackle the panzers.

Brigadier Dunphie, who had been on the battlefield all day, right up front, only two miles away from where Rommel had made his appearance, now ordered his artillery to fire smoke. He was withdrawing the battered survivors of his Lancers and Lothians to refuel inside the security of the Leicesters' perimeter.

Around seven o'clock, three hours after the Germans had opened the battle, the battered, weary survivors, with Dunphie personally bringing up the rear of the column, began to move into the Leicesters' positions. They converged from both sides of the road into single file to pass through a minefield, watched by the Leicesters who had dug themselves in on a rocky ridge, three miles south of Thala. But this evening there were no jeers or cries from the tankers about "getting some time in" or "when yer gonna get yer knees brown, mates!"

They were too weary, too shocked, too sad at their high losses to want to taunt the new boys this evening. Up ahead, "A" Echelon of the Lancers waited to collect the survivors from the abandoned tanks and to fuel up the rest. It seemed as if the smoke had done the trick. The Germans had been afraid to venture into the thick white fog in case it hid British anti-tank guns.

Now the first column had passed through the minefield, leaving the perimeter to the Leicesters. They watched and waited, knowing that it would soon be their turn; sooner or later the Germans would be coming. The evening was electric with tension.

The clatter of tank tracks startled them. They peered into the glowing gloom, sweaty hands tight on the butts of their rifles, hearts thumping in alarm. *Was it the Jerries?*

But then a familiar shape rumbled into view. They relaxed. It was one of the Lancers' Valentines! Even the new boys could not mistake its distinctive shape. On its deck slumped soldiers in dusty khaki, smoking easily, like men coming home from a hard day's labor, enjoying the first leisurely "spit-and-a-draw" of the evening.

The Valentine came closer. Behind it other tanks loomed up, advancing in the same slow fashion as the first tank. By now more experienced troops would have woken up to their danger. Not the new boys. They watched in passive inactivity —for which crime they were going to pay with two years behind barbed wire in far-away Germany.

Suddenly and surprisingly, the smoking men were tossing away their cigarettes and flinging themselves to the ground, already unslinging their rifles. The Valentine, captured earlier in the campaign from the Lancers, swung to the right. It was an old German trick, one they would use right to the end of the war. Its machine gun burst into frenetic activity, while the Mark IVs hurried up behind it. Almost at once their long overhanging 75mm cannon opened fire.

The ammunition truck of the Lancers burst into flames. Ammunition started to explode furiously. Captain George

Ponsonby, the Lancers' adjutant, jumped back into his tank
and rapped out his orders. At that range he couldn't miss.
Within the first few moments he had knocked out three German tanks. The battle between the leading German tanks and
the Lancers would last for several hours until, after losing
seven tanks, the Germans withdrew at midnight. But the
damage had already been done.

The remaining German tanks and trucked infantry were
through the gap in the minefield. Their vehicles swerved to
left and right of the burning panzers. Machine guns hammering, they raced for the infantry positions.

The Leicesters, according to contemporary accounts, had
hardly seen one of their own tanks before, never mind a
German one. It was a terrifying ordeal for these poorly
trained troops as the Mark IVs came surging toward the
rough holes they had managed to scrape in the rock. A German loudspeaker truck now came forward and a harsh metal-
lic voice rasped: "Come out, Englishmen! . . . Hands up! . . .
Surrender to the panzers—you haven't a chance!"[8]

The scared Leicesters started to come out of their holes,
hands raised in the air, crying, "Don't shoot, mate! . . .
Kamerad, nicht schiessen!"

The gunners, who were supposed to give the Leicesters
close support, were infected by their fear. They started to
make preparations to withdraw, while a furious mêlée
raged between the two tank groups below, cannon barking,
bright flames stabbing the darkness, tracer burring back and
forth.

But the gunners hadn't reckoned with Brigadier Cameron
Nicholson. He soon steadied them—and they began to do
battle with the triumphant panzers.

One mile within the perimeter, "F" Troop of the Royal
Horse Artillery now opened fire. One of their officers had
pinpointed a Mark IV by creeping toward it and firing a flare
directly above the steel monster. As it burst and bathed the
ground below in its bright white incandescent light, blinding
the crew momentarily, his sergeant opened fire at point-

blank range. He couldn't miss. There was that great, hollow boom of metal striking metal and the Mark IV rumbled to a sudden stop, bursting into flames immediately. Another German tank came charging toward the gunners. It, too, was stopped at a hundred yards' range. Then another followed, and another . . .

But the situation was becoming desperate. Everywhere the Leicesters, over 500 of them, were surrendering, completely overwhelmed by the ferocity and speed of the German attack. One by one, the Lancers and Lothians were being knocked out.

The artillery commander, Brigadier Parham, hurried around inspecting and placing every remaining gun for the last defense. He told the sweating, overworked crews, faces lit up and desperate in the ruddy glow from the burning tanks, that they had to hold on. American gunners were on their way to help them. They had to stick it out!

The colonel of the 2nd Lothians summoned his last tank commanders, sergeants, and young subalterns, ten in all, and told them they were going to counterattack. It would be the last desperate attempt to restore the Brigade's position. "I'm sorry," he said, "but we've got to go out on a forlorn hope." He paused momentarily as the artillery boomed and there was the vicious stab and thrust of small-arms fire on all sides. "I doubt whether any of us will come back. Good hunting, chaps . . . *Mount up!*"[9]

General Harmon was facing General Ward. They were complete opposites in appearance and in nature. Harmon was burly, barrel-chested and outgoing. Ward was thin and upright, looking more like a college professor than a cavalry officer.

"Ward," announced Harmon, "I'm about one thousand files behind you"—meaning that his own name was far below Ward's on the U.S. Army's promotion rolls—"but these are my orders and that's how it is."[10]

Ward said he understood. He would cooperate fully.

Harmon laid it on the line. Their troops were running away. o their first task was to turn them around and make them ght. His motto for this day was to be: "We are going to hold day and counterattack tomorrow. Nobody goes back from ere."

Ward agreed. He issued an order to what was left of the 1st rmored stating that "All units will be alerted at dawn for ovement in any direction—except to the rear."

Harmon liked that. So now he set out for Thala and his first onfrontation" with the British, as he phrased it. As he rode Thala he considered his situation. He realized he had not en handed a particularly attractive assignment by Ike. If e battle were won, he'd get no credit for it. If it were lost, 'd get the blame.

But Harmon need not have worried. Within the next sixty inutes he would have made an outstanding contribution to ctory at the Battle of the Kasserine Pass.

The Germans were shelling Thala when he arrived, and he d to dodge down alleys and backstreets, hugging the walls the shells exploded all around him on his way to Nicholson's llar headquarters.

Harmon was a little apprehensive about his appearance. e knew British spit-and-polish from the Old War and he was rty and unshaven, weary from having no sleep. Predictably, icholson was washed and shaved and crisply uniformed.

Harmon identified himself and told the British brigadier s position and orders; then he asked Nicholson his situation. "Well," Nicholason said crisply, "we gave them a bloody se yesterday, and we are damned ready to give them other one this morning!"

That was the kind of fighting talk Harmon liked. As he corded later,[11] "I knew that he and I were going to get along gether just fine."

But what Harmon didn't know was just how perilous icholson's situation really was. Most of his infantry was ne; all the tanks he retained from the two decimated regi- ents, the Lancers and the Lothians, were now engaged in

combat; and it was only thanks to the artillery, which wa
firing mightily at the advancing Germans, that his line wa
still holding steady.

Basically Nicholson was whistling in the dark.

Harmon told the Britisher that more American tanks wer
on their way and that if they could hold this new day, then h
was determined to counterattack and drive the German
back through the pass at Kasserine.

Suddenly there came a loud commotion from outside: angr
voices, British and American. A moment later a tall red
headed man burst into the cellar. Harmon recognized hir
immediately. They had been at West Point together in th
Class of '17. It was "Red," otherwise Brigadier General S
Leroy Irwin, the artillery commander of the 9th Infantr
Division.

Irwin had just marched his men—three artillery battalion
and a cannon company—800 miles in four days non-stop t
reach the front. Now, he told the others, he had received a
order from General Anderson to leave Thala and head for th
village of Le Kef, 50 miles away, which was being threatene
by a German attack.

Nicholson exclaimed in horror, "You can't do that! If m
men see your brigade pulling out it will be a terrible blow t
their morale."

It was now that Harmon made his battle-winning decision
He knew from his visits to Fredendall and Ward just how
terribly shaky the morale on the II Corps front was. "Indeed i
will," he broke in. "Irwin, you stay right here."

With these words, as he recorded later, "I countermande
an order of the commander of the Tunisian campaign. I fig
ured that if I won the battle I would be forgiven. If I lost, th
hell with it anyway."[12]

Irwin broke into a broad smile of relief. "That's just what
wanted to hear," he declared happily. Moments later Irwi
was on his way with Brigadier Parham to dig in his guns. Th
tide was beginning to turn.

thirteen

The last ten tanks of the Lothians, led by Colonel ffrench Blake—who had told them previously that he doubted if any of them would come back—rumbled forward toward the ridge where the Leicesters had surrendered. It was dawn and the front was strangely silent.

The "Green Jackets" of the Rifle Brigade had preceded them at Brigadier Dunphie's command and had taken possession of the lost ground. Obviously, cooperation between the tanks of the 10th Panzer and their panzer grenadiers was not too good. Now ffrench-Blake's antiquated tanks pushed even further forward up a ridge, the only sound the clatter of their own tracks. The going became steeper. Everywhere in the pale light of the false dawn, there was the litter of battle: wrecked infantry bren-gun carriers; charred, holed Mark IVs; shells and shell-cases; cans of compo rations; abandoned equipment—and the dead.

The dead were everywhere, the khaki-clad bodies of those of the Leicesters who had not surrendered but had fought it out with the panzers. Crumpled in wild, eloquent postures, they seemed all boot: those big clumsy British ammunition boots with the regulation thirteen studs and the instep still polished black, "bull" still lingering and triumphant in death. "Ten forty-twos" they were to a man—called up in 1942 and given the serial number of that year—trained and drilled for one long year to die out here in this barren waste at a place whose very name they had not been here long enough to learn. But they had *not* surrendered.

The Valentines started to top the ridge. Still all was silent. Behind them on the road, every available man, cook or clerk, was now dug in. Rifle in hand, Brigadier Parham, reputed to be the best gunner in the British Army, was personally surveying the forty-eight guns of the U.S. 9th Division for the battle to come. If they were going to stop Rommel this day, everything would depend on Irwin's and Parham's gunners.

Suddenly the first Lothian breasted the ridge. As one of the survivors would tell correspondent A. B. Austin later that day, he had never been so frightened in all his life as when he "saw the crosses on the great row of German tanks ahead in the dawn light." The Lothians had run straight into the tank laager of the whole of the 10th Panzer!

The Germans reacted swiftly. Surprised as they were and even in that bad light, the German gunners could not miss the Lothians silhouetted a stark black on the false ridge (as they now found out it was). The first seven Lothian tanks were knocked out in as many minutes. Instantly the ridge was ablaze with escaping gasoline as the survivors leaped from their wrecked tanks and started to run, bullets flying all around them, rushing to board the last three Valentines before they too were destroyed by that furious barrage of high explosive and AP shells.

It was "absolute Gilbert and Sullivan," they told Austin later; "all that stuff flying around and there was I trembling like an aspen..." "They said hold on at all costs and we were stuck out front, so we supposed that was where they meant..." "Old George was popping off at anything and everything..." To Austin they seemed to be "chattering, as if they had been enjoying a bath after a polo match."[1] But those particular chukkas were played for high stakes—life or death.

Death was the fate of some of the last of the Lothians. The regiment was virtually wiped out—but the gamble had paid off. The sudden appearance of these antiquated tanks right in the middle of the 10th Panzer convinced its commander, von Broich, that the Allies were preparing to counterattack in strength. It tallied with the information he had been receiving during the night from his Arab spies. They had reported the arrival of Irwin's guns, and they had also stated they had seen British troops of the Guards Brigade leaving Sbiba and hurrying toward Thala.

Now von Broich ordered his artillery to start pounding the Anglo-American positions and asked for air support to stop Allied reinforcements reaching Thala. Victory was almost within grasping distance. But, even though Anderson had already given the order to evacuate Thala if it proved necessary, even though the line to his front was held only by cooks and clerks, Dunphie's two armored regiments shattered and left with a handful of tanks, von Broich now went into a defensive position.

As Colonel ffrench-Blake was to write many years later: "The situation seemed to be hopeless; the morning was spent waiting to make a last stand, but the attack never came." And, he concluded, "The battle of Thala was a fine example of the fact that it pays never to give up hope, however desperate the situation!"[2]

Now the German guns thundered and the Anglo-Americans replied with a will. That day Irwin's gunners fired a whole peacetime year's allotment of shells at the 10th Panzer's positions.

Oberleutnant Schmidt, who had advanced so confidently back on the 15th, now found himself and his men at the end of their tether. "Yank guns began to hammer us as the light grew," he wrote afterward. "The day grew wilder. Shells seemed to rain on us from all directions . . . Our battalion's position became untenable. An order to withdraw reached us in the afternoon, but it was impossible to carry out in daylight."[3]

All that day the British and American guns pounded the German line. Indeed the Canadian officer, Captain Buchanan, spotting for the British at his forward OP, himself under constant German shellfire, had to shout so loud above the thundering guns that he lost his voice afterward for three whole days. By the end of that long February day the only way he could direct the 25-pounders' fire onto German positions was by firing tracer bullets from his rifle in their direction!

Watching Buchanan's efforts, Major Fyffe of the Rifle Brigade reported, "From time to time their guns [the British] were hidden by an enemy stonk and it was almost unbelievable that their crews could remain alive. No sooner, however, did the enemy shelling slacken than the Gunners leapt from their slit trenches and carried on with their interrupted programme, firing like mad until they were again doused by the enemy. Gunners serving their guns was a sight that will always remain in our memories."[4] That day, in one British battery alone, three Military Medals, a Distinguished Conduct Medal and one Military Cross were won.

Rommel came up to the front personally as the guns of both sides kept up their frenzied tattoo, roaring at each other in an elemental fury. The shelling was as bad as anything he had ever experienced in the trenches. Montgomery's barrage at El Alamein had been little worse, in his opinion. He retired to the safety of his armored command truck, for once not risking his life with his forward troops, and slumped back in his seat, face as sombre as his thoughts.

His men had let him down. They had thrown away the victory he had presented them with this day by failing to attack with their usual zeal and vigor. Now the Anglo-Americans were rushing in reinforcements. Soon, he knew, Montgomery would be launching his attack on the German line at Mareth. He was vitally needed down there to take over command before it was too late. Suddenly he was deflated, without energy or ability to make decisions. Sitting there and brooding to himself as the raindrops drummed on the steel roof of the command car, he gave in to that fatal German weakness: blaming failure on others.

The fault, Rommel decided, lay with his commanders—they had not been aggressive enough. And with the muddled Italian-German command structure that had deprived him of the speedy decisions he needed. And with von Arnim, who had not given him enough support. And with those spies in Rome, who had betrayed the details of his supply ship sailings so that the English could sink the transports.[5]

As the hours passed and the cold bitter rain increased its fury, lashing the sides of the command car in sudden angry squalls, Rommel told himself that he had not failed, the others had. But now it was too late. There was no alternative but to call off the offensive.

When he told them of his decision, Kesselring and his chief-of-staff Colonel Westphal were aghast. Together they worked on a glum Rommel, trying to persuade him to change his mind. They praised him. They reminded him of his past glories. They insisted that the *Amis* were in a worse state than his men; they were on the run.

But Rommel simply sat there shaking his head despondently, ignoring the urgent shrilling of the field telephone at his elbow. He started to rationalize his decision. He blamed the weather, the troops—and von Arnim, his pet hate. If von Arnim had sent him the Tigers under his command and more infantry battalions, he might well have succeeded, Rommel said.[6]

"That may be true," Kesselring replied, "but you had the authority to overrule von Arnim. Why didn't you?"

Rommel gave him a sulky reply. He maintained that von Arnim just didn't understand "how to take a calculated risk."

In the end "Smiling Albert" Kesselring, unsmiling this wet day, gave up. He let Rommel have his way, though why he had changed his mind would remain a mystery to him; only the night before, Rommel had radioed him a jubilant and confident report on the battle. A little while later, Rommel gave the order to withdraw.

Two weeks later Rommel was on his way back to Germany. A twentieth-century Hannibal, he had fought his last battle in Africa close to where that famed warrior had fought his (Zama is not far from Kasserine). In just over a year from now he would be dead, killed not by the enemy but by poison—administered to him in retaliation for the support he gave to the conspirators against Hitler's life.

Curiously enough, the man who would trigger off the chain of events that would result in Rommel being forced to kill himself at Hitler's command was presently a mere 100 yards away from where Rommel's command car stood, bogged down in the Tunisian mud: Colonel Klaus von Stauffenberg, chief-of-operations of the 10th Panzer Division.[7]

At ten in the morning of that same day of decision, Alexander issued an order-of-the-day to the "Soldiers of the Allies." It stated: "The enemy is making a desperate bid to break through. . . . Stand firm. Fight and kill the enemy. A great Allied victory is within our grasp if every soldier does his duty!"[8]

But the Germans did not come again; they had already begun their retreat under cover of darkness. Next day, knowing now that the threat was over, Nicholson gave up what was left of his battered "Nickforce" to return to his division. As a parting gift he gave his men some soccer balls "to take their minds off the ordeal." It was all very British.

A. B. Austin was following the route of the German retreat towards Kasserine that day. The scenes that met his eyes were, he noted later, more like the conventional idea of a battlefield than anything else he had seen so far in Tunisia: "Two wrecked Bren-carriers lay nose to a German Mark III tank with its turret blown off, just as it had come round the corner in the dusk that Sunday evening."[9] The road and slopes to either side were "covered with shells and shell-cases, tins of

erman food, scattered papers, bits of personal equipment—
ess-tins and knives and forks. An Arab lay dead up on the
ope, flung from his lean white horse as he was caught in the
ossfire. A dead German lay on his face beside his tank. They
ere digging a grave for him and an Army chaplain was
tting a surplice over his uniform to read the burial service."

Further on, Austin met some young Lancer officers laugh-
g and excitedly recounting their tales of the recent action: "I
y, wasn't it a shame they beat up that German motor cyclist?
uld have got a bloody good motor bike if only everybody
dn't shot him to pieces!" Austin knew the incident they were
ferring to; Parham's artillery had blown the man to bits as
e came forward to rescue German wounded. Parham's men
d been aghast and shamed. "Not so long ago," noted Austin,
ou had to have a private income and to be able to play polo if
u wanted a commission in that regiment."

Then Austin came upon that wretched Valentine tank that
d betrayed a whole battalion. It had been captured in an
rlier action from those same unfeeling Lancers, with Ger-
an markings now scrawled over its old name of "Apple
auce." He clambered inside the tank that had occasioned the
eicesters' surrender and found some half scorched letters
ritten in German. One was addressed to Alfons, thanking
m for the shoes: "We need these. The soap also will be useful
us." Alfons had not lived long enough to complete his reply,
t he had managed to scribble a few lines. He had seen
ommel up front, he said, "so everything will be all right."

But everything had not been all right. Rommel was gone
w and Alfons lay dead in the mud, his wife a widow, his
ildren fatherless, the cold rain beating down on his unfeel-
g face.

Austin went on. Above him on the heights the Grenadier
uards of the 3rd Battalion started to plod through driving
eet toward the Kasserine Pass. . . .

hirty-six hours later it was all over. Robinett's Combat
ommand B, the only outfit of the U.S. 1st Armored Division

to survive intact, and the infantry of "the Big Red One's" 16th
Infantry pushed into the Pass itself. Above them the Grenadiers took the heights. Both did so without a shot being fired,
the only danger being the mines that still lay everywhere.

The Germans had fled, leaving a wake of death and destruction. Shattered tanks and trucks, German, British, and
American, mingled with the halftracks and jeeps abandoned
in running order by the Americans on that first day of panic.
There were so many of them that the 3rd Grenadiers became
the first British Army unit to equip themselves completely
with those much sought after vehicles. Everywhere, like dead
stalks in the mud, rifles were thrust upright to mark the
position of a corpse. Inside the shattered tanks there was
putrid blackened paste plastered to the walls—all that
remained of men hit by armor-piercing shells. These were the
details of that lunar landscape, repeated over and over again;
a gigantic trash-heap of twisted torn metal and human flesh.

Sitting on his tank amid this scene of death and destruction
was Colonel Gardiner of the CCB. He was a veteran now; he
had seen it all before. He just sat there in the thin February
sunshine, enjoying the luxury of having his boots off for the
first time in six days. Just then a jeep drove up and his
commanding general, Orlando Ward, stepped out.

Ward wanted to know what the situation was up front.
Gardiner told him the pass was theirs; the Krauts had fled.
Ward heaved a sigh of relief. Then, since his own radio wasn't
working, Gardiner—still in his stockinged feet—escorted the
general to another tank. From there Ward put in a personal
call to Fredendall, still eighty miles behind the line in his
underground headquarters.

Very simply Ward told him: "The pass is ours."[10]

General Harmon was on his way to Fredendall's headquarters bearing glad tidings for the commanding general. But as
soon as he entered the underground HQ late that evening, he
could tell by the looks on the staff officers' faces that the news
had preceded him. Nevertheless, Fredendall was roused from

his bed to receive him. It was immediately apparent that Fredendall had been celebrating the occasion already; he was, as Harmon put it, "showing the effects of several helpings of whiskey."[11]

Now that Harmon had confirmed the good news, the drunken Fredendall put in a call to Anderson, telling him that Kasserine was back in American hands. Then he abruptly turned on Harmon and asked him if he was going to sack Ward.

Harmon shook his head. "If you will let General Ward command the division and you command the division through Ward," he replied, "I think you'll find he will give you good cooperation."

Fredendall did not like this reply. Brusquely, he said: "Well, if you're not going to relieve Ward, you might as well go back home."

Harmon stared at him for a moment, barely able to conceal the disgust he felt at his commanding general's condition and behavior, then turned and left. Minutes later he was on his way, accompanied by a single aide, heading for Morocco where his men would line the road for five miles to greet him, cheering and waving as the Old Man drove past. "It was a fine welcome and one of the most rewarding commendations I got for my labors at the Kasserine Pass," wrote Harmon long afterwards.[12]

But before Harmon returned to his old division in Morocco, he called in at Eisenhower's HQ and asked to see his chief.

"Well," Eisenhower asked him when they had exhausted the subject of the recent battle, "what do you think of Fredendall?"

Harmon didn't pull his punches. "He's no damned good!" he growled. "You ought to get rid of him."

"Do you want to take command of the II Corps?" Eisenhower asked next.

Harmon was tempted, but he knew it would be unethical to accept. "I have reported to you that my superior is no good," he told Eisenhower. "It would look like I had sold him down the river to better my own assignment. My recommendation would be to bring Patton here from Morocco. . . . Let me get back to my 2nd Armored. That's the best way out of this mess."

And that's what happened. Fredendall was relieved— though the great American public could not be told why. He was officially sent home to train troops, and promoted to boot. As Marshal Joffre once remarked cynically in World War One, "It takes 16,000 dead to train a major-general." In Fredendall's case, that training had taken some 6,000 dead, wounded, and captured. Not bad by World War Two standards!

So on his return to the States, Lieutenant General Fredendall was given a hero's welcome . . .

ENVOI

When we get old and wear dark baggy suits and slightly greasy bowler hats ... we'll order more beer and begin painting this bitchy trull of a war until it looks like a latter-day saint.

—Cassandra (alias W. Connor) 1943

In the end, those old men, who had almost led the young men under their command into disaster, all returned home, promoted, wounded, or simply fired. A new force swept through the tired, sad U.S. II Corps. Patton might have been as old in years as Fredendall, Ward, McQuillan, and all the rest of them, but he had ten times their fire and spirit.

Alexander had already briefed him on his new command. He had told Patton that the II Corps was "a frightful mess." His troops were "mentally and physically soft and very green." They desperately needed toughening and discipline.

So discipline is what Patton gave them, applying methods

that war correspondents thought "undemocratic and un-American." He stopped his staff arriving late at their desks in the morning by closing the breakfast mess at seven-thirty. Stringent dress regulations were introduced. Ties and helmets would be worn at all times. When his men failed to comply, he rounded up as many officers and enlisted men without helmets as he could find and snorted, "I will not tolerate any sonovabitch who fails to carry out my orders promptly and properly. For the last time I give you the choice: you either pay a 25-dollar fine or face a court-martial."[1] The men paid up. Thereafter his soldiers wore their helmets even to the latrine—Patton checked to see that they did—and his GI nurses kept them on miles behind the lines in their field hospitals; again Patton checked.

"Each time a soldier knotted his tie, threaded his leggings, and buckled on his heavy steel helmet," wrote his bemused second-in-command, General Bradley, "he was forcibly reminded that Patton had come to command the II Corps and that the pre-Kasserine days had ended. . . . A tough new era had begun."[2]

Bradley was right. For the rest of the campaign, even when Patton had gone again, the II Corps proved its fighting ability, in spite of the fact that it had absorbed 5,000 green replacements. It withstood von Arnim's last counterattacks launched by some of his best troops—men who had been fighting the Eighth Army for years; it never again lost ground that it had captured; and it was in there at the kill (if only on the sidelines) when von Arnim's 250,000-strong Army finally surrendered in May 1943.

On the thirteenth of that month, von Arnim surrendered personally to Alexander. Alexander treated him with courtesy, gave him supper and a tent for the night. "I felt he was expecting me to say what a splendid fight he and his men had put up, but I'm afraid I disappointed him," Alexander wrote later. Instead he sent a cable to Churchill stating, *"Sir, it is my duty to report that the Tunisian campaign is over. All enemy resistance has ceased. We are the masters of the North African shores.*"³

In the British Army they received one day off to celebrate the great victory—and almost immediately started preparing for the invasion of Sicily. It was little different for the Americans; they were sent back to the desert.

Lieutenant Neil McCallum was one such soldier. He returned with his infantry battalion through the Kasserine Pass, past the rusting relics of that grim St. Valentine's Day, reflecting on how often this land had been conquered and lost by rival armies. Their convoy passed through Constantine, the headquarters there already closed. The flags were out to celebrate the end of the war, but there was little sign of jubilation among the Arab population. After all, "Why should they care about the war fever of the white overlords?" as McCallum commented in his diary.⁴

They set up camp near a French farm. The French farmer was pleasant, but apprehensive. There might be damage to his farm.

"The war has not troubled you here?" the soldiers asked.

"Trouble!" snorted the Frenchman. "Ah, there has been nothing but trouble! The damned Boche!"

But there was no sign of warfare, the soldiers noted. Had there been much fighting?

No, no, that was elsewhere. It had been peaceful here, thank God. And now that it was all over, why, dear gentlemen, should we be disturbed? There were the crops, the vines. The war was finished . . . And perhaps the officers would care to stay to lunch?

They did not stay. As McCallum wrote in his diary that day, "We had not bargained for this plump, scented farmer. We had not pictured the local and national politics of him and his kind—the occupation of the Germans, the arrival of the Allies, Vichy, de Gaulle, the farm, Giraud, the harvest, the money in the bank, the next crops, and the future. Which side to back, what enthusiasm to show—the crops, the good living, the money in the bank . . ."

In July, Africa got rid of them at last. These young Britons and Americans vanished as speedily as they had arrived, going to fight another war in another continent, leaving only a handful of their kind to gather up the dead and bury them. The French were left in peace to gather their crops and put their money in the bank.

But their time would come too. Within a decade the French *colons* and *pieds-noirs* would themselves be engaged in battle—a desperate battle to quell rising Arab nationalism. It was a battle they would lose. In the end they would have to go as well.

Today there is hardly a trace of those young men who fought and died for a forgotten cause in North Africa, save for their graveyards in Tunisia: the 9,000-odd British, the 3,000 American, the 2,000 or so French—with the Free French even in death separated from the men of that army which had once served Vichy.

Yet somehow, although those Anglo-Americans did not leave behind them the temples, the amphitheatres, the memorials of previous invaders like the Romans or Arabs or French, something still lingers. Get away from the beaches, crowded with package-tour visitors from half of Europe; leave the teeming modern coastal cities and go out into those barren wadis and djebels flanked by jagged daunting peaks. Listen on a still day, with only the faint, cold breeze blowing, and once again you can imagine the cries of alarm, the hiss of machine guns, the harsh orders rapped out by the commanders of those young men, British, American, French, and German, who fought—and died—there once in another time. Men who are old now, or dead these forty years . . .

NOTES AND SOURCES

UTHOR'S NOTE

See Measure for Measure, Act I, Scene i, line 33:
> Heaven doth with us as we with torches do
> Not light them for themselves. For if our virtues
> Did not go forth of us, 'twere all alike
> As if we had them not.

"We are American soldiers! We are your friends!"

RELUDE TO A BATTLE

See Hilary St. George Saunders, *The Green Beret: The Story of the Commandos, 1940–45*. p. 125.

M. Clark, *Calculated Risk*, p. 84.

See Charles de Gaulle, *War Memoirs*, 3 volumes, Vol. II Unity 1942-1944.

The author is indebted in this account of the dinner party to General Mark Clark's book, *Calculated Risk*, p. 55.

U.S. diplomats were still accredited to Vichy France, which remained neutral in the new conflict between the U.S. and Nazi Germany.

6. Under the terms of the armistice, Germany had agreed
   respect unoccupied France as a sanctuary for escap
   prisoners.
7. M. Clark, pp. 85-91.
8. General Clark's trousers were later returned to hi
   cleaned and pressed, but they had shrunk so much th
   barely reached his knees! The money belt full of gold
   understandably—was never found.

PART I: THE LANDINGS
ONE
1. See Kay Summersby's book, *Eisenhower Was My Boss*,
   2.
2. M. Clark, p. 35.
3. M. Clark, p. 36.
4. Ralph Ingersoll, *The Battle is the Pay Off*, p. 184.
5. "John Thomas": military euphemism in World War II
   penis.
6. Dwight D. Eisenhower, *Crusade in Europe*, p. 94.
7. M. Clark, p. 96.
8. See Summersby, p. 36.

TWO
1. L. Farago, *Patton: Ordeal and Triumph*, p. 195.
2. L. Farago, p. 196.
3. C. Whiting, *Patton*, p. 8.
4. C. Whiting, p. 8.
5. Mason-MacFarlane was the former military officer a
   Intelligence officer who had once suggested to his su
   riors in London that he should assassinate Hitler from t
   balcony of his flat in Berlin with a sniper's rifle. T
   suggestion was turned down.
6. *Abwehr:* the wartime German Secret Service.
7. Dwight D. Eisenhower, *At Ease*, p. 255.
8. M. Clark, p. 98.

9. M. Clark, p. 99.
10. M. Clark, p. 99.
11. "Compo char": a new, ready-mix of tea, milk, and sugar.
12. Ladislas Farago: p. 194.
13. "Hello Morocco... Hello Morocco... The President of the United States speaks to you tonight..."
14. E. Harmon, *Combat Commander*, p. 85.
15. M. Clark, p. 101.
16. M. Clark, p. 102.

THREE
1. H. St. George Saunders, *The Green Beret*, p. 131.
2. H. St. George Saunders, *The Green Beret*, p. 131.
3. H. St. George Saunders, *The Green Beret*, p. 132.
4. P. Murphy, *Diplomat Amongst the Warriors*, p. 165.
5. *Purnell's Illustrated History of 2nd World War*, p. 1228.
6. M. Blumenson, *Rommel's Last Victory*, p. 57.
7. Lucian K. Truscott, *Command Missions*.
8. Lee became General Patton's cook for the rest of the war.
9. Truscott.
10. Whiting, p. 11.
11. Harmon, p. 95.
12. L. Farago, p. 216.
13. In addition to the 1,000 dead, more than 1,000 other British and American servicemen were wounded and some 600 taken prisoner by the French. The latter, of course, were soon released—in many cases, their places in jail being taken by Frenchmen who had supported General Mast.

PART II: THE FIRST TEAM
FOUR
1. P. Carrel, *Die Wustenfuchse (Foxes of the Desert)*, p. 318.
2. Murphy, p. 152.
3. Clark, pp. 116–17.

4. *Merde:* French for "shit."
5. Blumenson, p. 38.
6. Blumenson, p. 107.
7. H. St. George Saunders, *Red Beret,* p. 84.
8. H. St. George Saunders, *Red Beret,* p. 85.
9. H. St. George Saunders, *Red Beret,* p. 85.
10. H. St. George Saunders, *Red Beret,* p. 86.
11. Blumenson, p. 62.
12. Blumenson, p. 63.
13. "The Death or Glory Boys" might have been the British public's name for them, but the men of the 17th/21st Lancers called themselves the "Tots"—after the German word for "Death's Head," *Totenkopf.*
14. See R. L. V. ffrench-Blake: *The 17th/21st Lancers,* p. 126.
15. Blumenson, p. 67.

FIVE
1. See Kay Summersby, p. 43.
2. General Bedell Smith, Eisenhower's Chief of Staff.
3. Kay Summersby, p. 49.
4. Commander Harry Butcher, Eisenhower's personal aide and PR man.
5. CG: commanding general.
6. General Hughes defined a WAC as "a double-breasted GI with built-in foxhole."
7. Dwight D. Eisenhower, *Crusade in Europe,* p. 147.
8. Dwight D. Eisenhower, *Crusade in Europe,* p. 150.
9. Dwight D. Eisenhower, *Crusade in Europe,* p. 151.
10. A. Moorehead, *The African Trilogy,* p. 85.
11. A. B. Austin, writing in the *Daily Herald,* compared the supply situation with a soldier in Aberdeen being supplied from Portsmouth. He forgot to add that there were two seas to be crossed, too—the Atlantic and the Mediterranean.
12. C. Ray, *Algiers To Austria: The History of the 78 Division,* p. 34.

13. *Stars and Stripes.* January 1943.
14. See R. L. V. ffrench-Blake. Based on material from the **17th/21st** Lancers and personal information.
15. *Ibid.*
16. Cyril Ray, p. 35.
17. John Guest, *Broken Images*, p. 105.
18. John Guest, p. 104.
19. See Kay Summersby, p. 49.
20. H. Butcher, *Three Years with Eisenhower*, p. 194.

SIX

1. A. B. Austin: *Birth of An Army*, p. 52.
2. E. Taylor, personal interview.
3. Butcher, p. 195.
4. R. Murphy, p. 181.
5. Later, when de Gaulle took over in Algiers, Giraud asked him for ten divisions of French troops. De Gaulle's answer typified his whole attitude to the war: "Why should any Frenchman give his life for liberating France when her allies can do the job leaving France stronger?"
6. See Clark, p. 130.
7. Personal knowledge.
8. See Howard and Sparrow. *The Coldstream Guards, 1920-1946*, p. 116.
9. G. Thaxland, *The Plain Cook and the Showman.*
10. G. Thaxland.

SEVEN

1. C. Whiting, p. 20.
2. Lucien K. Truscott, *Command Missions.*
3. Butcher, p. 196.
4. Butcher's diary was published as *Three Years with Eisenhower*, p. 199.
5. Carrell, p. 313.
6. Personal knowledge.

7. "Führer's Reserve": the line of generals and field marshals awaiting a new command.

PART III: THE KASSERINE PASS
EIGHT
 1. Blumenson, Ch. 9., p. 88.
 2. "Land of Boundless Possibilities": a mocking German nickname for the United States.
 3. Irvine, p. 243.
 4. Stalingrad had surrendered on February 2, with the loss of the entire Sixth German Army and its commander General von Paulus.
 5. David Irving, *The Trail of The Fox*.
 6. Due to bad weather, of course, von Arnim's attack had to be delayed (as we shall see) until February 14, so it was in fact seven more days that they had to wait.
 7. H. Butcher, p. 224.
 8. Kay Summersby would end the war a captain in the American WACs, holding the British Empire Medal, the U.S. Legion of Merit, and sundry campaign medals.
 9. See Kay Summersby, Description p. 55.
10. Kay Summersby, p. 64.
11. Truscott.
12. Truscott.
13. In *At Ease: Stories I Tell to Friends*, Eisenhower gave the impression that he had been under fire from enemy paratroopers. In fact, as Truscott later wrote, their attackers were "trigger-happy U.S. sentries."
14. See Kay Summersby. A rather different description of events can be found on p. 57 of Summersby's book.
15. Kay Summersby, p. 60.

NINE
 1. Carrell, p. 342.
 2. Blumenson, p. 142.

3. Blumenson, p. 144.
4. Blumenson, p. 152.
5. Blumenson, p. 166.
6. Blumenson, p. 169.
7. Blumenson, p. 169.
8. Austin, p. 87.
9. Blumenson, p. 197.
10. Blumenson, p. 200.
11. Fortunately these losses were later scaled down as considerable numbers of survivors managed to struggle back to U.S. lines.

TEN

1. Blumenson, p. 159.
2. Blumenson, p. 162.
3. This was according to General Harmon, who later took over command of the 1st Armored.
4. Blumenson, p. 316.
5. Irving, p. 245.
6. To the average German, Swabian sounds something like a Yorkshire accent does to an Englishman or hillbilly to an American.
7. Truscott.
8. See Nigel Nicholson's biography of him: *Alex*, p. 177.
9. For more information on this subject see Nicholson, p. 177.
10. See Heinz Schmidt, *With Rommel in the Desert*, p. 199.
11. Schmidt, p. 204.

ELEVEN

1. Irving, p. 246.
2. Irving, p. 246.
3. Blumenson, p. 218.
4. Irving, p. 246.
5. Schmidt, p. 210.

6. Blumenson, p. 231.
7. Nigel Nicholson, p. 176.
8. Blumenson, p. 229.
9. Blumenson, p. 109.
10. Blumenson, p. 242.
11. Blumenson, p. 236.
12. Irving, p. 249.
13. Blumenson, p. 253.
14. Blumenson, p. 253.
15. Fredendall lived on to die a peaceful death in his old age.

TWELVE

1. E. Harmon, p. 112.
2. E. Harmon, p. 112.
3. E. Harmon, p. 113.
4. E. Harmon, p. 117.
5. Austin, p. 90.
6. Irving, p. 249.
7. Cyril Ray, p. 96.
8. Austin, p. 89.
9. Austin, p. 91.
10. Blumenson, p. 291.
11. E. Harmon, p. 117.
12. E. Harmon, p. 117.

THIRTEEN

1. Austin, p. 93.
2. ffrench-Blake, p. 56.
3. See Schmidt, p. 215.
4. ffrench-Blake, p. 59.
5. Rommel, of course, was unaware that, because of Ultra, the Allies knew every detail of such movements as soon as Rommel himself.
6. Irving, p. 250.
7. Klaus von Stauffenberg was the man who attempted to

kill Hitler. After being severely wounded by an exploding mine and being sent back to Germany, he joined the
group of plotters planning Hitler's death. It was he who
placed the bomb in Hitler's bunker in July 1944—and
thus indirectly caused Rommel to commit suicide for
being "a fellow conspirator."

Documents I. W. M.
Austin, p. 92.
Blumenson, p. 295.
E. Harmon, p. 119.
E. Harmon, p. 120.

VOI
Farago, p. 243.
Farago, p. 244.
Nicholson, p. 192.
Austin, p. 138.

INDEX

Date_____19 7

M_____

Address_____

Reg. No.	Clerk	Account Forward		
1	2 PB Hisloy		3	6l
2				
3				18
4				
5				
6			3	79
7				
8				
9				
10				
11				
2				

1040-11

Stated to Date—If Error Is Found Return at Once

Read ahead for the introduction to

Charles Whiting's

DEATH OF A DIVISION

the shocking story of America's worst
battlefield defeat in Europe in World
War II.

Available from Jove Books in August 1991

On a snowy day in the second week of December 1944,
a convoy moved through the Belgian village of Schoenberg. It took the steep road heading east to the front.
The trucks, filled with young men in new uniforms,
passed the big signboard announcing: YOU ARE ENTER-
ING GERMANY. BE ON YOUR GUARD.

The road wound higher and higher through thick,
snow-laden firs. Behind them Belgium lay stretched out
like a relief map. But their eyes looked only to the
front, to Germany, to the country they had come so far
to conquer. The trucks finally halted and the NCOs
ordered the men out. Stiff with cold after the long journey, the soldiers, each with the Golden Lion shoulder
patch on his sleeve, formed up in columns on either side
of the road for the two-mile hike to the forward combat
positions. Their guide from the division they were
relieving asked the colonel if they were ready. The colonel snapped an order.

'All right, you guys,' the NCOs shouted, 'move out!'

The young men began to 'move out'. The 16 000
men of the 106th US Infantry Division, the newest
division on any Allied front, were going into the line.

If the young men were apprehensive as they moved into position, at the point where the deepest penetration into Germany had occurred the previous September, they comforted themselves with the knowledge that this was now the 'Ghost Front', to which new troops were sent to be prepared for 'real combat'. Visiting the Ghost Front two months before, the Ninth US Army historian, Robert E. Merriam, described it in almost pastoral terms:

> All was peaceful; farmers in the fields along the road were ploughing their fields for the winter fallow and some were taking in the last of the summer harvest; cattle were grazing lazily. I was green and my guide knew it, so he said suddenly with a dramatic flourish of his hand, 'See that ridge line over there just across the valley?'
> I nodded.
> 'That's it.'
> 'What?' I naïvely inquired.
> 'The German line,' he replied.
> We were riding along the top of a huge ridge, silhouetted in plain view of an enemy no more than eight hundred yards away, guns of the West Wall supposedly bristling behind every bush and nothing happened.
> 'Have to be careful at night,' my talkative guide continued. 'Krauts like to sneak over patrols, just to make a social call. ... But the only shelling we get is when a Jerry goes to the latrine; seems like they have a machine gun and a mortar there, and each one fires a burst – hope they don't get diarrhoea!'

This, then, was the Ghost Front, where the only casualties were those caused by trench foot and VD contacted in the rest centres. Nothing ever happened here. The eighteen-year-olds of the 106th could look forward to a calm – if very cold – Christmas without fear. In 1945 all was uncertain. But the papers back home were already calling this 'The last Christmas of the war in Europe'. The Germans were well nigh beaten.

But the young men were in for a great shock. Before the week was out their division would be destroyed, and out of the 16 000 men who had gone into the forests, only some 4000 would return. The rest would be killed, wounded or captured, victims of the greatest US defeat in Europe in the Second World War.

Naturally, the events of that week were afterwards glossed over, perverted or conveniently forgotten. General Omar Bradley, to whose Twelfth Army Group the 106th Infantry Division belonged and the commander who had taken the 'calculated risk' (as he called it) of leaving the Eifel–Ardennes so thinly defended, wrote long after the event:

> Troy* was entitled to pride in his VIII Corps, for his divisions had rallied nobly in a furious delaying struggle that emphasized the resourcefulness of the American soldier. Though surprised and disorganized, part of the 106th fell back to the crossroads of St Vith. There it was joined by the 7th Armoured Division in the defense of that road junction.

Brave words, but far from the truth when one learns that that same Troy Middleton, shaken and worried by the events in the hills, was telling the 'hero of Bastogne', General McAuliffe, on 18 December, 'Certain of my units, especially the 106th Division, are broken.' And General Bruce Clarke, who led the 7th Armoured Division 'in the defence of that road junction', gained the impression on his arrival there that 'the 106th no longer existed as an effective division'.

Major Don Boyer of the 7th Armoured also remembers it differently. Leading the 7th Armoured's column towards St Vith, he saw the retreat at its height:

> Here would come an empty two and a half ton truck, then another two and a half, but this time with two or three men

*General Troy Middleton, commander of VIII Corps, to which the 106th belonged.

... in the rear, perhaps an engine crane truck or an armoured car, then several artillery prime movers – perhaps one of them towing a gun, command cars with officers up to and including several full Colonels in them, quarter-tons – anything which would get the driver and the few others he might have with him away from the front. It wasn't orderly; it wasn't military; it wasn't a pretty sight. We were seeing American soldiers running away.

Colonel Dupuy, the historian of the 106th Infantry Division, pulled no punches either in his account of the events of that December. He wrote:

Let's get down to hard facts. Panic, sheer unreasoning panic, flamed that road all day and into the night.* Everyone, it seemed, who had any excuse and many who had none, were going west that day – west from Schoenberg and west from St Vith too.

After the war Major Boyer wrote:

There was one of the biggest tragedies of St Vith, that American soldiers fled, and by fleeing they crowded the roads over which the reinforcements were coming and prevented those reinforcements from arriving in time to launch a counter-attack to save the 422nd and 423rd Infantry Regiments.

In essence, the cold official prose of the Department of the Army's published account of what happened in the Ardennes to the 106th Infantry Division is much closer to the truth than General Bradley's version. It states:

The number of officers and men taken prisoner on the capitulation of the two regiments of the 106th Division and their attached troops cannot be accurately ascertained. At least seven thousand were lost here and the figure is probably closer to eight or nine thousand. The amount lost in arms and equipment, of course, was very substantial.

*The day and night of 16 December 1944.

The Schnee Eifel battle, therefore, represents the most serious reverse suffered by American arms during the operations of 1944-45 in the European theatre.*

Indeed, with the exception of Bataan, it was the biggest surrender of American troops since the Civil War nearly a hundred years earlier.

'It is as great a mistake to return to old battlefields,' someone once wrote, 'as it is to revisit the place of your honeymoon or the house where you grew up. For years you have owned them in your memory. When you go back you find the occupants have re-arranged the furniture.'

The charred hull of the Sherman tank, surrounded by its little cluster of makeshift crosses which marked the graves of its crew, is no longer there. The long, shell-pitted road, draped with white ribbons to indicate that the engineers had swept the verges clear of mines, which once took a week to cover, can be walked now in a leisurely ten minutes. The bunker that held up a whole regiment for eight hours until some young men, 'eager for some desperate glory', took it in the end at a cost of fifty per cent casualties, is now simply a gentle mound. Time, progress and the green earth itself have drawn an almost impenetrable cloak over those scenes of desperate action where young men fought and died over thirty years ago.

Normally this is so; but not in the woods of the Snow Eifel where the 106th US Infantry Division came to such a shameful end. Those dark forests are still heavy with the 'feel' of the frightened young men who fought and died there. The foxholes and the rotting remains of the 106th Division are everywhere -- the gas masks; the

My italics. C.W.

hardly recognizable bits of combat boots and webbin
equipment; the rusty rifle clips and ammunition boxe
the shell holes near the road along which the 589t
Artillery fled; the lonely grave of Lieutenant Wooc
The shame of the 106th Division is still palpable in th
forest.

Military history is often written as a mere chronolog
– a series of moves and counter-moves made b
omnipotent, impersonal generals sitting in remot
headquarters; generals with the same backgrounds an
the same training, looking at the same maps of the sam
terrain, matching their moral strength and their tactic
ingenuity against their antagonists a hundred mile
away. But war isn't like that. War is a great traged
made up of the dramas and tragedies of many humbl
men, who have not been consulted on the length of th
preliminary softening-up bombardment, the prope
manner of isolating the battlefield, the appropriate tim
for throwing in the reserves. In this book I have attemp
ted to examine the drama and the tragedy of one sma
segment of that great army America sent overseas i
the Second World War: the 106th US Infantry Div
sion. Sixteen thousand young men who, between 1
and 22 December 1944, fought, died and surrendere
in the Eifel–Ardennes border area of Germany an
Belgium. This is their story.

234

TRUE ACCOUNTS OF VIETNAM
from those who returned to tell it all . . .

__PHANTOM OVER VIETNAM: FIGHTER PILOT, USMC John Trotti
0-425-10248-3/$3.95

__MARINE SNIPER Charles Henderson
0-425-10355-2/$4.50

__THE KILLING ZONE: MY LIFE IN THE VIETNAM WAR Frederick Downs
0-425-10436-2/$4.50

__AFTERMATH Frederick Downs
Facing life after the war
0-425-10677-2/$3.95

__NAM Mark Baker
The Vietnam War in the words of the soliders who fought there.
0-425-10144-4/$4.50

__BROTHERS: BLACK SOLDIERS IN THE NAM Stanley Goff and
Robert Sanders with Clark Smith
0-425-10648-9/$3.95

__INSIDE THE GREEN BERETS Col. Charles M. Simpson III
0-425-09146-5/$3.95

__THE GRUNTS Charles R. Anderson
0-425-10403-6/$4.50

__THE TUNNELS OF CU CHI Tom Mangold and John Penycate
0-425-08951-7/$4.50

__AND BRAVE MEN, TOO Timothy S. Lowry
The unforgettable stories of Vietnam's Medal of Honor winners.
0-425-09105-8/$3.95
